THE NATIONAL

pastime

THE NATIONAL

EDITED BY JOHN THORN

For the
Society for American Baseball Research

BELL PUBLISHING COMPANY
New York

This 1988 edition is published by Bell Publishing Company,
distributed by Crown Publishers, Inc., 225 Park Avenue
South, New York, New York 10003, by arrangement with
Warner Books.

Printed and Bound in the United States of America

Library of Congress Cataloging-in-Publication Data

The National pastime / edited by John Thorn for the
    Society for American Baseball Research.
    p.   cm.
    Reprint. Originally published: New York : Warner
    Books, 1987.
    ISBN 0-517-66202-7
    1. Baseball—United States—History.   I. Thorn, John,
    1947-   II. Society for American Baseball Research.
    GV863.A1N393   1987
    796.357′0973—dc19   87-33379
                                                CIP

h g f e d c b a

Table of Contents

Editor's Introduction

John Thorn

When Roger Clemens struck out 20 Seattle Mariners, he summoned from the cobwebs of 1884 the dimly remembered names of Charlie Sweeney and One Arm Daily, the pitchers who first set the record he broke. Pete Rose chased but failed to capture the ghost of Ty Cobb, much as Roger Maris and Henry Aaron did battle with the Babe. And the World Series Champion Red Sox of 1918 eerily prefigured the ill-starred crew of 1986: in 1918, the last time Boston won the Series, they did so in six games, winning the opener 1-0 behind southpaw Babe Ruth; that opening shutout was matched in 1986 by southpaw Bruce Hurst, whose name is an anagram for Ruth's, and Hurst's Red Sox came within one strike of winning in six games.

Baseball history lives. It is a seamless web in which every act on the field or off connects with a myriad of others, enriching the storehouse of legend that nurtures the game and the nation.

This collection of articles, essays, stats, and lore is dedicated to the proposition that baseball's past is every bit as exciting as its present. That past is not merely what happened in 1886 or 1936—it is also the events of today;it is yesterday's box scores perused this morning; it is today's game, history aborning. In the eternal hot stove league of the mind, Branch Rickey and Rickey Henderson are soulmates, Christy Mathewson and Tom Seaver duel at checkers, and Fred Merkle wraps a consoling arm around Bill Buckner.

These flights of fantasy are hardly less fantastic than some of the game's historical verities, such as the astrological keys to baseball success (no fooling: read John Holway's "Diamond Stars") or the weirdly kindred couple of Hack Wilson and Roger Maris (see Don Nelson's "A Tale of Two Sluggers"). If the 1986 Cy Young Award winner in the National League, Mike Scott of the Astros, has had a fantastic season by winning 18 games, what adjective does Webster's hold for the year when Hoss Radbourne won *60*? (See the piece by Frederick Ivor-Campbell.) If great hitting is what turns you on, get a hold of this one from Bill Mead's "The Year of the Hitter": In 1983 Lonnie Smith, then with the Cardinals, missed the National League batting championship by a scant .002; if he had been warped back to 1930 with his .321 average, he would have found himself ranking seventh—not in the league, *but on his own team.*

History is not all that's on display in these pages. There is analysis by such giants of sabermetrics—Bill James' coinage for the mathematical and statistical study of baseball— as David Neft, Pete Palmer, and James himself. There is nostalgia (remember Harry Perkowski? Van Lingle Mungo?). There is opinion (let's go back to eight-team leagues; today's players are better than the old-timers; old-time ballparks were better than today's). There are amusements (a ballparks quiz, an acrostic puzzle). And there is outstanding research underlying the whole volume.

When I developed *The National Pastime* for the Society for American Baseball Research (SABR) in 1982, the organization had been splendidly served for a decade by *The Baseball Research Journal*, created and edited by L. Robert Davids. It was Davids whose idea SABR was and whose untiring efforts made that idea take hold. A masterful researcher, he is represented in this volume with a piece on the youngest major leaguers, one of several articles reprinted from SABR's original annual publication.

What is SABR, anyway? It is a group of over 6,000 people of diverse backgrounds, united by their love of baseball and their desire to know more about it. Some are active researchers who pursue their areas of interest through one or more of SABR's committees, like minor leagues, or statistical analysis, or records, or biographical. Others simply like the SABR publications or the camaraderie of the regional and national meetings.

A rediscovered interview, taped in 1963 for "The Glory of Their Times."

Ladies and Gentlemen, Presenting Marty McHale

Lawrence S. Ritter

Damon Runyon once wrote a story about me, saying this fellow McHale, who is not the greatest ballplayer that ever lived, is probably the most *versatile* man who ever took up the game. This was in the 1920s, after I had left baseball. So Johnny Kieran of the New York *Times* asked Babe Ruth about it, knowing he and I had been on the Red Sox together. Johnny said, "Marty played in the big leagues, he played football in college, he was on the track team, he was on the stage, he wrote for the Wheeler Syndicate and the *Sun,* he was in the Air Service"—and so forth. He went on listing my accomplishments until the Babe interrupted to say, "Well, I don't know about all those things, but he was the best goddamn singer I ever heard!"

You see, I sang in vaudeville for 12 years, a high baritone tenor—an "Irish Thrush," they called it then, and *Variety*

LAWRENCE S. RITTER teaches economics and finance at New York University. He has authored or co-authored (with Donald Honig) three baseball books besides *The Glory of Their Times.*

1

called me "The Baseball Caruso." But even before vaudeville, before baseball even, I used to work in a lot of shows
around Boston and made trips down to Wakefield, Win-
chester—minstrel shows, usually—and sometimes these little two-act sketches.

So when I joined the Boston club, a bunch of us—Buck
O'Brien, Hughie Bradley, Larry Gardner, and myself—formed
the Red Sox Quartette. After a while Gardner gave it up and
a fellow named Bill Lyons stepped in. This Lyons was no
ballplayer, but Boston signed him to a contract anyway, just
to make the name of the act look proper. We were together
three years, and when we broke up I was just as well
satisfied because it was quite an ordeal keeping the boys on
schedule. They just couldn't get used to that buzzer that tells
you you're on next. They'd be a couple of minutes late and
think nothing of it, but you can't *do* that in vaudeville, you
know—you're *on*.

I did a single for about another three years, which was
not very good—just good enough so that they paid for
it—and then Mike Donlin and I got together. Now, you may
not remember Mike, but he was—well, he was the Babe
Ruth of his day. "Turkey Mike," they called him, because
when he'd make a terrific catch or something he'd do a kind
of turkey step and take his cap off and throw it up like a
ham, a real ham; but he was a great one, he could live up to
that stuff in the field or at the bat. His widow gave me some
of his souvenirs: a gold bat and ball that were given to him
as the most valuable player in 1905, some cufflinks, and
a couple of gold cups, one from the Giants and the other
from the Reds. He hit over .350 for both of them.

Mike and I were together for five years, doing a double-
entendre act called "Right Off the Bat"—not too much
singing, Mike would only go through the motions—and we
played the Keith-Orpheum circuit: twice in one year we
were booked into the Palace in New York and that was when
it was the Palace, not the way it is now! They had nothing
but the big headliners. When Mike left for Hollywood, I
went back to doing a single. He made a bunch of pictures
out there, and that's where he died.

Which did I like better, baseball or vaudeville? Well, I'd call it about 50-50. The vaudeville was more difficult, the traveling. Sure, you had to travel a lot in baseball, but you always had somebody taking care of your trunk and your tickets and everything; all you had to do was get your slip, hop onto the train, and go to bed. When you got to the hotel your trunk was there. In vaudeville you had to watch your own stuff. I used to say to Mike, you're the best valet I know, because he was always on time with the tickets and had our baggage checks and everything all taken care of, right on the button all the time.

Of course, Mike and I wouldn't have been such an attraction if it hadn't been for baseball, so maybe I ought to tell you how I came to sign with the Red Sox in 1910. First of all, Boston was almost my home town—I grew up in Stoneham, that's nine miles out and if you took a trolley car and changed two or three times, you could get to the ballpark. Which I'd done only once—I only saw one big-league game before I played in one, and Cy Young pitched it; I wasn't really a Red Sox fan. But here comes the second reason for my signing: they gave me a *big* bonus. How big? Two thousand dollars, and back then that was money!

You see, that year for Maine University I had thrown three consecutive no-hitters, and the scouts were all over. I had a bid from Detroit, one from Pittsburgh, one from the Giants, and another from the Braves. And there was sort of a veiled offer from Cincinnati, which is an interesting story.

This Cincinnati situation, Clark Griffith was down there managing and when I reported to the Red Sox, which was in June, following the end of the college term, his club was playing the Braves, over at Braves Field across the tracks from the Huntington Avenue park. Now, the Red Sox were on the road when I and some other college boys reported. We had signed, but the Red Sox didn't want us with them right away: they had to make room for us, they could only have so many players. So I remember that Griffith came over to the Red Sox park one morning to watch the boys work out. The clubhouse man told us we were all being watched—like you'd watch horses, you know, working out each morning, and he said if we wanted to stay with the club, better take it easy and not put too much on the ball and so on. See, the club usually asks waivers on the newcomers immediately upon reporting to see if anybody else is interested in them, and if so they can withdraw the waivers after a certain time.

I remember very definitely—I went out there and I was pitching to the hitters and I put everything I had on the ball, because after looking over that bunch of Red Sox pitchers I could see there was not much chance for a young collegian to crack that lineup.

At any rate, Griffith must have put in some claim, you see, because two days later I was on my way to Chicago to join the Red Sox. They had withdrawn the waivers. I joined them in Chicago and we went from there to Cleveland. I remember my pal Tris Speaker hurt his finger in Chicago and he was out for a few days, and Fordham's Chris Mahoney, who was an outfielder, a pitcher, and a good hitter, took his place.

He and I weren't the only college boys on that team, you know: Bill Carrigan, Jake Stahl, Larry Gardner, Duffy Lewis, Harry Hooper...even Speaker went to—not the University of Texas, but Texas Polyclinic, Polytechnic or something of that kind out there; only went for two years, but he went. And Ray Collins and Hughie Bradley, too. Buck O'Brien, he came the next year, he said, "I got a degree, I got a B.S. from Brockton." He said B.S. stood for boots and shoes, meaning that he worked in a factory.

Now on this day in Cleveland, we had Chris Mahoney playing right field, Harry Hooper moved over to center, and Duffy Lewis stayed in left, and Patsy Donovan put me in to pitch my first game in the big leagues against Joe Jackson and those Cleveland boys.

I wasn't what you'd call sloppily relaxed, but I wasn't particularly nervous, either. You see, I was one of the most egotistical guys that God ever put on this earth: I felt that I could beat anybody. I struck out ten of those Naps, including Jackson. The first time he was up, I had Joe two strikes, no balls, and I did something that the average big-league pitcher would never do. Instead of trying to fool him with a pitch, I stuck the next one right through there and caught him flat-footed. He never dreamed I'd do that.

So the next time up there the same thing happened. He hit a foul, then took a strike, and then Red Kleinow, an old head who was catching me, came out for a conference. He said, "What do you want to pitch him, a curve ball?" And I said, "No, I'm going to stick another fast one right through there."

He said, "He'll murder it." Well—he did! Joe hit a ball that was like a shot out of a rifle against the right-field wall. Harry Hooper retrieved it in *left* center!

Yes, I had ten strikeouts, but I lost the ballgame. It was one of those sun-field things: a fellow named Hohnhurst was playing first base for Cleveland and, with a man on first, he hit a long fly to left-center field. Harry Hooper, who was in center this day, was dead certain on fly balls, but when Speaker was out there, as Harry said afterwards, he used to let Speaker take everything within range. Harry said he and Duffy Lewis didn't exactly get their signals crossed, but they were not sure as to who was going to take the ball.

Finally Duffy went for it, and just as he made his pitch for the ball the sun hit him right between the eyes and he didn't get his hands on the thing and the run, of course, scored, and Hohnhurst, the fellow who hit the ball—he got himself to second base. Ted Easterly got a single on top of that, and anyway, the score ended up 4-3. That was it.

I was supposed to be a spitball pitcher, but I had a better overhand curve, what they called a drop curve—you'd get that overspin on it and that ball would break much better than a spitter. I had what they call a medium-good fastball, not overpowering but good enough, and if you took something off your curve and your spitter, your fastball looked a lot better. For my slow one, the changeup as they call it now, I tried a knuckler but never could get any results with it, so I stole Eddie Karger's slow-breaking downer. He and I used to take two fingers off the ball and throw it with the same motion as we used for the fastball.

They still have those fellows today that throw spitters, but it doesn't make much difference—because even when the spitter was legal in my day, in both leagues you couldn't pick six good spitball pitchers. You'd take a fellow like Ed Walsh with the White Sox, the two Coveleskis, Burleigh Grimes, and the lefthanded spitter in the National League, who has since lost both legs, Clarence Mitchell.

Now, Clarence was a good spitball pitcher, but Walsh was the best. He worked harder at it, had a better break, had better control of it, and he pitched in more ballgames than any pitcher in either league over a period of years.

Eddie Cicotte, he was with us in Boston, you know, he was going with a spitter for a while. He used to throw that emery ball, too, and then he developed what we call the "shine" ball. He used to have paraffin on different parts of his trousers, which was not legal, and he would just go over all the stitches with that paraffin, making the other part of the ball rougher. It was just like the emery situation, but in reverse, and an emery ball is one of the most dangerous, not like the spitter, which can be controlled. But Cicotte's main pitch was the knuckleball, and he used that to such an extent that we called him Knuckles.

Joe Wood was with the Red Sox when I joined them, too. Now there was a fellow who could do nearly everything well. He was a great ballplayer, not just a pitcher, he was a good outfielder, he was a good hitter, he was a good baseman, he would run like blazes, he used to work real hard before a ballgame, he was just a good all-around ballplayer and a great pitcher. And he was a fine pool player, too, and billiards. He could play any kind of a card game and well; also he was a good golfer. I think that he could have done nearly everything. If he were playing football he'd be a good quarterback.

Joey was a natural—and talking about egotistical people, there's a guy who had terrific confidence, terrific. Without being too fresh, he was very cocky, you know. He just had "the old confidence."

I wasn't with Boston the year they won the World's Championship and Joey won those 34 games and then three more against the Giants, but I was at the Series and wrote a story about that final game. I saw the Snodgrass muff—he was careless, and that happens. But right after that he made a gorgeous running catch.

Earlier in that game Harry Hooper made the best catch I ever saw. I hear from Harry twice a year or so; he lives in California, and he's got plenty of the world's goods. Harry made this catch—he had his back to the ball—and from the bench it looked like he caught it backhanded, over his shoulder. After I sent my story to him, he wrote to me. "I thought it was a very good catch, too," he said, "but you were wrong in your perspective. When I ran for that ball, I ran with my back toward it and you guys with your craning necks were so excited about it, when I ran into the low fence"—you see the bleachers came up from a low fence in Fenway—"the fence turned me around halfway to the right and I caught the ball in my bare right hand." Imagine!

In 1913 I joined the Yankees—they weren't called the Highlanders any more—and then three years later I went back to the Red Sox. Bill Carrigan, who was the Boston manager then, said, "Now that you're seasoned enough you can come back and pitch for a *big-league* team." The Yankees in those days were a terrible ballclub. In 1914 I lost 16 games and won only 7, with an earned-run average under three. I got no runs. I would be beaten one to nothing, two to nothing, three to one, scores like that. You were never ahead of anybody. You can't win without runs. Take this fellow who's pitching for the Mets, Roger Craig, what did he lose—22, something like that? What did he win—5? One to nothing, two to nothing, terrible.

When I got to New York Frank Chance was the manager, a great guy. He had a reputation as a really tough egg, but if you went out there and worked and hustled and showed him that you were interested in what you were doing he would certainly be in your corner, to the extent that he would try and get you more money come contract time.

I have a watch, one of these little "wafer" watches, that Chance gave me in 1914 after I guess about the first month.

I had won a couple of games for him, one of them was the opening game against the World Champion A's, and one day, just as a gesture, he said, he gave me this watch.

Frank and I were such good friends that late in 1914, when we were playing a series in Washington, after dinner, one evening he said, let's take a little walk. So we went out to a park across from the hotel and sat down. "I'm going to quit," he said. "I can't stand this being manager, can't stand being the manager of this ballclub."

He said, "We're not going to get anyplace. I've got a good pitching staff"—and he did have a good pitching staff—"but you fellows are just batting your heads against the wall every time you go out there, no runs." The owners wouldn't get him any players, see, and he said, "I just can't take it—I'm going to quit."

He had already talked it over with the front office in New York and one of the reasons he took me out to the park was that he had told them which men he thought they should keep, and I happened to be one of three pitchers along with Slim Caldwell and Ray Fisher, and he said I know that you'll be working in vaudeville next winter and I would advise you to get yourself a two- or three-year contract, if you can, before you leave New York on your tour, which was very good advice—which advice I didn't take. I was too smart—you know how it is, very smart—so Mike Donlin and I went out on the Orpheum circuit that winter after opening at the Palace.

So Mike, before we left New York, he said, you better go over to the Yankee office and get yourself signed in before we leave for Chicago. He said, you never can tell what's going to happen. I, being very, very smart, I said, "No, I'll be worth more money to them in the spring than I am now after the publicity we will get in vaudeville this winter."

But I was wrong, because during the winter, while we were in Minneapolis at the Orpheum Theatre, Devery and Farrell sold the team to Ruppert and Huston. I'm quite sure I could have made a deal with Frank Farrell for a two- or three-year contract before leaving, but as I say I wasn't very smart.

When we got back east Bill Donovan (that's Bill, not Patsy) had been appointed manager of the Yankees, and he was not in favor of anybody having a long-term contract. I didn't even last out the year with him.

It seemed every time I pitched against Washington I had Walter Johnson as an opponent, or Jim Shaw, either one. Griffith, he used to... I don't know... I had an idea he didn't pitch them against Caldwell. It seemed that every time Slim pitched, the team would get him three or four runs—though he didn't need them, he was a great pitcher.

Was Johnson as great a pitcher as they say? Let me tell you, he was *greater* than they say. He was with one of the worst ballclubs imaginable, not quite as bad as the old Yankees but almost as bad.

When I got out of the Air Service, after the War—you see, I quit baseball on the 4th of July, I think, in 1917 and went into the Air Service—when I came out I went to work for the New York *Evening Sun*. I wrote articles, and the *Sun* used to run them every Saturday. The Wheeler Syndicate used to sell them to—wherever they could sell them, Boston, Philadelphia, Newark, anywhere they could, you know, and I used to get five, two, four, eight dollars apiece for them, and one of the stories that I wrote was about Walter Johnson.

I wrote one about Joey, too, and about Cicotte, and Mathewson, oh, so many of them. In the story about Johnson, I wondered what would have happened if he had been pitching for the Giants, who could get him five or six runs nearly every time he started, and I'm wondering if he'd *ever* lose a ballgame. I found out from Joe Vila, who was the sports editor for the *Sun,* that Matty didn't care very much for that.

Matty was a very good friend of Mike's, and so was McGraw, who was my sponsor into the Lambs Club. He was a Jekyll and Hyde character. Off the field he was very affable, but the minute he'd get in uniform, he was one of the toughest guys you'd ever want to know. Mike used to tell me a lot of inside information which of course helped me when I was writing these stories.

Do you know about the movie Speaker and I made? In 1917, just before I went into the service, we produced a motion picture of the big stars in both major leagues. We had $80,000 worth of bookings for the picture, and then they declared baseball during the War not essential, so all the bookings were canceled. We sold the rights to the YMCA to use it in the camps all over Europe, in the ships going over and back, and in the camps here.

After the War was over I showed the film to my friend Roxy, God rest him, and he took the thing over and showed it at the Rivoli and the Rialto and down to Fifth Avenue, and then I happened to come into Wall Street to work as a stockbroker—in 1920 I started my own firm, which I still run today—and I forgot all about the film.

It was put in the morgue some place up at the Rialto or the Rivoli, and the YMCA lost their prints somewhere over in France, but I had left in the tins some cuts and out-takes of the shots of—well, Speaker, Hooper, Ruth, Wood, Matty, and Johnson and all, and I still have them. I showed the clips only about two years ago at the Pathé projection room one day and they still look pretty good.

The game's a lot different today from what it was when I played. The biggest change—and the worst one, in my opinion—is the home run. Now, let's first talk of the fellow going up to the plate. Seventy-five percent of the time he goes up there with the thought of hitting the ball out of the ballpark, and it's not too difficult to do, because they have moved the ballpark in on him. Now in right field and center field and left field, you've got stands. They used to have a bleacher, way out, in the old days, but the only home run you'd get would be if you hit it between the fielders. "In grounds," they'd call it, a home run in grounds: if a ball got in between those fielders and if you had any speed, they wouldn't be able to throw you out. Today, if you hit a good long fly it's in one of these short stands.

In the old days they juiced up the ball some, but when they talk about the dead ball—there *never* was any dead ball that I can remember. I've got a couple of scars on my chin to prove it. I saw Joe Jackson hit a ball over the top of the

Polo Grounds in right field—*over the top of it*—off one of
our pitchers, and I have never seen or heard of anyone
hitting it over since, and that was around 1914-15, in there.

Today's ball is livelier, no doubt of that. They are using
an Australian wool now in winding the core of the ball. In
the old days they used wool but not one that is as elastic as
this wool. The bats are whippier, too. But the principal
reason for all these homers is the concentration of the hitter
on trying to hit the ball out of the park.

The fielding today? Well, any of these boys in the big
leagues today could field in any league at any time. I think
the better equipment has more to do with the spectacular
play. You take this here third baseman up with the Yankees—
Clete Boyer—he's terrific, just terrific. Larry Gardner, who
played third on the Boston team with me, he was a great
third baseman, and he had that "trolleywire throw" to first,
but Larry was not as agile as Boyer. I think Boyer is a little
quicker. But, if you want a fellow to compare with Boyer,
take Buck Weaver of that Black Sox team. He would field
with Boyer any day, and throw with him, and he was a
better hitter. He would be my all-time third baseman.

Players of my day, give them the good equipment, and
they would be just as good or better. Now, you take a fellow
like Wagner—I don't mean the Wagner we had with the Red
Sox, but the Pirates' Wagner, Honus Wagner, who came to
see us in Pittsburgh at the theatre, and he took up the whole
dressing room with that big can of his. There was one of the
most awkward-looking humans you ever saw, but he made
the plays, without the shovel glove. And Speaker—could
a big glove have made him any better?

As an outfielder, Speaker was in a class by himself. He
would play so close to the infield that he'd get in on
rundown plays! Then the next man perhaps would hit a long
fly into center field and he would be on his bicycle with his
back to the ball—not backing away, he'd turn and run—and
you'd think he had a radar or a magnet or something
because just at the proper time he'd turn his head and catch
the ball over his shoulder.

Those fellows, Speaker, Lewis, and Hooper, they used to

practice throwing, something that you don't see anymore. Those fellows would have a cap down near the catcher and they'd see who would come closest to the cap when they'd throw from the outfield. They all had marvelous arms. Nobody would run on them and I think that most of the people who ever saw them play would say there was no trio that could compare with them.

Mike and I, in our act, we used to do a number called, "When You're a Long, Long Way From Home." In it I used to do a recitation, and the last two lines were, "When you're on third base alone, you're still a long, long way from home." It was serious, about life being like a game of baseball. Times have changed—a boy can't peek through a knothole in a concrete fence—but that's still true.

"Maybe Evers got the ball and touched the base afterward. If he did it didn't prove anything."

The Merkle Blunder:
A Kaleidoscopic View

G. H. Fleming

On September 23, 1908, as I wrote in The Unforgettable Season, *"the Giants and Cubs played the most celebrated, most widely discussed, most controversial contest in the history of American sports. The game was declared a 1 to 1 tie." This was, of course, the game of the "Merkle blunder." As Kurosawa's film masterpiece* Rashomon *beautifully illustrated, the same event may be seen in different ways by different people; and so it was with what took place at the Polo Grounds on that momentous day. What is the truth, and what is illusion? You be the judge. As in* The Unforgettable Season, *everything below is presented exactly as it appeared in the original accounts of 1908.*

MONDAY, SEPTEMBER 21

Here is something for the fans to consider. Suppose Fred Tenney should be crippled. That would be a calamity,

G. H. FLEMING is the author of *The Unforgettable Season*, a reconstruction of the 1908 National League pennant race.

13

wouldn't it? Yes, it would in one way, but it wouldn't keep
the Giants from winning the pennant. There is a young
fellow on the bench named Fred Merkle who can fill that
job better than nine tenths of the first basemen in the league.
He is crying for a chance to work, but with Tenney playing
like a youngster just out of college it would be silly to take
him out of the game.

—BOZEMAN BULGER, Chicago *Tribune*

WEDNESDAY, SEPTEMBER 23

There were rumors afloat last night to the effect that Mr.
Tenney had injured his back and might not play today.

—Chicago *Tribune*

"Take nothing for granted" is the motto that hangs over
the desk of President Pulliam. Evidently McCormick has
never seen it. When he cracked a grounder to centre in the
fifth inning of the second game [of a doubleheader which
the Giants lost to the Cubs] he loafed a little, thinking it a
sure hit. Evers went over for a fine stop and his throw just
nailed McCormick. It should have been an infield hit.

—New York *Globe*

THURSDAY, SEPTEMBER 24

Censurable stupidity on the part of Merkle yesterday
placed the Giants' chances of winning the pennant in jeopardy. His unusual conduct in the final inning perhaps deprived
New York of a victory that would have been unquestionable
had he not committed a breach in baseball play that resulted
in Umpire O'Day calling the game a tie.

With the game tied in the ninth inning and two outs, and
New York having a runner, McCormick, on third base
waiting for an opportunity to score and Merkle on first
looking for a similar chance, Bridwell hit into centre field, a
fair ball sufficient to win the game had Merkle gone on his

way down the base path while McCormick was scoring. But instead of going to second base, Merkle ran toward the clubhouse, evidently thinking his share in the game had ended when Bridwell hit the ball into safe territory.

Manager Chance quickly grasped the situation and directed the ball be thrown to second base, which would force out Merkle.

Manager Chance ran to second base and the ball was thrown there, but immediately Pitcher McGinnity interfered in the play and a scramble of players ensued, in which, it is said, McGinnity obtained the ball and threw it into the crowd before Chance could complete a force play on Merkle, who was far from the base line. Merkle said he had touched second base, and the Chicago players were equally positive he had not done so.

Chance then appealed to Umpire O'Day for a decision. The crowd, thinking the Giants had won, swarmed on the playing field in such a confusion that none of the fans seemed able to grasp the situation, but finally their attitude toward O'Day became so offensive that the police ran into the crowd and protected the umpire.

Umpire O'Day finally decided the run did not count, and inasmuch as the spectators had gained such large numbers on the field the game could not be resumed O'Day declared the game a tie. Although both Umpires O'Day and Emslie, it is claimed, say they did not see the play at second base, Umpire O'Day's action was based upon the presumption that a force play was made on Merkle.

The singular ending of the game aroused intense interest throughout the city, and everywhere it was the chief topic of discussion.

—New York *Times*

Hofman threw the ball to Evers, but before the latter could step on second base McGinnity, who had been on the coaching line and was on his way to the clubhouse, took a hand and grabbed the ball away from Evers. Evers and Tinker then grabbed McGinnity and wrestled with him trying to get the ball. They weren't successful, for the next minute the ball was sailing over toward the left field bleachers. Some Chicago player rescued it and brought it in. Merkle in the meantime had been trying to go back to second base before the ball could be brought there, and two or three Chicagoans were hanging on to him trying to keep him from the bag.

There were excited cranks surging around the grouped and tussling players and many more swarming around the umpires, on their way to the exit beneath the stand. The Chicago players chased the umpires to find out what ruling had been made, and the cranks gathered around both, jostling, elbowing, and rubbering. The police jumped in quickly and scattered the crowds right and left as the umpires slowly made their way to the exit, the players following at their heels. The umpires made their escape finally and then a crowd tagged on to the heels of Capt. Chance and other Cubs who had been in the wrangling and turmoil. The police blocked off the crowd as the players moved across the field.

Everywhere in the stands and on the field spectators were all at sea as to what had happened and as to the status of the game. The cops were too active for anything in the way of violence to break loose. It was the general impression, too, that New York had won, and there was a feeling of satisfaction over that. Herzog, who had made the first run for the Giants, was carried off the field on the shoulders of a shouting string of admirers.

Charles Murphy, president of the Chicago club, came down from his box in the upper stand to find out what the umpire's decision had been. When O'Day was asked how the game stood he replied: "Emslie says he didn't see the play at second base, and it's no game I suppose."

—New York *Sun*

When Bridwell slammed his hit in the ninth, Merkle, instead of starting promptly for the second bag, made a move toward the clubhouse. Warned by the yells of Little Johnnie Evers, the boy orator, who was entreating Hofman to chuck the ball to the infield, Merkle changed his course and waddled toward second base. The crowd, at this time, was surging out onto the field, and exactly what happened no man can say. But this much is certain: Hofman threw the ball to the infield, it bounced off Evers' back, rolled toward Kling and was finally corralled by Joe McGinnity. When three or four frantic Cubs tried to tear the ball from Joseph's grasp, it disappeared from the scene and plays no further part in the interesting narrative.

Merkle, when he had touched second base, wanted to stay and see the fight out, as Frank Chance, Evers, Steinfeldt, and a few other invaders were making frantic protests to Emslie and O'Day, but Mathewson dragged him away and they went on a run to the clubhouse.

The writer wishes to assure the fans that neither Emslie nor O'Day saw the play at second base, and neither Emslie nor O'Day knows whether Merkle went to second base ahead of or behind the ball. As a matter of fact the ball never got there.

The moment that both umpires started for their little coop, and the crowd started for the "L" and surface cars, members of the visiting club rushed toward Emslie and shouted, "Merkle hasn't touched second base." Emslie kept on going, remarking, in reply, "I didn't see any such play." O'Day also hurried to the shelter of the stand, though Chance tried nobly to get within slugging distance and the gathering thousands from stands and bleachers began to threaten the impetuous Chicago leader in rather ugly fashion.

Hank O'Day and Robert Emslie stayed in that little coop for many moments, talking it over. Emslie, seeing that he has a wig, was the judge, and Hank was the attorney. Many and learned were the arguments going back and forth, because neither of the worthy arbitrators had seen the play, and they were to make up in talk what they lacked in vision. When they finally came out of the gloom, and were braced by a gathering of baseball scribes, Emslie declined to be interviewed and O'Day muttered something about "no game."

—WILLIAM F. KIRK, New York *American*

Never was a victory more cleanly won. The Giants and Cubs gave one of the most brilliant exhibitions of baseball in the history of the game, and all the way the Giants had just that shade of superiority that wins games and pennants. First of all credit must go to Mathewson, who outpitched Pfiester, the southpaw who has bothered the Giants all season, but there was brilliant work all around, and McGraw's men fully justified the confidence of the crowd that went up to the Polo Grounds sure that New York would hold the lead so splendidly earned.

No matter what the ultimate decision as to the game may be, and that decision may determine the ownership of the pennant, yesterday's was a glorious victory.

New York was without the services of Tenney, who has a bad leg, and Merkle, who was to acquire notoriety soon enough, took his place. He played well, but Mathewson dominated the struggle and pitched a game that he has never surpassed in his wonderful career.

—New York *Tribune*

The facts gleaned from active participants and survivors are these: Hofman fielded Bridwell's knock and threw to Evers for a force play on the absent Merkle. But McGinnity cut in and grabbed the ball before it reached the eager Trojan [Evers, who came from Troy, New York]. Three Cubs landed on the Iron Man from as many directions at the same time and jolted the ball from his cruel grasp. It rolled among the spectators who had swarmed upon the diamond like an army of starving potato bugs.

At this thrilling juncture "Kid" Kroh, the demon southpaw, swarmed upon the human potato bugs and knocked six of them galley-west. The triumphant Kroh passed the ball to Steinfeldt, after cleaning up the gang that had it. Tinker wedged in, and the ball was conveyed to Evers for the force-out of Merkle. . . .

Some say Merkle eventually touched second base, but not until he had been forced out by Hofman to McGinnity to six potato bugs to "Kid" Kroh to some more Cubs, and the shrieking, triumphant Mr. Evers, the well-known Troy shoe dealer. There have been some complicated plays in baseball, but we do not recall one like this in a career of years of monkeying with the national pastime.

Peerless Leader Chance ran at O'Day to find out what Hank had to say, but the sparrow cops, specials, 200 cops, and Pinks—slang for Pinkertons—thought Chance was going to bite Hank on the ankle. Half a hundred men in uniform surrounded the P.L. and thousands of bugs surrounded them. Bill Marshall [the utility player usually known as Doc], who is an expert on bacteria, and Del Howard rushed in to help the Peerless Leader. Another squad of cops had O'Day in tow some yards away.

Hank didn't know Chance wanted to converse with him, and they couldn't get together anyhow. Finally the cops got O'Day into a coop under the stand and tried to slam the door in the face of the Peerless Leader. He jammed his robust frame in the opening and defied the sparrow chasers. Chance later got to O'Day, who said Emslie, working on the bases, did not see the second base play because of the crowd, but Hank informed Chance that McCormick's run didn't count.

Still later Hank submitted gracefully to an interview by war scribes. He said Merkle was forced at second and the game ended in a tie. None of the Giants remained to make public statements. Part of the crowd lifted a player in white to their shoulders and bore him to the clubhouse. The Giant thus honored was not Mr. Merkle. He left long before the trouble started.

—CHARLES DRYDEN, Chicago *Tribune*

Merkle lost his head. He started for the clubhouse, but only took a few steps when Matty, waiting his turn at bat, yelled to him. Chance was watching Merkle and frantically called to Hofman to field the ball to second. Hofman was also in the air and began to hunt for the ball. Evers ran down the field waving his arms and legs at Hofman like a guy gone daffy.

The crowd, thinking the game was won, poured over the stands in a surging mass that swept some of the players off their feet.

Just then Chance and Steinfeldt got to second on the run, and those two, with Evers, surrounded McGinnity and began to wrestle with him for possession of the ball. Seeing he was outnumbered, and getting wise to why they wanted the ball, Joe threw it into the left field bleachers.

Where that ball is now no one knows, except perhaps the fan who captured it and has it in a frame over his pillow.

One thing is certain, it never got to second. Merkle got to second. He started late, but he got there. The ball never did.

Chance tore after Emslie, but the crowd blocked his way, not really knowing why they did it, but blocking him all the same.

Chance fought like a real bear, and a grizzly at that, to get to the umpires. He's a husky guy, that Chance, and from the way he almost got through he'd do well on a football team. But you can't buck a line of thousands, and Chance was stalled. He had his lungs with him, however, and did some yelling. This was partly drowned by the yells of the crowd, which had become a mob.

It began to look ugly. Chance was packed in the center of a push that didn't even give him elbow room. And O'Day was in a like predicament.

The near-cops were spectators on the outside fringe of affairs. Then the real blue boys got busy. They formed a flying wedge, and got to the center of the maelstrom. It took a few pokes with their night sticks to do it, but when did a cop hide his stick when it was handy?

They rescued Chance, and the umpires were locked up behind the grand stand for safekeeping until such time as the crowd could be scattered to their homes.

—GYM BAGLEY, New York *Evening Mail*

The Cubs are right, under every rule of baseball law and common sense, and entitled to win their protest. Rules are rules, and clubs having boneheaded mutts on the basepaths deserve only to be penalized.

All honor to Hank O'Day. There has been much roasting of Hank, both on account of the exactly similar Pittsburgh affair some weeks ago [on September 4], and because he seemed to be handing the lemons to the Cubs in all close decisions. But Hank has shown the genuine goods, and has put himself on record as an honest umpire and a game man—all honor and praise to Hank O'Day!

—W. A. PHELON, Chicago *Journal*

It is high time that the league took a decided stand on the rules which are not specific enough for the controversial play of yesterday. It has long been an unwritten baseball law that as soon as a home player crossed the plate with a run that breaks a tie after the eighth inning the game is over that instant. A batter runs out his hit and that is all. If a batter singles and scores a runner from second base, it is necessary for him to touch only first base.

If a game does not end when the winning run scores, then, pray, why does not a batter who makes a long hit get full credit for it? If it is a three-bagger, and a man scores from third, why does not the batter get as many bases as he can take? If a ball is lifted into the bleachers, thereby scoring a runner ahead of the batter, no credit is given for a home run. [Since 1920 a ball thus hit has been ruled a home run.] Then why should base runners be compelled to run around the sack after the winning run has been scored?

If the National League throws out the game on such a technicality the organization does not deserve any more of the splended patronage it has had in this city. When games are played in an office with technicalities by politicians of the game, it is time for ping-pong to be chosen for the great American game.

—SID MERCER, New York *Globe*

"When I saw Merkle leave the base path," declares Christy Mathewson, "I ran after him and brought him back to second base, so as to make our lead unquestionable. He was on second base after McGinnity tossed away the ball, following his tussle with the Chicago players. Maybe Evers got the ball and touched the base afterward. If he did it didn't prove anything. I can state positively that no force play was made before Merkle got to the base. He wanted to stick there when he saw the scrapping on the diamond, but I pulled him away, and we went to the clubhouse.'' [A myth later developed, and continues to receive support in print, that because Mathewson, unable to tell a lie, informed National League President Pulliam that Merkle had not touched second base, Pulliam ruled the game a tie.]

—New York *Globe*

FRIDAY, SEPTEMBER 25

Following a sleepless night of agony throughout the length and breadth of Manhattan haggard bugs waited all morning for President Pulliam's decision on the riotous windup of Wednesday's game. War scribes from far and near assembled in Pulliam's outer office, where he conversed on general topics in his usual affable manner. Then he retired to the inner sanctum and sent out a neatly typewritten ruling, which in effect ruled the game a 1 to 1 tie.

Barring himself within the inner precincts, Mr. Pulliam declined to see anybody, nor would he come forth to reveal the future. Questions sent in by scribes came back in the original state—unanswered. Nothing was said about playing off the tie game, as provided by the league constitution, which says such games shall be played. As this is the last day the game could be played, the Giants are subject to a fine. It rests with the home club to arrange such matters but McGraw announced last night the contest would not be played over.

Umpires O'Day and Emslie were present in Pulliam's office when the decision was rendered. Secretary Williams of the Cubs notified these officials the Chicago team would be at the Polo Grounds at 1:30 today [September 24], the regular hour for starting double headers. Hank and Bob were dumb as clams. All they did was do a looking listening part.

Thinking the Giants might assemble on the field at 1:30 and attempt to put something over, the Cubs swallowed a quick lunch and hiked to the scene of combat. A dozen

Giants were there in uniform, with a crowd pouring in, but the locals made no effort to line up in battle array. At 1:30 the Peerless Leader put a complete team on the field, with Coakley pitching and Kling behind the bat. Tom Needham kindly stood at the plate with a pestle in his hand while Coakley pitched four balls. There were no umpires to tell Needham whether he struck out or got a pass.

The bugs howled derision, but Chance had made his little play and will claim the game by forfeit.

—CHARLES DRYDEN, Chicago *Tribune*

I have never seen local lovers of the game so fairly boiling over with anger as they were yesterday when President Pulliam's decision was announced. Eddie Tolcott voiced the opinion of all true lovers of the game when he said to me yesterday: "There was never a more hideous outrage committed. It is a slur on the great national game, the sport we all love and admire above all others for its heretofore absolute cleanliness and absence of all taint of dishonesty or unfairness.

"That the foundation of the sport should be undermined by such a contemptible trick is shameful. If the Cubs win the pennant by that one game they stole from the Giants, the streamer would amount to nothing but a dirty, dishonored dishrag. The Cubs' title to the championship would be discredited and the name Champions would be an empty honor. It is simply a disgrace that any gentleman connected with the national game should stoop to such unsportsmanlike methods as I understand President Murphy has. If the Giants are robbed of their fair victory I shall be ashamed to say I was ever connected with baseball."

—SAM CRANE, New York *Evening Journal*

One of the remarkable things in this baseball race is the attitude of Mr. Fan and all his family and friends toward the late disaster at the Polo Grounds. Truly, John McGraw should feel grateful for the sympathy of almost the entire baseball world in the controversy over that memorable battle with the Cubs.

For doing what is right Umpire Hank O'Day and President Pulliam are being condemned all over the country, while Frank Chance and his Cubs are everywhere being branded as poor sportsmen because, forsooth, they acted with intelligence and took advantage of the rules to gain an edge in a race that is so close that every fraction counts.

The game of baseball takes nothing for granted. Because the play happened to be a final one does not make it excusable to slur the rule. It is just as much a crime against the baseball code to fail to complete a play at the end of a game as in the middle. Merkle was asleep and worked his little dab of gray matter very poorly. He paid the penalty of thoughtlessness, just as he must have paid the penalty had he been caught asleep off base.

Frank Chance was a man on his job. He saw the mistake and took advantage of it, and for this he deserves not condemnation but praise for his watchfulness and thoughtfulness.

As a matter of fact, the Giants deserved not merely to have the game declared a tie, but to forfeit it. McGinnity's effort to stop the play by throwing away the ball is distinctly interference, the penalty for which is loss of the battle. And if you probe that cautious mind of John J. McGraw, you will probably find him secretly satisfied that no worse result followed the indiscretions of Merkle and McGinnity.

—JOHN E. WRAY, St. Louis *Post-Dispatch*

SATURDAY, OCTOBER 10

During the last few days many veteran ball players have come to the front and spoken in behalf of Fred Merkle, the young Giant who has been unmercifully roasted by many fans for his alleged failure to touch second base at the finish of the memorable September 23 contest. Seasoned ball players like Joe Kelley, Bill Dahlen, Billy Gilbert, Willie Keeler, Frank Bowerman, and manager Billy Murray of the Philadelphia Club, are among them. They call attention to the fact that ever since the rule was adopted under which a game ends when the team last at bat scores the winning run, players have run for the clubhouse as soon as the runner crossed the plate, without advancing to the next base.

—New York *World*

Hot shots and the 3-1 drill.

The Pitcher as Fielder

Jim Kaplan

Several members of the Texas pitching staff were sitting in the clubhouse one afternoon discussing the importance of fielding. They were quick to agree with Los Angeles manager Tommy Lasorda's assertion that a good-fielding pitcher can help himself with another two games a year. "It's really very simple," said Burt Hooton. "It's a question of a pitcher's very function: not putting too many runners on base."

"As soon as you release the ball," put in Dave Schmidt, "you're a fielder."

"When Ed Halicki was with the Giants," said Charlie Hough, "he was told he'd be sent down after his next start. Then he found himself protecting a one-run lead in the ninth. Somebody hit a liner at him, and he barehanded it and threw to first for a double play. He went on to win the game. He wasn't sent down."

"Fernando Valenzuela is the best I've ever seen at fielding grounders hit right at him," said Hooton. "Unlike most of us, he gets his glove all the way down. He's not as great at covering first."

JIM KAPLAN is the author of the soon-to-be published *Playing the Field* from Algonquin Books; this essay derives from it.

"But that's the most important thing a pitcher can do on defense!" said Dave Rozema.

Hence, the critical and evocative drill that starts every spring training. The play is the very essence of spring: grounder to first, pitcher covering. It's as simple as three to one.

"It's gathering time, like a class reunion," says former major league pitcher Jim Kaat (see box). "All of a sudden, you're in the home room, with nineteen or twenty pitchers talking about what happened during the winter."

And working on the 3-1 play. It's a drill pitchers practice before they work a single game, a play they repeat until they see it in their dreams. That's because Lasorda and the Rangers were right about pitchers winning games with their gloves, and there's probably no play they make more often than the 3-1 putout.

The drill takes longer than any other because of the number of players involved. All the pitchers—veterans, rookies, minor-leaguers up for a quick look—participate, along with three or four first basemen. A weathered coach bats out grounders.

"It's a more difficult drill for the pitcher than for us first basemen," says Chris Chambliss, who starred for the Indians, Yankees and Braves, "because none of them run it as often as each of us does. They're not as accustomed to the play. Besides, during the game they're thinking of getting the batter out, and I'm thinking of playing defense."

Games can turn on how fast a pitcher reacts. "I learned to break for first on any ball hit to the right side of the infield," says Kaat, who won more Gold Gloves (16) than any pitcher. "When a hitter beats a pitcher, nine times out of ten it's because the pitcher didn't get a jump." Kaat used to head for a spot ten to fifteen feet down the line from first base. Then he'd turn sharply left and race parallel to the line. If all went well, he'd catch the first baseman's toss a couple of steps ahead of the base. Then he'd look for the base and touch it with his right foot to avoid colliding with the runner. "If you practice it enough," says Kaat, "you'll get your footwork down like a hurdler."

Of course, the play is not as simple as the neat 3-1 on our scorecard. For one thing, the throw doesn't always go from first baseman to pitcher. A bunt or slowly topped grounder can be fielded by either player. (If both converge on the ball, the second baseman should cover first, but for some reason, he rarely participates in the spring-training drill.) Also, the first baseman's throw to the pitcher may not be perfect. "I look for bad throws because I know I can handle the good ones," says Phil Niekro of the Indians. Niekro also doesn't panic about tagging the bag. Pitchers usually err when they look for the base before they have the ball.

The play looks simple enough when the ball is hit sharply to the first baseman, who then flips an underhand throw, chest-high, to the pitcher a couple of steps before he reaches the bag. Things start getting complicated, both in practice and games, when a ball is hit any distance to a first baseman's right. An underhand toss won't get the job done in such instances; the throw must then be sidearm or overhand and may not be right on the money.

A 3-1 play figured in the most exciting Series finale ever played. The Yankees were leading the Pirates 7-5 in the eighth inning of the 1960 Series' seventh game, with Pittsburgh runners on second and third and two outs. When Roberto Clemente hit a chopper to the right of first baseman Moose Skowron, a standard 3-1 should have ended the inning. Unfortunately for the Yankees, Bobby Shantz, the best-fielding pitcher of his time, had been replaced by the sluggish Jim Coates. When Coates was slow covering first, Clemente was safe, a run scored and the stage was set for a three-run homer by Hal Smith. The Pirates eventually won 10-9. Yankee fans are still fuming over manager Casey Stengel's decision to replace Shantz with Coates.

Fielding would be tough enough for a pitcher if the 3-1 play were all he had to make. It's not. The pitcher has to break to his left fast enough to cut off a drag bunt down the first-base line; if the ball gets by him, it's invariably a hit. Sometimes the 3-1 play doesn't occur because the first baseman doesn't get to a slowly hit ball in the hole. The second baseman does, and the play goes to the pitcher, 4-1.

Another corollary to the 3-1 play is the 3-6-1 double play. The first baseman fields a ball in the hole and throws to the shortstop covering second. With the first baseman out of the play, the shortstop then relays to the pitcher covering first. In this case, the pitcher somehow catches the ball as he's looking back over his left shoulder. Then he has to find the bag. Strange things can happen. On May 24, 1985, Hough induced Boston's Rich Gedman to hit a double-play ball with the Rangers leading the Red Sox by one run in the ninth, one out, and men on first and third. Gedman hit a one-hopper to first baseman Pete O'Brien, who threw to shortstop Curtis Wilkerson covering second. Then Wilkerson relayed to first. Hough caught the ball, stepped on first to end the game—and tripped over the bag.

Most of the time a pitcher's fielding is no laughing matter. There's often a direct correlation between good fielders and big winners. Consider some of the most respected fielders to pitch in the last ten years. Tom Seaver. Jim Kaat. Fernando Valenzuela. Phil Niekro. Ron Guidry. By no coincidence, all of them may be Hall of Fame candidates.

Here's what a pitcher can do to help his team win a game. On June 28, 1974, the Cubs were leading the Expos 2-1 in the ninth, with Montreal runners on first and third and one out, when Ron Hunt tried to lay down a suicide squeeze bunt. He popped it up along the first-base line, and Cub pitcher Rick Reuschel dove for the ball and caught it just a few inches off the ground. Then he threw to first to double up a runner and end the game. Not for nothing is Reuschel considered the best-fielding active pitcher in baseball.

Here's what a pitcher can do to win a big game. In the fifth game of the 1964 World Series, the Cardinals' Bob Gibson, a righthander who always twisted toward the first-base line on his follow-through, was hit on the buttock by a liner off the bat of the Yankees' Joe Pepitone. The ball caromed over to the third-base line. After spinning around Michael Jackson-style, Gibson ran the ball down, retrieved it, and threw out Pepitone in what became the game's pivotal play. "It didn't seem like much at the time, but I still don't know how I did it," says Gibson. Other pitchers often contribute to losses by dropping throws from their first basemen. That's what happened to the Cardinals' Dave LaPoint in the 1982 World Series.

The only play a pitcher is likely to make as often as the 3-1 putout is the throw to first, second, or occasionally third on a bunt situation. It's a play that doesn't come easily. After all, the pitcher is accustomed to being totally in charge before throwing the ball. Look at him out there: standing on the rubber, taking a deep breath, assuming the proper grip, throwing when ready. Suddenly, the ball's in play and he must field it, turn, sight the base, and throw quickly—all without getting a good grip on the ball. Often his throw is hurried. Often it's off. In one of baseball's strangest ironies, the man who holds the ball and initiates the action comes unglued.

"On a bunt situation the most important thing is the first three steps," says Kaat. "Coming off the mound the pitcher should take three strong strides. The closer he gets to the ball, the smaller his strides should be, so that he can get his body under control. While listening to his catcher tell him which base to throw to, he should get his hand up to the throwing position as quickly as possible. That way the fielder he's throwing to can see the ball, and the pitcher can make a better throw. Finally, he should spin off his back foot and take a little crow-hop before throwing. That gets his body under control and his momentum going toward the base."

There are other defensive jobs a pitcher must familiarize himself with. Like backing up third or home if a play is being made there. The idea is not to stand near the catcher or third baseman, but near the fence; that way, a pitcher can reach overthrows that kick to the side as well as those that go through the fielder.

Holding runners on base is another defensive skill the pitcher must master. Actually the term "pickoff" is misunderstood. The idea isn't as much to pick off a runner as it is to keep him close to the base. To put it another way, a pitcher who picks off fifteen runners a season but allows thirty to steal may not be as valuable as a pitcher who picks off two or three but allows none to steal.

Not that a pickoff can't be useful. Tied 3-3 with the Blue Jays, the Orioles were forced to use a reserve infielder, Lenn Sakata, as their tenth-inning catcher. Three Toronto players reached first. None stole second, or even tried to. Tippy Martinez picked off each one.

White Sox great Wilbur Wood would throw to first so many times the runner would be lulled to sleep. Most often the key ingredient isn't the throw to first as much as the quick throw home. The pitchers who do this best are those who don't waste time. They come to the "stop" position on their windup with their weight on their back foot, so they won't have to rock back before throwing. And they minimize the leg kick and throwing motion. A quick delivery invariably follows. A pitch that reaches the plate in 1.2 seconds or less won't yield many stolen bases because the average catcher can get the ball to second in 2.0. The total of 3.2 is quicker than most baserunners with a lead can get from first to second.

Finally, there's the business of handling grounders like any other infielder. Hall of Famer Whitey Ford was so adept at fielding balls up the middle that his shortstop and second baseman could play unusually wide of the bag. In short, Ford affected the entire Yankee infield. Tom Seaver often takes 30 minutes of fielding practice, working not only on catching the ball but making the difficult turnaround throw to second. The most difficult fielding play a pitcher makes on grounders is the high bouncer hit over his head. Bob Gibson made one of these back-to-the-plate plays, turned almost all the way around in midair and threw a basketball chest pass to first. Hall of Fame pitcher Dizzy Dean called it the best fielding play he ever saw. "You have to think about the ball being hit to you, want it," says White Sox scout Bart Johnson, a former big-league pitcher. "Then you have to know what to do with it. Look at how well-trained the Detroit and Baltimore pitchers are; after they've fielded the ball, they get rid of it as quickly as anyone."

All of which is mere prelude to the real blood and guts of

fielding the pitching position: staying alive. Let Johnson describe the starkness of it all. "We pitchers always get a kick out of third base being described as the hot corner," he says. "Hot corner? If the third baseman crept in fifty feet from home plate, people would say, 'He's nuts: He'll get harelip.' We pitchers are fifty feet from home every time we follow through!"

Every pitcher has been hit on some part of his anatomy by a line drive or hard-hit ground ball. Most escape without serious injury. All live in fear of experiencing the same fate as Cleveland's Herb Score. Once boasting a fastball reminiscent of Bob Feller's, Score was hit in the face in 1957 by a line drive off the bat of the Yankees' Gil McDougald. Score was never the same again. Nor was the White Sox' Wood after his kneecap was shattered by a Ron LeFlore liner in 1976.

Pitchers have their best and worst moments contending with these shots. Before fielding Luis Salazar's sharp one-hopper early in 1985, Yankee reliever Dave Righetti made a 180-degree turn on his follow-through. Then he caught the ball between his legs. "All that was," Righetti said truthfully, "was protecting myself." Even more memorable was a play Gibson made on Orlando Cepeda. A Cepeda line drive shattered Gibson's leg. Gibson picked up the ball and threw out Cepeda. Then Gibson was carried to the hospital. Talk about profiles in courage. For years there's been a lively debate about how a pitcher should prepare for hard-hit balls at him. "You show me a pitcher following through in good fielding position and I'll show you a pitcher who ain't following through," said Dean. Actually, there have been some pitchers like Seaver who naturally finish the delivery square to the hitter and glove held high. "It's a delicate balance," says Kaat. "You don't want to alter a pitcher's motion to the point where he isn't throwing his best stuff, but you do want him to protect himself." For his part, Kaat resisted the temptation to wear a huge glove. He might have better protected his face that way, but he probably would have restricted his mobility. Kaat wore a small but supple mitt and took his chances.

The bottom line is that every pitcher can protect himself only so much in the face of 150-mph liners. He needs some luck, too. That's why pitchers think less about their hospital bill and more about the 3-1 drill. It's straightforward. It's sociable. And it's safe.

Kaat's Poise

In 1959 a big, teenaged kid out of Michigan named James Lee Kaat ambled onto a major league field for the first time, wearing the uniform of the Washington Senators. In 1983 a 43-year-old Jim Kaat played his last major league game, for the St. Louis Cardinals. In between he made an excellent case for selection to the Hall of Fame. Kaat had pitched an unprecedented twenty-five years over four decades in the big leagues, won 283 games, helped to popularize the quick-pitch delivery, and revolutionized training methods by continuing to throw between starts. But Kaat will be equally well remembered for his fielding. He won 16 Gold Gloves—more than any other pitcher. He could make all the plays in the field, and he could explain how to do them, too. That's why he went on to coach the Cincinnati Reds pitching staff in 1985.

"A pitcher's got to be aware that almost every time the ball is hit, there's someplace he's got to be other than the mound," says Kaat, who is now in broadcasting. "Ball hit to the right side: Cover first. A single: Back up the second baseman so that the first baseman can stay on the bag and prevent the runner from taking liberties. Base hit with a man on first: Back up third. Base hit with a man in scoring position: Back up the plate."

Among the greatest-fielding pitchers of all time, you can make an equally strong case for either Bob Gibson or Jim Kaat. Gibson is celebrated for spectacular plays; Kaat prided himself on perfecting the more routine but also more frequent plays. No one made the

3-1 putout better. No one moved faster to his right coming off the mound. And certainly no one thought more intelligently about fielding. Asked which play he remembers most fondly, Kaat cites the three 3-1 plays he and Minnesota first baseman Harmon Killebrew made on the Dodgers' speedy Willie Davis in a 1965 World Series game. He's also proud of the many grounders that he turned into double plays.

Not that Kaat couldn't make spectacular plays, too. He once raced over to the dugout to make a sensational grab of a foul ball his catcher had lost sight of. And a memorable series of events brought Kaat's fielding to the world's attention in the first place.

"There was a game in 1962 when I was hit in the mouth by a high-bouncing grounder," he says. "The play cost me six teeth. The next time I pitched, two ground balls were hit back to me—sharp one-hoppers— and I got them both. People took note." He won the first of his 16 consecutive Gold Gloves that year.

Like most of the good-fielding pitchers, Kaat was an excellent athlete. "Growing up, I was always one of the smaller kids, and I had quick reflexes and good coordination," says Kaat, who excelled in basketball, golf and handball as well as baseball. "When I reached my full height (6'5"), I still had these qualities." Of equal importance, Kaat had an agile mind. Long before it was fashionable, he was giving up red meat and stressing strength, flexibility, and stretching exercises in his training. While other pitchers were haphazard in their fielding practice, Kaat rehearsed every play he'd have to make until it became second nature. And as a coach he made sure his pitchers did likewise. "We had a drill," he says, "in which pitchers used a cloth-covered 'Incrediball.' They hit it at each other as hard as they can from 50 feet. It sharpens their reflexes."

It's obvious that Kaat's influence on fielding will be felt long after the end of his playing career.

Was Rickey Henderson born to run?

Diamond Stars

John B. Holway

Jiminy Christmas! By the great heavenly stars! Was Rickey Henderson *born* to steal bases?

You bet your sweet ephemeris he was.

Henderson was born Christmas Day 1958, a good day to be born if you want to grow up to be a big league base-stealing champion. For that makes him a Capricorn (Dec. 22-Jan. 19). In fact, he was born almost exactly 99 years after Hugh Nicol, the flying Scot, who set the old record (that still stands) of 138 back in 1887. Nicol was born New Year's day 1858. Another Capricorn speedster, Max Carey (born January 11, 1890), led the league in steals ten times, a record.

Since 1876, 195 big league stolen-base crowns have been won, and Capricorns have captured 29 of them, well above their fair share of 16.

But look at Pisces (Feb. 19-Mar. 20) like Bert Campaneris: They've won 31, twice as many as they should be expected to win.

Down at the other end of the list, the poor Cancers (June

JOHN B. HOLWAY is co-author of *The Pitcher* and author of *Voices from the Great Black Baseball Leagues*.

20-July 22) have won only three of the 195 titles. Latest to do it was Willie Wilson in 1979. Now there's a man who seems to have figuratively outrun his stars.

BASE-STEALING CHAMPIONS

Sign	Dates	Titles	
Pisces	Feb. 19-Mar. 20	31	Campaneris 6, Wagner 5, Reiser 2, Ashburn
Capricorn	Dec. 22-Jan. 19	29	Carey 10, Henderson 7, Taveras, Nicol
Sagittarius	Nov. 22-Dec. 21	24	Cobb 6, Minoso 3, Bruton 3, Moreno 2
Taurus	Apr. 20-May 20	24	Aparicio 9, Mays 4, Lopes 2, North 2, Otis
Gemini	May 21-June 20	19	Brock 8, Werber 3, Galan 2, LeFlore
Virgo	Aug. 23-Sept. 22	20	Raines 4, Cuyler 4, Dillinger, 3, Frisch 3, Coleman 2
Libra	Sept. 23-Oct. 22	13	Wills 6, Patek, Murtagh, Crosetti
Aquarius	Jan. 20-Feb. 18	11	J Robinson 2, Schoendienst
Scorpio	Oct. 23-Nov. 21	11	Case 6, Stirnweiss 2, Rivers, Tolan
Aries	Mar. 21-Apr. 29	6	Sisler 4, Milan 2
Leo	Jul. 23-Aug. 22	4	Reese, Frey, Isbell
Cancer	Jun. 21-Jul. 22	3	W Wilson, Rivera, Hartsel

Total: 195

What are the chances of such a distribution—31 on the high side, three on the low—occurring by chance? To find out, I asked Edgar "Pete" Palmer, statistician and co-author of *The Hidden Game of Baseball*. Pete punched some numbers into his computer and came up with the answer. This could indeed have happened by chance—once in ten million times.

Note that the top six signs account for 75 percent of all titles, the bottom six only 25 percent.

Note also that winter babies (Pisces, Capricorn, Aquarius) account for 71 titles, summer babies only 27, or about one-third as many.

Why?

I don't know why, I just know that they do.

Palmer questions whether repeat winners should be allowed, saying they skew the averages unfairly. Personally, I feel that a Luis Aparicio, with nine titles, deserves more weight than a Topsy Hartsel, with one. So we decided to do it both ways—total championships and total individual champions—and let the reader take his choice.

Pisces leads the total titles list with 16 percent. It also leads the total individual champions list with 14.5 percent. However, since the second list is less than half as large, the odds go down dramatically. It is far harder to toss 90 heads out of 100 than to toss nine heads out of ten. The percentages are the same, but the odds are vastly different.

Anyway, the odds on individual winners came to 40-1. Statisticians say anything over 20-1 is "significant." So, using even conservative numbers, the data pretty well rule out chance as an explanation.

Numbers like these intrigue me. A stubborn Scorpio, I began checking data in a dozen categories—Presidents, Congressmen, Academy Award Winners, Nobel laureates, Pulitzer Prize winners, and on and on.

Of course, I was especially anxious to check the old wives' tale that Scorpios make the best lovers and wrote to Masters and Johnson to see if they had any data on that. They replied huffily that they don't lend themselves to such research. A pity. Science will always be the poorer for it.

Meanwhile, you don't have to believe in astrology to read statistics, and the data I found made me pause and scratch my head and ask "why?"

I should say that I also did a thorough study of biorhythms and sports, checking over 1,000 performances in baseball, football, tennis, track and field, boxing, and swimming. I must report that I found absolutely no statistical confirmation of this seemingly scientific but—I'm convinced—actually fraudulent theory. If anyone wants to bet on the World Series, the Super Bowl, or a heavyweight title fight on the basis of biorhythm alone, let him see me. I'll be glad to take all the money he has.

On the other hand, astrology, which smacks of unscientific magic, produces numbers far outside what the law of averages says is normal. It seems downright unfair that a man's birthday can give him an advantage in stealing bases or hitting home runs, but then life has always been unfair. Athletes are not typical of the rest of us. They're taller, heavier, have better eyesight, better muscle tone, superior hand-eye coordination, etc. They also differ, I now must add, in their birthdays.

BIG LEAGUE STARS

Palmer was also skeptical, so like a good SABR member, he decided to do some scientific checking. He ran a massive computer study on all 9,388 men who had played major league baseball from 1909 through 1981. His readout produced an almost perfect sine curve of births arranged along the calendar year:

If you want to grow up to be a big league player, Palmer found, you'd be wise to plan to be born roughly between July 20 and Christmas, that is, from Leo through Sagittarius. The best time of all is late summer. Virgo (Aug. 24-Sept.23) has produced 921 players, or 18 percent more than normal. In fact it leads at every position except shortstop and third base.

The worst time to be born is early spring, as an Aries

(March 21 to April 20). Only 681 big league players were born then, 11 percent below normal, and 35 percent less than those born Virgos.

Incidentally, this is almost the same result I got in a study of pro football players in 1977. Virgo was way out in front, Aries next to last.

Suppose you throw 9,388 darts at a large round dart board divided into 12 slices and spinning furiously. Assuming that all the darts hit the board, what is the chance that 921 will land in one section and only 681 in another?

The chance, Palmer found, is over 700 million to one!

Of course, not all slices of the zodiacal pie are exactly the same size. Cancer has 32 days, Pisces 29.

And births are not distributed equally throughout the calendar. However, authorities disagree on which are the high-birth months and which the low. One study says Gemini (May 22-June 21) has the fewest births, Aquarius (Jan. 21-Feb. 19) the most. But another study is just the other way around.

At any rate, the difference is not great, 15 percent at the most. It hardly explains why Pisces has more than ten times as many stolen-base championships as Cancer.

But, strangely, Palmer found, although Virgos get on the team more than anyone else, once they're in uniform, they don't particularly excel. They're about average in combined batting average and home runs among hitters, as well as earned run average and won-lost records for pitchers.

About the only outstanding Virgos in big league annals are Ted Williams, Roger Maris, Frank Robinson, and Larry Lajoie. Virgos are supposed to be painstaking perfectionists. If that's true, it certainly describes Williams at least. And if there is any validity to these data, then Ted, who had to overcome so much—five years at war, a difficult home park, a variety of injuries—apparently had to overcome his stars as well.

BATTING CHAMPS

Palmer's study reveals another anomaly. Aries, the least likely to get on a team, are collectively the best hitters once they do land a job. Their combined batting average is .267. The average for all signs is .262. Leo (mid-summer) has the worst average, .259.

In fact, the batting average curve is almost the exact opposite of the total players' curve, with above average figures in the late winter and early spring (Pisces through Taurus) and average or below-average figures for the rest of the year.

My own study of 206 big league batting champs, 1876-1986, confirms Palmer's finding: Two spring signs, Aries and Taurus, are among the tops in producing batting champions. Late winter and early spring are the high periods. All other signs, except Sagittarius, are average or below.

BATTING CHAMPIONS

Sign	Titles	
Taurus	26	Hornsby 7, Brett 2, Mattingly, Gwynn, Mays
Sagittarius	25	Cobb 12, DiMaggio 2, Buckner, Kaline, Kuenn, Garr
Aries	23	Rose 3, Waner 3, Sisler 2, Appling 2, Speaker
Pisces	21	Wagner 8, Ashburn 2, Reiser
Libra	17	Carew 7, Foxx 2, Oliver, Hernandez, Mantle
Leo	15	Clemente 4, Heilmann 4, Yastrzemski 3
Cancer	15	Oliva 3, W Wilson, Torre, Boudreau
Virgo	15	T Williams 6, Lajoie 3, F Robinson, Carty, Raines
Aquarius	14	Aaron 2, Lansford, Lynn, Ruth, J Robinson

Scorpio	13	Musial 6, McGee, Terry
Gemini	13	Boggs 3, Simmons 2, B Williams, Gehrig
Capricorn	9	Madlock 4, M Alou, Mize
Total:	*206*	

Don Mattingly and Tony Gwynn gave Taurus a sweep in 1984 and put their sign into first place, for the first time overtaking Ty Cobb and the other Sagittarians.

However, if Scorpio Stan Musial had been born one day later, his seven titles would have put Sagittarius out of reach—for the present, at least.

Stan is not the only champ to overcome his stars. The 1985 king, Willie McGee, is also a Scorpio. Wade Boggs has won three titles so far for the next-to-last Geminis. And Bill Madlock won three for last-place Capricorn, which proves, perhaps—as the astrologers admit—that the stars impel, they don't compel. Long shots do come in. I just wouldn't bet on them, that's all.

Let's look at the favorites. Taurus, Sagittarius, and Aries make up 25 percent of the zodiac but account for 36 percent of all batting championships, over half of all .400 hitters, and more than half of the lifetime 3,000-hit men. Two of the three, Sagittarius and Aries, have produced the six longest batting streaks of this century—Sagittarians Cobb (twice) and DiMaggio, and Aries Rose, Sisler, and Holmes.

The quintessential baseball Aries is Pete Rose. Who can forget the image of Rose barreling into catcher Ray Fosse to win the 1974 All-Star Game, a scene as indelibly engraved into the baseball psyche as the famous photo of Cobb flying into third with spikes flashing?

Aries are the "I am," take-charge egotists of the zodiac; they supposedly love the spotlight and usually hog it in conversation and everything else. Aries lead all other signs in winning Academy Awards (Marlon Brando, Gregory Peck, Paul Newman, Spencer Tracy, William Holden, Bette Davis, Joan Crawford, Liza Minelli).

Capricorns come next to Sagittarians in the calendar, but they rank at the bottom among batting champions, with only nine. One of those was Elmer Flick, who won in 1906 with a .306 average, second lowest winning average ever.

HOME RUNS

Home run champions show a strong preference for being born in the autumn and winter. All of these signs, except Capricorn, are average or above. All the spring and summer signs, without exceptions, are average and below.

The best sign of all for power hitters is Libra. Out of 224 home run titles won or shared since 1876, Libras have won 34, five times as many as last-place Gemini. Libra Mike Schmidt alone has won eight crowns. Mickey Mantle, Jimmie Foxx, and Chuck Klein each won four, and Ed Mathews two.

Thanks to Schmidt, Libra has now vaulted into first place, overtaking the mighty Aquarians—Babe Ruth, Hank Aaron, Ernie Banks, and Ben Oglivie—who had been kings of the sluggers until Schmidt brought the age of Aquarius to an end.

HOME RUN CHAMPIONS

Sign	*Titles*	
Libra	34	Schmidt 8, Mantle 4, Foxx 4, Klein 4, Mathews 2
Aquarius	28	Ruth 12, Aaron 4, Banks 2, Oglivie
Pisces	28	Ott 6, Rice 3, Murphy 2, Stargell 2, Allen 2, Baker 2, Murray
Sagittarius	27	Kingman 3, Foster 2, DiMaggio 2, Thomas, Bench
Taurus	18	Jackson 4, Mays 4, H Wilson, 4, Hornsby 2

Scorpio	18	Kiner 7, Barfield, Sievers
Cancer	17	Killebrew 6, Armas
Virgo	15	T Williams 4, Maris, F Robinson, Cepeda, Snider
Aries	14	Cravath 6
Capricorn	13	Mize 4, Greenberg 4, McCovey 3, Conigliaro, Grich
Leo	8	Howard 2, Nettles, Yastrzemski, Colavito
Gemini	6	Gehrig 3, Darrel Evans
Total:	*224*	

Darrell Evans is another one who overcame the accident of birth. He's not only the oldest home run champ, he's a Gemini, the least likely sign to lead the league.

The greatest slugger of all, Josh Gibson (962 home runs), was a Sagittarius. Sadaharu Oh is a Taurus.

As the chart shows, autumn through winter (Libra through Pisces) is the best time to be born if you want to grow up to be a home run champ. But the month-to-month swings are too erratic to sustain any simple seasonal theory. Aquarius, with 28 home run titles, for example, comes right after Capricorn, with only 13. There is obviously something else at work here besides the earth's journey around the sun. If it is not astrology, whatever it may be deserves some serious study.

April 8, 1974, was a particularly good day for Aquarians. If Hank Aaron had let his eye stray from the sports pages for a moment, he would have read in Sydney Omarr's syndicated horoscope column the following forecast for himself:

> Advancement indicated. Views are vindicated. You receive compliments from professional superior. You make significant gains. Profit potential increases. . . . Standing in the community is elevated.

* * *

That night Aaron went out and hit his million-dollar 715th home run, the one that broke Babe Ruth's lifetime record.

PITCHERS—ERA

Pitchers show a different profile altogether.

Palmer found that there have been more Virgo pitchers in the big leagues than any other sign, just as there are more Virgos in general. Capricorn has produced the fewest pitchers.

Yet strangely, Virgos are only average as a group once they get on the team. Sagittarians, like Steve Carlton, have the best combined won-lost record, as well as the best combined earned run average. Cancers have the worst won-lost mark, Geminis the worst ERA.

My own study of ERA champs shows that Pisces Steve McCatty and J.R. Richard have pitched their sign into first place among individual winners, edging Aries (Don Sutton, Phil Niekro, Cy Young) by 28 to 27. The two signs incidentally come next to each other on the calendar—late winter and early spring.

Yet, again, the month-to-month differences are so large they rule out an easy seasonal explanation. Aquarius comes right before Pisces on the calendar, but it's dead last in ERA titles, with only seven.

Aquarian Nolan Ryan was really bucking the stars when he won in 1981. However, Aquarians are the only sign to produce one man who won all three titles—ERA, home runs, and batting. His name, of course, was Babe Ruth. (But note that Babe gave up pitching and took up slugging full-time. Did his stars impel him?)

For four straight years, 1982-85, Cancer produced one of the two ERA kings—Rick Honeycutt, Alejandro Pena, Rick Sutcliffe, and Dave Stieb.

ERA CHAMPIONS

Sign	Titles	
Pisces	28	Grove 9, Alexander 5, McCatty, Richard
Aries	27	Joss 2, Young, Sutton, P Niekro, Hunter
Libra	20	Palmer 2, Capra, McCormick, Podres, Waddell
Scorpio	20	Johnson 5, Seaver 3, Gooden, Rogers, Candalaria, Gibson, Marichal*
Cancer	19	Hubbell 3, Covaleskie 2, Stieb, Pena, Sutcliffe, Tanana, Lopat
Leo	19	Mathewson 5, Wilhelm 2, Blue, Fydrich, Clemens
Capricorn	16	Koufax 5, R Jones, Wynn, Lyons
Virgo	14	Guidry 2, Chandler 2, McDowell, Hoyt
Taurus	13	Spahn 3, Peters 2, Newhouser 2, Walsh 2, Scott
Sagittarius	12	Tiant 2, Gomez 2, Carlton, Swan, Burdette
Gemini	9	Chance, Parnell, Cicotte
Aquarius	8	Ryan, Hammaker, Bosman, Reynolds, Ruth
Total:	*205*	

*Marichal's birthday is variously listed as October 24 (Scorpio) and October 20 (Libra).

(Satchel Paige was a Cancer. Smoky Joe Williams, once voted the best pitcher in blackball history, was an Aries.)

PITCHERS—STRIKEOUTS

Power hitters differ astrologically from singles hitters. Do power pitchers, the strikeout kings, also differ from finesse pitchers, the ERA champs?

They sure do.

I haven't counted all the individual strikeout titles won, but on the list of the ten top strikeout pitchers of all time, four are Scorpios—Walter Johnson, Tom Seaver, and Bob Gibson. A fourth Scorpio, Bob Feller, would surely be on the list, perhaps at the top of it, if he hadn't lost his four best years in the Navy. Two Scorpio youngsters will probably join the list within 15 years—Dwight Gooden and Fernando Valenzuela.

Nolan Ryan, the all-time champ, is an Aquarius, the only one in the top ten. The entire list, as of Opening Day 1987:

ALL-TIME STRIKEOUT LEADERS

Pitcher	*Sign*	*SO*
Nolan Ryan	Aquarius	4282
Steve Carlton	Sagittarius	4006
Tom Seaver	Scorpio	3640
Gaylord Perry	Virgo	3534
Walter Johnson	Scorpio	3508
Don Sutton	Aries	3431
Phil Niekro	Aries	3278
Ferguson Jenkins	Sagittarius	3192
Bob Gibson	Scorpio	3117
Bert Blylever	Aries	3090

(The leading strikeout pitcher of all time, with 4490—Japan's Masaichi Kaneda—is a Leo.)

Will the day ever come when big league scouts will carry a book of horoscopes along with a stopwatch and the other tools of their trade?

Charlie O. Finley, boss of the Oakland A's, dabbled in

astrology, though perhaps he was more interested in the as-
trologer, a beautiful redhead named Laurie Brady, than
in astrology. At any rate, Brady predicted in 1970 that the
A's would win the division crown in '71 and then the World
Series three years in a row. They did. In '76 Finley asked
her to do daily charts on every player on the roster. Manager
Chuck Tanner promptly threw them in the wastebasket.
Perhaps he should have read them: That year the A's failed
to win the division for the first time in six seasons.

Only one player has ever admitted to using astrology:
Wes Ferrell, who won 20 games six different times for the
Red Sox and Indians in the 1930s. An Aquarius, Ferrell
"freely admits that his fortunes are governed by the stars,"
Washington *Post* columnist Shirley Povich wrote in July
1938. "Astrology rules his life. He is a confirmed disciple
and credits astrology with curing the soreness in his arm
when all other methods failed including the ministration of
medical and bone specialists, quacks and voodoo doctors."

Povich continued: "On the days the stars say they are in
his favor he will be the picture of confidence on the pitching
mound. He says that several years ago when he was with
Cleveland he had his horoscope read and a re-check of his
season's victories revealed that he had won ball games on
days when the stars were favorable and had lost games
when, according to the horoscope, the days were due to be
'bad.'

"He makes no bones about his faith in astrology. He
points out that it was more than a coincidence two years ago
at Griffith Stadium when, on the same day, Joe Cronin was
beaned and Rick Ferrell suffered a broken finger. 'It was a
bad day for people born in the sign of Libra,' said Wes,
'and the chart showed it. both Cronin and Rick were Libra
babies.' "

Did it work? Well, Ferrell won 193 big league games,
including 25 in 1935 to lead the league.

READING LIST

If astrology can predict the future, it should be able to predict the past. I went to two astrologers—Laurie Brady of Salem, Massachusetts, and Maude Chalfant of Washington—and gave them the birthdays of several athletes and asked them to describe the men, knowing nothing else about them. Then I asked them to tell what might have happened to each on a particular day in his career. Their readings follow. See if you can guess who the men were. Answers on page 52.

I

BORN: Feb. 6, 1895: A very emotional chart. He either had an explosive temper or explosive energy, so if he were a baseball player, I would think he was one of your home run hitters, or a heavy-weight boxer.

He had sort of a tormented life, lots of problems. There were definitely problems in his natal home. His father or mother sat on him real hard. There was probably quarreling in the home, or a separation or divorce or loss of parent. He was extremely independent and hard to manage.

There's a very heavy emphasis in the House of Show Business, and Sports in general. He probably loved kids, and I would imagine he had many love affairs.

EVENT: Oct. 1, 1932: I'm wondering, was this person having some health problems? It could be a chart where a person was retiring, or the end of his career was coming. It could have been home runs if this was a baseball player.

II

BORN: August 30, 1918: He is terribly independent, probably was very hard to manage. He might have been frustrated, had to control himself, or was made to control himself. He has a fiery way of thinking, and fire in his hands. Anything to do with the hands would be good for him. I'm sure he had emotional problems, probably drinking problems, although I could be very wrong. There's a strong emphasis on his House of Self-Undoing.

He's precise, a Virgo, very exacting in details about everything. He has a quick mind, but he might have been sarcastic in his speech. He could have acted like a dictator to his friends. This is a psychic person, I'm sure, very sensitive.

III

BORN: Oct. 25, 1923: A terribly intense person, fixed and stubborn, but very sweet-natured, likable, and very lucky. He might be a quarterback if he's in football. He would be a power hitter if he's in baseball.

EVENT: Oct. 5, 1951: I think this event was a very happy one. The moon was touching Venus, meaning that sweet things were coming to him or being stirred up. Jupiter in his House of Work also means good things. Uranus, the planet of Change and Surprise, was exactly over his Pluto (energy). So, whatever this was, it was probably unexpected and very strong and explosive. And very fateful. It's kind of hard to read whether it was pure luck or whether it wasn't.

IV

BORN: April 14, 1941: This is a strong, strong person. Super strong. A lot of self-confidence. He was born with it in the cradle. Even before he opened his eyes, he knew what he wanted.

He's aggressive. He was born with that, too. And stubborn. He wanted what he wanted when he wanted it. He rushes into things, just shoots out and does what he thinks he has to do.

When he's playing, he's totally into it. His whole being— his brain, his body—are all working for one thing.

He's got tons of physical energy. His friends would think

he's courageous. His enemies would consider him pushy.

Sometimes he can be very strong-willed, rebellious, anti-social, when Mars hits him. All of a sudden he can turn into a really raging person. These are tendencies from birth; he may have mellowed since then. If his energy were all kept inside him, he'd probably hurt people. But he releases it physically in sport.

I would think he's extremely dexterous. His timing is excellent. He moves like a panther. He moves beautifully.

He's got a quick mind, like a hair trigger. Really, really fast mental chemistry.

He had sort of a conflict with his relatives. He's quarrelsome and independent. He was kind of noisy as a child, or could have been.

He would also have to learn the value of sexuality. I think when he was younger he would rush into love affairs. But I think he's outgrown that. He's very charming and attractive. He may not be beautiful, but he's bewitching. He has this inner charm. It's more than just charm. I see a little gleam in his eye.

But he's better off when he does things on his own. Any mates would probably be jealous of him. He's dominating, and he attracts people who have a lot of needs, especially females, very sexual, who want a lot and are very demanding.

He's sort of restless at home, a high-tension person, lots of nervous energy.

He's creative, though he might put it all into his sport. He's intellectual. He's a lot more intellectual than people know.

I think he has a powerful position, because he has such drive, such energy. He needs power. He likes to be on top. If he were in politics, look out!

I like him, whoever he is. I would want to stay away from him with a ten-foot pole, as a female. But I think he's dynamite. He's a real power.

EVENT: Aug. 1, 1978: I get the feeling there has been a lot of strife going on. He may have been very aggressive in the few days just before this. He's so damn strong, you'd think he could overcome almost anything that goes wrong. But he may have been a little disappointed. Things may not have turned out the way he wanted them to.

V

BORN: May 18, 1946: He's a Taurus, which is a fixed, sort of placid, slow-moving person who is very interested in money. He's very lucky with money. He might be a little erratic with it, but I think he will make good money.

He probably has tremendous energy and heavy hands.

I'm sure he's very charming. Probably women like him. He could be flirtatious and have lots of affairs.

He's really introverted, except for his moon that brings him in front of the public. I think he's ambitious and driving hard for what he wants, and the public pulls him out.

I suspect he's a little hard to handle because of that stubborn Taurus sun: "Don't tell me what to do." He probably loses his temper very easily. He might have a tendency to flare up and speak more angrily than he means to. He's probably impulsive and quarrelsome.

EVENT: Oct. 18, 1977: A terrific massing of planets in his House of Work. The north node of the moon—the lucky part—the moon itself, the sun, Pluto, and Venus—which usually means nice things and gifts—are all in his House of Work. This was just a fantastic day with all those planets— half of all his planets—all in one place. On the whole, I would think this was a fortunate event.

VI

BORN: Nov. 22, 1950: I'd say he's a sweet person, talks sweetly and thinks sweetly, perhaps idealistically. He probably likes to talk a lot, is jovial, likes people. He could be a good storyteller. Women like him.

A lot of energy. And he has the Saturn-Mars square found in a lot of boxers, so I would say he has power also.

EVENT: Sept. 23, 1978: This is so complicated, I can't

make a flat statement whether it was good or bad. But it was of great significance, because there were aspects after aspects (of the stars) hitting his chart that day. There could be something very surprising about this event.

Saturn is right on the edge of his House of Career. Saturn is the planet of the ending of things, so this was very significant in his career and his life.

Was he hurt, or could there have been anything involving a hospital in this situation?

There was something mysterious, something about this whole thing. It may be that he had a sense of mysterious things happening around him that he felt very strongly. I sort of lean to something very disappointing, but I can't quite back it up.

But there's a strong emphasis on hospitals and health.

ANSWERS TO READING LIST

I. Oct. 1, 1932: Babe Ruth's "called the shot" home run. **II.** Aug 30, 1918: Ted Williams (I didn't give an event date). **III.** Oct. 5, 1951: Bobby Thomson's "shot heard round the world." **IV.** Aug. 1, 1978: Pete Rose's hit streak ends. **V.** Oct, 18, 1977: Reggie Jackson's three World Series homers. **VI.** Sept. 23, 1978: Lyman Bostock is shot to death.

Just an exhibition?

"The First World Series"

Al Kermisch

Some historians would have you believe that the major leagues' first World Series took place 100 years ago when the Cincinnati Reds, the first champions of the American Association, played host to Cap Anson's Chicago club, National League winners. The clubs played two games, the Reds winning 2-0 before 2,700 on Friday, October 6, 1882, and Chicago winning 2-0 the next day before a crowd of 4,500. As the story goes, Denny McKnight, president of the American Association, then stepped in and notified the Cincinnati club that it would be expelled if the games continued and as a result the series was abandoned. This makes a good story but it is not based on fact. Although supporters of the Cincinnati club were anxious to see the Reds in action against National League opposition, there seemed to be little chance of it happening since it was against the constitution of the Association and could result in expulsion.

A wealthy Cincinnati booster came up with an idea that would make exhibition games with National League clubs

AL KERMISCH, a retired colonel, had his first baseball article published in 1939.

possible. Since the Cincinnati players' salaries ran to October 15, the gentleman made an offer to assume responsibility for the remainder of the players' salaries after October 1 (amounting to about $4,000) if the club would turn over all the players to him, including release of the players. This proposition looked good to the club officials, since it would produce a big saving, and they readily agreed. The players also agreed to take their releases on October 1 and for two weeks remain in the employ of the wealthy benefactor. Thus the Cincinnati club had no official status and was enabled to circumvent the American Association ban on playing NL teams.

Exhibition games were then arranged with Cleveland and Chicago. The Reds lost two out of three to Cleveland before Chicago came in for the two games as mentioned above. There wasn't any abrupt ending to this series. Two games were all that were scheduled and the clubs could not have continued the series even had they wanted to. The Reds were scheduled to play an exhibition game in St. Louis on October 8, while Chicago had to depart for Providence, where they were to start a nine-game exhibition series against the second-place Providence club on October 10.

When the latter series was first proposed at a special meeting of the National League in September, it appeared it would be a series to decide the league championship. Earlier the National League had announced that the Troy and Worcester clubs were to be dropped in 1883, upon which these clubs threatened to drop out before the end of the season. This could have resulted in revision of the standings to exclude the games played with those clubs and could have deprived Chicago of the championship. Hence, the nine-game series for the title was planned. But Troy and Worcester did finish out the season, and Chicago was the winner by three games. Providence still wanted to have the nine-game series decide the title but finally agreed to play the contests as exhibitions. Three games were played in Providence, one in New York, four in Chicago, and one at Ft. Wayne, Indiana. The series was hampered by bad weather and was poorly attended. Chicago finally prevailed, five games to four.

"The Cardinals did NOT plan a strike against Robinson."

Remembrance of Summers Past

Bob Broeg

In my years as a traveling baseball writer, namely 1946 through 1958, I believe I bridged the gap between the yesteryear of hero worship and the modern adversary era. When I came along, writers were just beginning to find warts on athletes' faces. Now? Heck, they're apt to see nothing but.

Somewhere, of course, there is the proper balance between writing independently and writing arrogantly, between criticizing justly and unjustly. And I've never felt, by the way, that no matter how unpleasant an athlete might be, a writer was justified in teeing off on him. In other words, if it's germane to the story, let the man make an ass of himself, but don't look for or—most certainly not—originate criticism that isn't justified. As an epitaph, I believe a writer can qualify for only one: "He Was Fair." (That's fair as in "just," not as in "mediocre.")

BOB BROEG is sports editor of the St. Louis *Post-Dispatch* and author of *Super Stars of Baseball* and other sports books.

George Hendrick, the St. Louis Cardinals' right fielder, rarely speaks, though I suspect that underneath his silence lurks a man who would be direct and personable in conversation if he hadn't been singed somewhere along the line. Hendrick is helpful and supportive of young players and, more pertinently, one helluva fine outfielder. He can crank up for the long ball, hit behind the runner, field, and throw.

When I went around the circuit, I never met ballplayers who declared themselves off-limits or were invariably surly. But a generation ago, ballplayers weren't nearly so financially independent and, maybe, writers were more tolerant.

Although I proudly took out my BBWAA card in Boston late in 1941, shortly before I went into the Marines, I really didn't travel until 1946. That season, of course, provided an interesting mixture of established stars who had been away and the 4-Fs who had taken over.

Equally interesting—and often sad—was the effort of the returning vets to regain what for too many had been lost. Even though he'd missed the center cut of his career, Bob Feller came back with an impressive flourish. Obviously, Joe DiMaggio had been hurt. From a record standpoint, Ted Williams had been, too.

Others were hurt physically. The Cardinals' Johnny Beazley, a handsome 21-game winner as a rookie in 1942 and twice a World Series victor over the Yankees, ruined his arm through the caprice of a military superior's command to pitch when not ready. Cecil Travis, a superior-hitting infielder who went to war with a career batting average of .327, wound up with frostbite of his feet, and never again hit higher than .252. And the minor leagues' most promising pitcher in 1942, John Grodzicki, had been hit in the lower backside with a bullet as a paratrooper, giving him a dropped foot he couldn't offset.

I look back in amazement now that we ever tolerated a day without the blacks in the big leagues. Looking back, I can't understand how it never struck me as odd that I went through school without ever having a black in class. And I'd competed against just one, who couldn't hit a curve ball...but, then, hell, I couldn't, either.

As a writer, I believe I treated Jackie Robinson fairly in 1947, his rookie year. I subscribed to the theory expressed then by Eddie Dyer, manager of the Cardinals. Dyer had been a football star at Rice and an assistant football coach there. He admired Robinson as an all-around athlete. "Don't jockey him," cautioned Dyer. "He's like Frank Frisch. You make him mad and he'll beat the hell out of you all by himself."

The story about the Cardinals' planned "rebellion" against Robinson early in 1947 is a barnyard vulgarism. Some players grumbled about having to play on the same field with a black, just as did some of the Dodgers. Maybe here and there one popped off about how he didn't care to play against Robinson, but no one paid attention to it. Certainly not the captain of the Cardinals, Terry Moore, nor his infield alter ego, Marty Marion, the man to whom ballplayers are most indebted for their tremendous pension plan.

Sure, club owner Sam Breadon was worried about his team's reaction to Robinson. First, a little background. Mr. Breadon was a funny man. Personally generous, he was pretty tightfisted with his talent, though the sheer ability of the Cardinals made him pay close to top dollar even when the team failed to draw. The colorful Gas House Gang, for instance, needed the 100,000 paid admissions they attracted in the thrilling final week of the 1934 season to draw 334,863. The club's peak attendance until 1946 was 778,147 in 1928, a pennant-winning season of better financial times.

When the Redbirds went over the one-million mark in 1946, so did many other clubs. Breadon no longer had to pay the more than $80,000 in salary and profit percentage to Branch Rickey, but he writhed when that applecheeked, graceful outfielder, Stan Musial, wanted big money. Stan was paid $13,500 at the outset of the '46 season, in which he shifted to first base to shore up a hole and also hit .365. After all, Musial reasoned, wasn't Feller getting about $80,000 at Cleveland and DiMaggio and Williams doing extremely well, too? He had turned down $75,000 cash and an attractive contract from the brothers Pasquel, who, in effect, did almost as much for the players in their day as the

Federal League had earlier and arbitrator Peter Seitz much later.

The Man asked for $37,000 and settled finally for $31,000, which made Breadon fretful, to say the least. With his ballooning payroll Sam, who had grown up poor and had an abiding fear of coming up short again, was beside himself when his world champions lost 11 of their first 13 games in '47. Hmmm, were they worried too much about that black man in the Dodgers' lineup? He consulted with Moore and Marion about Dyer's control of the club. After all, Breadon had been, in part, an early-day George Steinbrenner. From 1926 through 1930, he'd had six managers even though the Cardinals won three pennants.

Moore and Marion checked out Dyer as A-OK, but Dr. Robert F. Hyland, the surgeon-general of baseball, as Judge Landis described him, expressed Breadon's concern to an old friend, Rud Rennie, baseball writer of the *New York Herald-Tribune*. Rennie told his sports editor, Stanley Woodward, who went to National League president Ford Frick. Frick did the only thing logical—yes, decent—and said he'd suspend any player who went on strike because of Robinson.

The *Herald-Trib* broke a copyrighted story and the monkey was on the Cardinals' back. I've always resented the story, not because I had to scramble at night to follow it up, but only because it put so many fine players in an unfavorable light.

The truth is, to repeat, the Cardinals did *NOT* plan a strike against Robinson, even though a few players grumbled in their beer about the athlete of a different color. But baseball history has labeled them unfairly.

I've got at my desk a picture that, as a photo often does, tells the story. It shows Robinson, ejected by Bill Stewart for his publicized chokeup sign in a key moment of an important game in 1949, walking through the Cardinals' dugout, grinning at St. Louis players who were smiling over something said by Robinson or by one of them.

Another postwar development was the establishment of

the baseball pension, in which the prime influence was Marty Marion and the Cardinals. I broke the story and watched the wire services pick it up and bounce it around the country. I was delighted over the years to watch the idea take hold and become a reality.

In 1946, as Boston lawyer Robert Murphy sought to form a players' union and Jorge Pasquel beckoned from Mexico, the teams asked management for rinky-dink improvements: more meal money . . . buses instead of taxi cabs after night games . . . personal luggage handled by the club instead of the players, etc.

Aided by trainer Weaver, Marion drew up the Cardinals' recommendation at the old New Yorker Hotel in Manhattan. Each player would make a modest daily contribution toward a pension and the club would match it. In addition, All-Star Game receipts and World Series radio rights would be used. If necessary, too, a midseason exhibition between natural rivals (Cubs vs. White Sox, Yanks vs. Giants, Red Sox vs. Braves, Athletics vs. Phillies) could be played.

Other clubs recognized a good idea when they heard one. So, too, did such management representatives as Larry MacPhail, Tom Yawkey, Phil Wrigley, and Breadon. Breadon had been giving the National League $100 a month to dole out to alcoholic Grover Cleveland Alexander, unwilling to let his role become public.

The World Series representatives, the Cardinals and Boston Red Sox, had to approve. The Redbirds did, unanimously. Veteran Bosox, moaning about a skimpy Series between two teams with small parks, didn't want to give up the radio money, but Yawkey offered to put up if they didn't shut up. And the Sox recognized a truly fine sportsman's *beau geste*.

So now, 36 years later, the original notion of $100 a month at age 50 has been transformed by the television windfall, aggressive player unionization, and ownership opulence. Today's pension setup spirals to more than $50,000 a year at 65—if any of the well-heeled present-day players will need it.

To get back to where we came in, as a traveling baseball

writer I saw the game go a l-o-n-g way, sometimes backward, more often forward. I don't like to sound too much like an oldtimer, much less a grouchy one.

The game has changed from trains to planes; from regional to national; from soggy, dirty flannel uniforms to clean, form-fitting polyesters; from smaller gloves that required sure hands to beartraps that often will snare a ball without the hand knowing it.

The players no longer wear cabbage leaves under their caps—dugouts are air-conditioned and, thank heaven, so are trains and hotel rooms. I used to make those three- and four-week trips with so much clothing that I had to take a treatrical trunk—and I wasn't a clothes horse.

When I was on the beat, they changed old ideas with new ones that made sense. They hauled players' gloves off the field, to avoid a mishap, and they began to drag the infield, a midgame boon for concessionaires, weak kidneys, and dented infielders cups. Now, of course, they've got artificial turf, which has done to game-canceling wet fields almost what night baseball did to the sport, as Breadon saw it: that is, made every night Sunday.

Personally, I like the ersatz fields, the development of the relief pitcher into a position of prominence, and the present-day combination by which the stolen base and home run, previously strange bedfellows, coexist if not cohabitate.

No newspaperman—I am not an exception—likes it if a player won't talk or sulks out of bounds in the trainer's room. I recognize, too, that fuller radio coverage, including clubhouse programs for which players often are paid, have made the job more difficult for print reporters. Television heading toward national cable coverage will have further impact. But the prophets of doom should look elsewhere than baseball. Funny thing, I have a 1932 *Baseball Magazine* in which a headline reads: "Will Broadcasting Kill Baseball?" Obviously, despite some of its own attempts to commit suicide, the grand old game is still pretty healthy.

The state of baseball writing is another matter. Yes, a reporter has to interview players and use the clubhouse for illuminating comments, but I honestly believe writers need to rely more on their own judgment, to review a ballgame as if they were reviewing a movie or a stage play. A film critic can't ask Burt Reynolds if he thought he'd had his stuff in this scene or that one—and when did you ever hear of any drama reviewer asking an actor his opinion of the audience on opening night?

Pointed questions, clarifying a situation for the writer and the reader, are extremely worthwhile, but I weary of, for instance, talk about the batter hitting a "hanging" slider or curve. Hell, I can see that. Besides, who cares? The question is banal, the answer insipid.

Writers today are generally better educated and as a whole write better. They ought to rely more upon their abilities: a well-written narrative, not peppered with quotes, can be an excellent change-of-pace.

The years in which I traveled regularly, until I became a sports editor in 1958 and merely picked my spots, were a joy and an education. Those ten-day barnstorming trips north from Florida every spring, each town a one-night stand, enabled a guy to see places he otherwise would have missed. Yet my most enjoyable trip was a 1960 season-opening tour from St. Petersburg to San Francisco which included a week's stopoff in the Phoenix area.

A highlight of the trip was the last confrontation of Stan Musial and Ted Williams as active ballplayers. The Red Sox, after all, trained then at Scottsdale. Both great hitters had suffered what appeared to be end-of-the-career seasons in '59 (Musial .255, Williams .254). But they put on a great show that day and then some. Williams hit a home run, Musial hit two.

That year Ted went on at 42 to hit .316. Stan, three years later at nearly 43, played enough to contend for an official batting championship, hitting .330. Musial was a delight to travel with as a player and as a person, before and after his 3000-hit railroad bandwagon trip from Chicago to St. Louis in May, 1958, the Cardinals' last train ride.

When the Cardinals made their first plane trip west to Los Angeles and San Francisco in 1958, it was, of course, an emotional tug, the loss of Brooklyn's Ebbets Field and New

York's Polo Grounds. But I looked forward to the Coast, where I'd spent two enjoyable springs with the Browns in 1950-51. They lived in Hollywood and trained near Burbank.

I'm glad that I got out there again when the Giants' home was Seals Stadium, the springboard to stardom for Joe DiMaggio, and the Dodgers played at the Coliseum where Roy Campanella, if he hadn't been hurt, would have used that open stance and uppercut swing to hit a ton of home runs.

At San Francisco, where the raw trade winds at night should have foretold the problem at Candlestick Park, Ty Cobb saw Musial play the first big-league game there. Stan went 4-for-4 and Cobb invited him to breakfast, chortling: "You still can run and you still can hit. Drink a little wine before dinner and you'll play for years."

At the Coliseum, where the right-field fence was in Siberia by contrast with the pitch-and-putt screen looming large in left, Duke Snider moaned to Musial at the batting cage before the game. Stan nodded, motioning to left field, "If you can't beat 'em, Duke, join 'em. Go the other way." So with a large crowd there to see Musial, as there had been in San Francisco, The Man broke in at L.A. the same way: 4-for-4.

After all, he was en route to 3000 hits then, past 37 years old, and he didn't want to waste time. "I might get hit in the can with a cab," he said. So he made it in just 22 games—with 43 hits!

Long shots perhaps, but with imposing track records.

For the Hall of Fame: Twelve Good Men

Bob Carroll

Back in the days when I could claim my local race track as a dependent, I always played long shots. Understand, a long shot wasn't a horse that just *might* finish ahead of the field—a good long shot was a splendid steed that was *bound* to win, despite having been overlooked by handicappers with less insight than I. The satisfaction of watching a correctly tabbed long shot cross the wire first was infinitely preferable to that of winning with the mob. The money wasn't bad either. At least, it wouldn't have been bad had any of my choices done what they were supposed to do.

I still think my reasoning was sound, although the horses never quite got the hang of it. I know they tried. In fact, many of them paused to think it over just before the homestretch. If there was a flaw in my system, it was that I had to make my bets *before* they ran the races.

All of which brings me to baseball's Hall of Fame. In effect, we can place our bets on the candidates for enshrinement

BOB CARROLL, artist, writer, actor, and teacher, was represented in the premier issue of TNP in 1982.

after the races are in the record book. We can wait until a guy has thrown his last pitch or swung at it before we say: "That man belongs in Cooperstown!" If baseball chose its Hall of Fame candidates the silly way race tracks rank their horses, we'd have to start casting plaques when a kid was still in AAA.

We can do a whole lot better picking baseballers than bangtails. Not only are most baseball players smarter than horses, but we can know much more about them. We can ask them questions and some of them will answer. More important, we can measure their performances in a greater variety of ways, under a wider diversity of circumstances, and on a larger number of occasions. Horses only run; ballplayers run, hit, throw, and field. And horses don't have a 162-race season.

Of course, ways of measuring player performance are older than my blue serge suit. Anyone who can't figure a batting average or an earned run average (and quote a whole passel, too) is unlikely to be reading these words.

We all grew up with the same magic numbers: .406, 60, 56, 25 (the used-to-be price of *The Sporting News*), and all the rest. I still remember an old telephone number with 5442 as the final digits because Ralph Kiner hit 40 and then 54 home runs in 1948 and 1949. I just put them in reverse order and add the number of seasons. I've forgotten whose number it was.

With the advent of Bill James in his *Abstracts*, Pete Palmer and his Linear Weights System, and the rest of the hardworking sabermetricians, we have X number of fascinating new measuring tools. And fascinating new measurements.

Let me define my terms, as Noah Webster once remarked. When I call a Hall-of-Fame long shot, I don't mean Smead Jolley or Mario Mendoza. I'm pointing to someone who deserves to be in Cooperstown before the next elephant gestates and—in the best of all possible worlds—would already be residing there had he but caught the fancy of a coterie of opinion-makers.

On these pages, I'll present my top twelve HOF long

shots. Why twelve? Not because I prefer keeping my shoes on while I count, but because twelve is a traditional and even mystical number, i.e., twelve apostles, twelve good men and true, twelve chairs, and the Dirty Dozen. With twelve long shots, we get the cream.

Although all my long shots are eligible for the Hall right now, none of them has been the recent recipient of heavy fanfares. Such present favorite non-enshrinees as Billy Williams and Nellie Fox are off my list because they've been plentifully trumpeted for election of late.

I'm not including Harry Stovey either. His candidacy has been presented so vehemently and convincingly by some SABR members he has to rate at even money.

However, now that I've brought old Harry up, I might as well throw in a little sidebar about Hall of Fame deliberations. Every year the time frame viewed by the Committee on Baseball Veterans expands. New veterans become eligible while those once passed over are reconsidered. The job is expanding like a runaway balloon.

It seems to me they should set a cut-off year—one that falls within the area of experience for most of the committee members—and say, "That's it! No one who retired before this year will be considered again." As a cut-off year, 1920 comes readily to mind, but I'm not locked into it; I just want to eliminate some of the clutter. If they'd like to hold one last giant election to take care of all the eligibles who retired before their chosen date, that would be all right with me.

As a matter of fact, four of my long shots are pre-1920 eligibles, and I'd hate to see them scratched. Nevertheless, something should be done to make the work of the Veterans Committee—an awesome and thankless task at best—at least theoretically possible.

But enough of improving the system! It's time to get on with my duty—presenting a dozen deserving long shots for the Hall.*

*This essay was first published in 1985. In the following year, two of the author's "twelve good men"—Bobby Doerr and Ernie Lombardi—were elected to the Hall of Fame.

DICK ALLEN

Rugged individualism is more admired at a distance than up close and personal. Had Dick Allen played fifty years ago, he might be lauded today as a shining example of American independence. Instead, his moodiness, self-absorption, and free-and-easy approach to baseball make him anathema to many. His plaque in Cooperstown will diplomatically avoid his personality quirks. Besides, there's more to say about his play than about his playing around.

From the time he won Rookie of the Year honors with the Phillies in 1964 through the mid-'70s, he was a slugger to make pitchers cringe. Six times he topped 30 homers in a season. His RBI totals looked like I.Q. scores for the smart class even though his teammates seldom clogged the bases in front of him. He was figuratively, and all too often literally, a one-man gang.

That was never more clear than in 1972 when his bat hoisted a very ordinary White Sox club into the thick of a pennant race. They gave him the MVP Award that year because there wasn't anything higher.

In the field, Allen was never a surgeon but hardly a butcher. He started at third with the Phils and ended up at first with the A's. In between, he played some second, outfield, and even shortstop.

He was special because of his bat. In an era of low batting averages, he finished with a fine .292. More important, his 351 home runs, 1,119 RBIs, and 1,099 runs scored have him up with the big kids who played longer.

In Palmer's Linear Weights System, Allen ranks 40th in overall player wins, just ahead of Bob Johnson, about whom more later. The next eight *below* these two are already in the Hall of Fame.

RICHIE ASHBURN

They said Richie Ashburn would have been the perfect player if he'd had home run power or a good arm. He never did do much for homers, averaging fewer than two a season, but ask Cal Abrams about his arm. In the ninth inning of the final game of the 1950 season—with the pennant on the line—Ashburn gunned down Abrams at the plate to preserve a tie. The Phillies won the flag in the tenth.

Abrams was in good company. Ashburn led NL outfielders in assists three times and averaged better than ten a season for his fifteen-year career.

Besides catching baserunners he caught base hits, or rather potential base hits. No modern centerfielder who played in more than 2,000 games ever went and got 'em like Richie. Palmer's LWTS ranks him 16th in defensive wins, ahead of all outfielders except Speaker and Carey. He led NL flychasers in chances per game every year from 1948 through '58 save '55 when he finished second by point-one. His career chances-per-game average of 3 is well ahead of his more celebrated and tuneful contemporaries Willie, Mickey, and the Duke. Put it this way: Over a 162-game season, Ashburn would catch about 50 balls that Mays wouldn't get to. That's a lot of base hits obliterated.

If we could add those hits to Richie's offense, he'd go off the scale. Not that he had to hide his head when it was bat time. He led the NL in hitting twice and finished with a career .308. His ability to draw walks—he led four times in free passes—pushed his career on-base average to nearly .400, marking him as one of the best leadoff men since Adam.

Had he hit home runs, he'd have been Roy Hobbs.

BILL DAHLEN

For a couple of months in 1978, everyone in baseball was saying, "Who's Bill Dahlen?" The occasion for all the head-scratching was Pete Rose's consecutive-game hitting streak. As Pete's total mounted, it was noted he was near to tying Dahlen's streak of 42 set in 1894. Once that landmark was passed, all eyes focused on Willie Keeler's 44 in '97, and Dahlen was dimly remembered as a slugger from the misty past.

That impression was wrong. Dahlen could hit all right. Although his most common batting average was in the .260's, he put together a couple of marks a hundred points higher early in his career. Over his twenty-two years in the Bigs he scored 1,589 runs and batted in 1,223, even leading in ribbies in 1904. He also stole 547 bases.

But, if Bad Bill is to be remembered correctly, it should be as a grounder-gobbling shortstop on four National League pennant winners between 1899 and 1905. Today, a shortstop who can hit is a bonus, but one who can't field is a DH. Fielding was even more important in Dahlen's day. The ball was deader than Caesar on March 16, and the surest route to first base was to smash that pill into the dirt. A premium was on an infielder's ability to grab and throw. Dahlen was top drawer all the way.

His figures are impressive. Among shortstops of all eras, he's 1-2 in career putouts, assists, and total chances. His 6.3 chances per game ranks him third—ahead of Honus Wagner.

BOBBY DOERR

The Boston *Globe* didn't stop their presses whenever Bobby Doerr made an error, but they probably got more stories about men biting dogs. Lots of players have gone three months without making an error—November, December, and January—but Bobby did it at the height of one of the American League's hottest pennant races. From June 24 to September 19, 1948, he handled 414 chances flawlessly.

In six different seasons, he led AL second basemen in fielding, and his putout, assist, and double play totals were always at or near the top.

However, any resemblance to the "good field, no hit" stereotype ceased when Doerr picked up the lumber. He packed his .288 lifetime batting average with 223 home runs and 1,247 ribbies.

Bobby was an integral part of the murderous Red Sox lineup of the late 1940s—one that featured Dom DiMaggio, Johnny Pesky, Junior Stephens, and Ted Williams. Perhaps the big bats that surrounded him kept Doerr from getting his full due. A single pearl seems less radiant in a necklace than alone on a satin pillow. Worse, the Red Sox necklace looked like a choker when Boston was nosed out of several AL pennants. All those frustrating second-places clouded Doerr's luster in some minds.

Needless to say, none of those minds belonged to the trembling pitchers who had to face him or the frustrated batters who tried to chop one past him.

Bobby ranks 26th overall in Palmer's LWTS. How many players with Hall of Fame eligibility rank higher?

None.

WILLIAM HULBERT

When William Hulbert died in 1882, the National League passed a resolution "that to him alone is due the credit of having founded the National League, and to his able leadership, sound judgment, and impartial management is the success of the league chiefly due." That's a lot to lay at any man's door. Still, it's true; without Hulbert, there wouldn't have been a National League, and we can all shudder at what might have been in its place.

For those who don't know the story, back in 1875 baseball had a sort of league called the National Association. It had a reputation that would embarrass the town harlot. Hard-drinking players were loaded on the field more often than the bases, gamblers knew tomorrow's standing this morning, and the whole mess was about as disciplined as the theater crowd when the Bijou burned down.

In stepped Hulbert, a part owner of the Chicago team, to outline for the western teams a new league brim full of integrity. Then he went to the wicked East and sold his idea to the clubs there. To make it more palatable, he let easterner Morgan Bulkeley act as figurehead president.

The clean league struggled through 1876. The public was wary. New York and Philadelphia saved money by skipping their final western tour. Bulkeley didn't even bother making the December league meeting. Pretense was put aside; Hulbert became prexy and immediately expelled the eastern spoilsports.

He'd cowed the clubs. The next year, he sent a resounding message to the players by barring for life four Louisville players who'd been fixing games. That kind of tough leadership during his remaining years proved to the public that baseball belonged up there with Mom and apple pie. The sport was on its way!

BOB JOHNSON

Consistency may be the hobgoblin of little minds, but it can also make certain ballplayers nigh unto invisible. Indian Bob Johnson never had one of those super seasons that make everyone sit up and whistle. While phenoms came, collected the MVP trophies, and faded, he just kept plodding along hitting .300, with a couple dozen homers and a hundred ribbies year after year. From 1933 through 1945, he ticked off those seasons like a guy punching a time clock. Ho-hum, another April. Time to start hitting.

Maybe someone might have noticed him had he played on a pennant winner or two. Johnson was stuck for most of his career with Connie Mack's Depression A's, a club that treated last place like swallows treat Capistrano. He hit with power and consistency, ran, threw, and fielded like a star, but his light was hidden under a bushel of Philadelphia losses.

Nevertheless, as though writ in that trick ink kids used to scrawl messages with, Johnson's name suddenly pops into full visibility when those career-total lists are examined: 2,051 hits, 1,239 runs, 1,283 RBIs, and a solid .296 BA.

He's exactly the kind of player sabermetrics benefits—an overlooked star whose accomplishments become manifest under the microscope of detailed analysis. The Ruths, Cobbs, Aarons, and Musials need a sabermetric imprimatur like Cosell needs a thesaurus. But did you know that Palmer's

LWTS ranks Indian Bob as the 41st best player ever? Of course, Palmer doesn't factor in the hype.

ERNIE LOMBARDI

Some heroes have feet of clay; Ernie Lombardi had feet of lead. He was the slowest great player in any sport except chess. Fortunately, flat-out sprinting isn't in the job description for catchers, and all the things a maskman is supposed to do Ernie did better than most.

He was the rock the Cincinnati pennant winners of '39 and '40 were built on. A quiet strong man with enormous hands, he nursed his pitchers, intimidated baserunners, delivered key hits. His contemporaries Dickey, Cochrane, Hartnett, and Ferrell are already ensconced in Cooperstown; big Ernie ranked with them, and sometimes he came out ahead.

In 1938, he was named NL Most Valuable Player when he became only the second catcher ever to win a batting title. Then, to prove it was no fluke, he took another batting crown in 1942. The list of catchers who've won batting championships since is as long as the list of battleships berthed in Kansas.

Even though he had to bounce the ball off the scoreboard to get a leg hit, Lombardi finished his seventeen-season career with a .306 batting average. Infielders, knowing they could throw him out on anything they could reach, played back an extra twenty to thirty feet. Nevertheless, he generated such power with his peculiar interlocked-finger grip that his cannon shots still got through.

He had the kind of power that breaks seats in the upper deck, but he specialized in line drives rather than moon shots, so his home run totals were only in the teens. But, had he possessed the blazing speed of a tortoise, he'd have hit .400.

BILL MAZEROSKI

You have to start with THE home run. When Bill Mazeroski smacked Ralph Terry's pitch over the Forbes Field wall in the ninth inning of the seventh game to win the 1960 World Series, he carved an ironic monument for himself. Remembering Maz for his hitting is like remembering Dolly Parton for her elbows.

Not that he was a cipher. His respectable .260 for seventeen years with the Pirates kept rallies alive, and he had a penchant for clutch hits, twice topping 80 RBIs in a season. Six times he managed double figures in homers. Still, a whole team of Mazeroskis would score fewer runs than a roster of Joe Morgans.

Maz purchased his ticket to Cooperstown with defense. He was simply the best second baseman who ever put glue in his glove, coupling the hands of a magician with the range of a Magellan. Five times he led his league in putouts, nine times in assists, eight times in total chances. His .983 lifetime fielding average is barely a bad hop under the record.

He was the da Vinci of the double play. Other second sackers caught the shortstop's toss and then threw; with Maz, the ball seemed to ricochet at lightning speed to first, earning him the nickname "No Hands." He set the major league record for twin kills in a season (161), years leading (8), and in a career (1,706). If we named baseball situations like diseases, we'd call double plays "Mazeroskis."

In LWTS, Maz ranks first in lifetime defensive wins. Of the top seventy-five seasons by a defensive player, Maz has six! Think of it this way: put Mazeroski on the same team with ANY second baseman in history, and the other guy gets to play the left field.

BID McPHEE

Sabermetrician Bill James lists as one of his criteria for Hall of Fame selection: "Was he (in any given season) the best player in baseball at his position?'' By that standard, John ''Bid'' McPhee qualifies for Cooperstown ad nauseam. In just about every one of his eighteen years before 1900, he ranked as the best second baseman around.

Cincinnatians turned down all bids for Bid and kept him in town for his full career, with teams in both the American Association and the National League. They knew they had a timely hitter with a sting in his bat. His 188 career triples would translate into a hefty heap of homers in a more modern era. All told, he batted in 1,067 runs and scored a bountiful 1,678.

But he was at his best when the other guys went to bat. From 1882 through 1896 he led his league's second basemen in putouts eight times, assists six times, double plays eleven times, total chances per game six times, and fielding average nine times. In every one of those years, he led in at least one category and usually in several—but he never led in errors.

And remember, he piled up a record that would turn a modern green without wearing a glove. Only in his final three years, long after the glove became standard equipment, did he begin to cover his left hand with leather.

In 2,125 games, Bid accepted 14,241 chances, and that comes to a greedy 6.7 per game. To put it another way, in the average Cincinnati game, he accounted for about one-fourth of their opponents' outs. The only one involved in more outs was the scorekeeper.

HAL NEWHOUSER

Like General Patton, Hal Newhouser peaked during World War II. But conventional baseball wisdom holds as an article of faith that diamond doings during The Big One don't count. In memory, major league rosters were peopled by one-armed geriatrics or pimply adolescents. If the Browns could win a pennant, *real* ballplayers would have won the Nobel Prize!

No one has yet suggested they take away Lou Boudreau's 1944 batting title, but Newhouser's brilliant 1944-45 record is always regarded as proof that the competition was strictly Little League. In case you've forgotten, Prince Hal left-handed his way to a 29-9 mark in '44 and backed that with 25-9, an ERA title, and a pair of World Series wins in '45. In both seasons, he carted off the American League MVP Award.

Ah, but those were the War Years! Forget that Hal's record would look good against even the girls from Sister Theresa's. Forget that a jeroboam of evidence exists that the quality of wartime play was better than the jokesters want to remember. Forget that no other pitcher ever bookended MVP trophies. What did he do when the big boys came home?

Well, in 1946 he "slumped" to 26-9 with a 1.94 ERA. For the five years after the war, he averaged 19.6 wins.

The man Ted Williams called one of the three toughest pitchers he ever faced was always a pretty good thrower. Back in 1940, at the ripe old age of nineteen, he put nine victories in the till for the pennant-winning Tigers. But, like a lot of lefties, he took a while to discover they only call strikes if the ball is over the plate. When he learned the knack in 1944, he blossomed into unbelievable.

Although a sore arm ended his career prematurely, his record—not even counting the War Years—makes him the best lefty of his decade.

DICKEY PEARCE

They're always putting up statues of people who did things first. Somebody ought to carve a couple of life-size, 5'3" replicas of Dickey Pearce.

The first should show him bunting. Dickey invented that little maneuver back in the days when they still spelled the name of the game with a space between base and ball. The rule then said the ball only had to land once in fair territory. He mastered the art of plopping the pellet down 'twixt the lines and then having it skitter off to God-knows-where. Reportedly, he collected numerous doubles while fielders retrieved the ball from under spectator's wagons.

When the National League was founded, Pearce was forty years old and had been one of baseball's few "name" stars for more than half his life, mostly with the famous Brooklyn Atlantics. The bunts were a nice touch, but what made Pearce an 1860s superstar was his fielding.

His second statue should show him shortstopping a grounder. He was, as a matter of fact, the first to play what we would consider the shortstop position. Until Pearce came along in 1856, the "shortstop" was a fourth outfielder whose job was to catch flares (or whatever they called them in those days) and to take short throws from the deep outfielders and relay them to the infield. (The early ball was so light that no one could throw it more than 200 feet or so.) Dickey noticed that many more base hits were bouncing safely between second and third than were pop flies coming into his grasp in the outfield. Accordingly, he moved himself into the breach.

He probably got a few quizzical looks, but he got a lot more groundouts. Pretty soon, every shortstop followed his example. Nevertheless, during his long career—spanning the amateur, early professional, and league eras—no one did it better than the original short stopper.

RON SANTO

Many good things come in threes: Faith, Hope & Charity; 'Reading, 'Riting & 'Rithmetic; Curly, Larry & Moe. But, for Ron Santo, being one of a terrific trio has thus far hexed his Hall of Fame chances. Not only was he the third wrecker in the Cub crew of Banks, Williams & Santo, but he was also one of the troika of great third basemen during the 1960s: Robinson, Ken Boyer & you-know-who. Some people seem to confuse the third slot with second-rate.

Because Robinson has already gone to Cooperstown, a few comparisons may be enlightening. Robinson played longer and won more Gold Gloves, but Ron played 2,243 games and picked up five Gold Gloves—despite having to compete with both Ken and Clete Boyer for the trinket.

Let's do some comparative math, using Bill James' idea of dividing games played by 162 and then dividing the result into career totals to get an "average" season.

	AB	R	H	2B	3B	HR	RBI	BA
Robinson	595	69	159	27	4	15	76	.267
Santo	590	82	163	26	5	25	96	.277

It doesn't take a genius to figure out that a team with Santo at third base would score more runs than the same team with Robinson at third. It would take an awful lot of third base defense—Robinson's strongest suit—to make up the difference. But remember, Santo was no slouch with the leather himself.

There are other factors to consider, of course. Some favor Robinson; some favor Santo. The point is, when all the evidence is added up, they run a photo-finish.

They'll never convince me Robinson doesn't belong in the Hall of Fame. I just say Santo should be there with him—along with my other long shots.

With two out in the ninth...

The Almost No-Hitters

Keith Sutton*

On April 15, 1983, pitcher Milt Wilcox of the Detroit Tigers came within one out of a perfect game when pinch hitter Jerry Hairston of the White Sox, batting for shortstop Jerry Dybzinski, hit a clean single through the middle with two down in the ninth inning. Imagine the deep disappointment for hurler Wilcox, who retired 26 batters in a row, and for the Detroit team, which fielded flawlessly and supported him with four runs. The more than 19,000 fans in Comiskey Park undoubtedly had mixed feelings about the Honolulu native's superbly pitched 4-0 victory over LaMarr Hoyt.

According to available information, there have been only three other occasions where hurlers came within one out of a perfect game (meaning no hits, walks, hit batsmen or errors). The first took place on July 4, 1908. New York Giant rookie Hooks Wiltse was locked up in a 0-0 battle with the Phillies George McQuillan. Wiltse retired the first two batters in the ninth inning, and Phils' manager Bill

KEITH SUTTON is a sportswriter for *The Wayne Independent*.
*Assisted by Paul MacFarlane

77

Murray permitted McQuillan to bat. Wiltse quickly registered two strikes against his opposite number, then for some inexplicable reason threw an 0-2 curve ball. This pitch slipped from his hand and struck the batter. Wiltse went on to record a ten-inning no-hitter, but the perfect game was gone.

The second was on August 5, 1932, and that game also involved a Tiger hurler. Tommy Bridges, the great curveball hurler of the 1930s, had a 13-0 lead over the Washington Senators, but he wasn't coasting because he had a perfect game within his grasp. He had set down 26 straight batters, seven of them on strikes, and only five balls had been hit to the outfield. Washington manager Walter Johnson called on Dave Harris, the American League's best pinch hitter in 1932, to bat for pitcher Bobby Burke, who two years before had hurled a no-hitter himself. Harris hit the first ball pitched to left field for a single and the spell was broken. The partisan Detroit crowd booed and continued to do so after the next batter, Sam Rice, was retired on a grounder.

Johnson was criticized for inserting a crafty pinch hitter like Harris in a hopelessly lost game, and Harris was booed for breaking up the string of outs. The latter's response was to the effect that "a batter gets paid for hitting like a pitcher does for pitching."

The third near-perfect game was on June 27, 1958, when Billy Pierce of the White Sox beat the Senators 3-0 at Chicago. Pierce went to two out in the ninth without a flaw, thanks to a spectacular play by shortstop Luis Aparicio in the fourth. He dashed behind second base to take a bouncer off the bat of Ricky Bridges and threw him out in a close play at first. In the ninth, Jim Lemon took three balls and a strike before flying out. Norm Zauchin then looked at a third strike. Ed FitzGerald came in to hit for pitcher Russ Kemmerer and rifled the first pitch down the right-field line for a double. When Albie Pearson fanned to end the game, the White Sox fans, who long admired Pierce, booed FitzGerald bitterly. Police took the precaution to go out to second base to escort him to the dugout.

In the three near-perfect games involving American League teams, all three batters breaking up the strings were pinch hitters swinging on the first delivery. Ironically, in all the other games where no-hitters were broken up with two out in the ninth, the spoiler was not a substitute batsman.

Research by SABR members has uncovered 26 other games which went down to the final batter before a no-hitter was spoiled. Two games are not carried on the accompanying list because they were not individual pitching efforts through 26 outs. On July 4, 1954, the pennant-winning Indians used three hurlers against the White Sox in a 2-1 victory. Mike Garcia, Ray Narleski, and Early Wynn worked the nine innings, with Wynn giving up a single to Minnie Minoso with two down in the final frame. Minnie then became the final out when he was thrown out stealing.

On April 18, 1964, Jim Maloney of the Reds, who was to hurl three no-hitters in his career, pitched six innings of hitless ball against the Dodgers before pulling a muscle in his side. John Tsitouris then took over and held the Dodgers in check until two were out in the ninth. Frank Howard then smashed the ball back of second base and beat the throw from shortstop Leo Cardenas. The Reds won 3-0 on Deron Johnson's three-run homer off Sandy Koufax.

In almost all of the games listed, the contest turned out to be a one-hit affair with the batter following the "spoiler" being routinely retired to end the game. It might be appropriate to describe briefly the rare exceptions, as well as some of the more interesting games.

On September 26, 1978, Mike Flanagan of the Orioles was pitching brilliantly with a 3-0 lead over the Indians. Then, with two down in the ninth, Gary Alexander suddenly blasted a home run. Then Ted Cox and Duane Kuiper followed with singles. In a twinkling, Flanagan had lost his no-hitter, a shut-out, and the tying run was at bat. Gone also was a complete game as manager Earl Weaver called in Don Stanhouse, who fanned the final batter and preserved a 3-1 victory.

Tom Seaver of the Mets, one of the greatest pitchers of his era, had great difficulty achieving a no-hit game. On

July 9, 1969, he retired the first 25 batters in a victory over the Cubs before Jim Qualls singled. On July 4, 1972, he again got one out in the ninth before Leron Lee of San Diego got the first hit. On September 4, 1975, he got two out in the ninth before Joe Wallis of the Cubs lined a single to right field. Seaver retired the next batter, but the Mets didn't get him any runs. The game was scoreless after nine, and, although Tom gave up two hits in the 10th, the score remained at 0-0. Skip Lockwood took over in the 11th and lost it 1-0. Seaver finally achieved a no-hitter with the Reds in 1978.

Al Milnar of the Indians had a similar situation on August 11, 1942, when he was engaged in a scoreless duel with Tommy Bridges of the Tigers. Milnar did not give up a hit until Doc Cramer singled with two out in the ninth. The game continued without a run until called after 14 innings. The Cleveland lefty yielded only two hits over that stretch but got no decision.

Of the 27 individual hurlers who lost a no-hit game with only one batter remaining, nine were able to achieve a hitless gem at some other time in their careers. They included John Clarkson, Cy Young, Bob Rhoades, Nap Rucker, Jeff Tesreau, Dazzy Vance, Ted Lyons, Tom Seaver, and Ken Holtzman. John Odom had a shared no-hitter with Francisco Barrios in 1975. Speaking of Holtzman (who had two no-hitters with the Cubs), he came very close to a third career no-hitter while with Oakland on June 8, 1975. With one out remaining, Tom Veryzer of the Tigers lofted a long fly to A's center fielder Bill North, who briefly lost the ball in the sun and it dropped behind him for a double.

Grover Alexander, the greatest pitcher never to pitch a no-hitter, came as close as possible. On June 5, 1915, which was a year when he hurled a record four one-hitters for the Phils, Alex was pitching a masterful game against the Cardinals in St. Louis. There was nothing resembling a hit against him and it looked like nothing was going to stop him from a Hall of Fame performance. With two out in the ninth, Cardinal leadoff batter Arthur Butler lunged at a curve ball well off the plate and tapped it weakly back of second base, just barely out of reach of second baseman Bert Niehoff and shortstop Dave Bancroft. Alex then fanned Bob Bescher for the final out.

Billy Rohr of the Red Sox came very close to a no-hitter in his pitching debut April 14, 1967, in Yankee Stadium. The Yankees were held hitless down to the final out, and the young southpaw got that far thanks to a great catch by Carl Yastrzemski of a drive to left field by Tom Tresh to open the ninth. Rohr got the next batter, but with a 3-2 count on Elston Howard, the latter connected for a single. It was still a tremendous win for the rookie, who beat Whitey Ford, 3-0. Ironically, Rohr won only two more games in his brief career.

Here is the list we were able to compile of individual pitchers who had no-hitters broken up with two out in the ninth inning. Asterisk indicates site of game. All spoiler hits were singles except for four doubles and one home run, which are so designated.

NO-HITTERS BROKEN UP WITH TWO OUT IN NINTH

"Perfect Games"

Date of Game	Pitcher and Teams	Score	Spoiler
†7/4/08	Hooks Wiltse, NY* vs. Phi. NL	1-0	George McQuillan
8/5/32	Tommy Bridges, Det.* vs Was. AL	13-0	Dave Harris
6/28/58	Billy Pierce, Chi.* vs Was. AL	3-0	Ed FitzGerald (D)
4/15/83	Milt Wilcox, Det. vs Chi.* AL	6-0	Jerry Hairston

Other Near No-Hitters

Date of Game	Pitcher and Teams	Score	Spoiler
5/26/92	John Clarkson, Bos.* vs Lou. NL	7-0	Hugh Jennings
7/23/96	Cy Young, Cle.* vs Phi. NL	7-0	Ed Delahanty
9/9/99	Doc McJames, Bkn.* vs Bos. NL	4-0	Hugh Duffy
9/27/04	Bob Rhoades, Cle.* vs Bos. AL	3-1	Chick Stahl
7/22/11	Nap Rucker, Bkn.* vs Cin. NL	1-0	Bob Bescher
5/16/14	Jeff Tesreau, NY vs Pit.* NL	2-0	Joe Kelly
4/14/15	Herb Pennock, Phi.* vs Bos. AL	2-0	Harry Hooper
6/5/15	Gr. Alexander, Phi. vs StL* NL	3-0	Arthur Butler

Date of Game		Pitcher and Teams	Score	Spoiler
8/16/15	(2)	Bernie Boland, Det. vs Cle.* AL	3-1	Ben Paschal
5/6/18		Dan Griner, Bkn.* vs Phi. NL	2-0	Cliff Cravath
6/17/23		Dazzy Vance, Bkn. vs Cin.* NL	9-0	Sammy Bohne
9/19/25		Ted Lyons, Chi. vs Was.* AL	17-0	Bobby Veach
6/13/33		Whitlow Wyatt, Chi.* vs StL AL	6-1	Tedd Gullic
8/11/42		Al Milnar, Cle.* vs Det. AL	0-0	Doc Cramer
7/8/43		Orval Grove, Chi.* vs NY AL	1-0	Joe Gordon (D)
4/26/52		Art Houtteman, Det.* vs Cle. AL	13-0	Harry Simpson
4/14/67		Billy Rohr, Bos. vs NY* AL	3-0	Elston Howard
6/7/68		John Odom, Oak.* vs Bal. AL	6-1	Dave Johnson
8/21/73		Stan Bahnsen, Chi. vs Cle.* AL	4-0	Walt Williams
6/8/75		Ken Holtzman, Oak.* vs Det. AL	4-0	Tom Veryzer (D)
9/24/75		Tom Seaver, NY vs Chi.* NL	0-0	Joe Wallis
9/26/78		Mike Flanagan, Bal.* vs Cle. AL	3-1	G. Alexander (HR)
9/23/83		Chuck Rainey, Chi.* vs Cin. NL	3-0	Eddie Milner
8/00/86		Walt Terrell, Det.* vs Cal. AL	4-0	Wally Joyner (D)

†Perfect game broken up by HBP, but no-hitter achieved.

Everything old is new again: a proposal

Let's Go Back to Eight-Team Leagues

John McCormack

At their 1983 winter meetings the major leagues instructed their long-range planning committee to consider the feasibility of expanding the National and American leagues to sixteen teams each. I believe the committee should recommend such an expansion, and moreover it should recommend that the National and American leagues be dissolved, to be replaced by four regional eight-team leagues.

The National and American leagues have long since outlived their usefulness. They are, in fact, detrimental to the game. As long as they exist, no sensible realignment of teams can be effected. And, only through such realignment—and expansion to thirty-two teams—can baseball regain undisputed supremacy in professional sports.

Before discussing realignment and expansion, however, it would be useful to review the transition of the National and American leagues from vital forces to their present meaningless states. Once things were different. Very different.

JOHN McCORMACK of Dallas is a past SABR vice president; he has written for the BRJ.

The American League was formed in 1901 as a rival to the National League, then in its twenty-sixth year. It soon had franchises in five of the National League's seven cities. Thereafter it was war, a nasty, bitter war for survival in which anything went. The resulting wounds were deep, the scars long-lasting. Though peace came with the 1903 season, the National League still regarded the upstart with scorn—so much so that in 1904 there was no World Series. The National League's New York Giants refused to play the American's Boston Pilgrims, surprise victors of the previous year's Series. Disingenuously, the Giants proclaimed themselves champions of the only major league: What could they gain through postseason play?

Although peace did not bring good fellowship, it did bring a great asset to the game: *league* fan loyalty. It was deeply ingrained by the war and was passed thereafter from parent to child. A fan was a National Leaguer or an American Leaguer—if his team didn't win the pennant, there was always the hope that his league could win the Series. It's inconceivable, for example, that a true Giant fan would ever have rooted for the New York Yankees in a World Series, even against the loathsome Dodgers.

Continental expansion, which brought the pillage of all but one of the two-league cities (Boston, Philadelphia, St. Louis, and New York—only Chicago remained) just about killed league loyalty. Fans in one-league cities have no feel for the other league. Little attention, let alone passion, is given to it. And, how could it be otherwise? There is no longer animosity between the leagues. Even churlishness is rare. The leagues are, in effect, business partners who put on a display of mock-combativeness at the All-Star Game and the World Series.

Contrast Connie Mack's approach to the 1933 All-Star Game with Whitey Herzog's to the 1983 game. Mack was there to win. He wanted to humiliate his old antagonist, John McGraw, the National League's manager. He told his squad that if some did not play, it was unimportant so long as the American League won. Among those who rode

Mack's bench all day were future Hall of Famers Bill Dickey and Jimmie Foxx. His future colleague at Cooperstown, Earl Averill, was luckier. He got to pinch-hit. But the American Leaguers won.

In 1983 Herzog's pregame position toward victory was, "Who cares?" His National League team reflected its leader's indifference, being battered, 13-3—whereupon Herzog announced to one and all that he was *glad* the American League had won! John McGraw, Barney Dreyfuss, and Charlie Ebbets must have spun in their graves. Unfortunately for baseball, however, the American League's victory had little emotional impact on the game's fans. If the leagues didn't care who won, why should the fans?

Even if interleague rivalry is a thing of the past, would tradition warrant retaining the two leagues? Hardly. The Organized Baseball Establishment has given the back of its hand to tradition at every opportunity. What happened to tradition when such hallowed franchises as the Brooklyn Dodgers, Boston Braves (a charter National League member), and Philadelphia Athletics were callously uprooted when greater profits beckoned elsewhere? Where was tradition when greed produced the 162-game schedule that would surely (and did) destroy the game's records? Where was tradition when the American League corrupted the game with the designated hitter? ("The outlook wasn't brilliant for the Mudville *nine* that day."—*Casey at the Bat* [emphasis added].) Tradition has long since been laid to rest. It's no grounds for keeping the two leagues.

The National and American Leagues should be replaced by four regional, eight-team leagues. Since a major purpose of the realignment would be to create fan loyalty—though to a region, not to a league—and thereby develop new, real fans, each league would be named for the region in which its teams were situated. Thus the Northeast, Midwest, Southern, and Western leagues, composed of these teams:

Northeast: Toronto Blue Jays, Montreal Expos, Boston Red Sox, New York Yankees, New York Mets, Philadelphia

Phillies, Baltimore Orioles, and (new) a team from Washington, Northern New Jersey, or Buffalo.

Midwest: Pittsburgh Pirates, Cincinnati Reds, Cleveland Indians, Detroit Tigers, Chicago Cubs, Chicago White Sox, Milwaukee Brewers, and Minnesota Twins.

Southern: Atlanta Braves, Houston Astros, Texas Rangers, Kansas City Royals, St. Louis Cardinals, and (new) three teams from among Tampa, New Orleans, Miami, Memphis, and Birmingham.

Western: San Diego Padres, California Angels, Los Angeles Dodgers, San Francisco Giants, Oakland Athletics, Seattle Mariners, and (new) two teams from among Vancouver, Phoenix, Portland, and Denver.

Each league would play a balanced 154-game schedule, i.e., twenty-two games against each other team, eleven at home, eleven away. Once again there would be true pennant races. No longer would contenders meet for the last time in midsummer. No longer would there be unbalanced (and hence unfair) schedules; the best team would win on its merits. There would be no divisions, no split seasons, no Shaughnessy playoffs, or any other bush practices. Just an old-fashioned, honest-to-goodness pennant race, the kind that used to grip the whole country, that was talked about into the winter. The winner would advance to postseason play; the losers would go home. To contend that baseball could not survive commercially if twenty-eight of thirty-two teams (87.5 percent) do not make the playoffs is nonsense. From 1903 through 1960 fourteen of sixteen teams (87.5 percent) did not make the World Series. Baseball got along very nicely financially with, it should be noted, nowhere near the television and radio income now received.

As is the case today, there would be three postseason series. Realignment, however, would admit only true champions into championship play. No longer would there be a ludicrous League Championship Series pitting one team against another it had beaten eleven out of twelve times during the regular season. To enhance the chances of the better team winning, all postseason series would be on a best-of-seven-games basis.

First-round matchups would be constant: Northeast vs. Midwest and Southern vs. Western. These pairings would maximize the possibility that at least one warm-weather city would host the World Series. In any event, they would eliminate such present potential World Series climatic horrors as, among others, Chicago vs. Toronto and Milwaukee vs. Montreal. (Were these teams to meet in the first round under the suggested realignment, the shorter regular season would increase the chance of comfortable weather over what it would be if the teams met in a World Series as now constituted.)

With four regional leagues and no gimmicks for deciding the winners, baseball would have *bona fide* champions competing for the game's ultimate crown. No other professional sport, with its wild-card teams or everyone-into-the-pool playoffs, could make that claim. (Nor can baseball now: The divisional setup permits mediocre teams to reach the World Series. Remember 1973? The New York Mets won the National League East with a disgraceful .509 mark. They caught a good Cincinnati Reds team looking the other way and stumbled into the Series.)

It would be easier for several reasons to stock new teams now than it was during prior expansions. First, the players' right to free agency won in 1976 would annually give to the six expansion teams the opportunity to sign some of the game's greatest stars. Second, the Caribbean area now sends more players to the major leagues than it formerly did, and it will continue to grow as a player source. Last, the United States population is quite adequate to support a slightly smaller increase of teams now, from twenty-six to thirty-two (23 percent) than occurred in 1961-62, from sixteen to twenty (25 percent). In 1983 the United States population was estimated at 234.2 million, or about 9 million per team. Expansion to thirty-two teams would reduce the per team number to 7.3 million. That's a decrease of about 19

percent per team. Sounds bad? Not really. It is insignificant
when baseball's golden age (1920-1941) is considered. In
1920 the United States population was 105.7 million, or
about 7.7 million per team. That's 5 percent more than the
7.3 million per team realignment would bring. Few fans
would complain if major league play were miraculously to
achieve 95 percent of the golden age's standard. One must
conclude that a well-managed, well-financed expansion franchise could reasonably expect to become competitive quite
quickly.

A 154-game schedule would be economically feasible.
Two attributes of the regional leagues would more than
offset the revenue loss of eight games: natural rivalries and
reduced travel expenses.

There's no doubt that the New York Yankees are a
tremendous attraction. Their mystique lures customers to the
ballpark regardless of how the Yankees are doing. But they
alone have that mystique. Other teams draw exceptional
crowds only because of their current success. The Cincinnati
Reds of the mid-1970s had fans everywhere flocking to see
them. The Cincinnati Reds of 1982-84 were not even an
average attraction. If the Seattle Mariners were burning up
the Western League, they would draw as many customers in
San Diego as did the Big Red Machine. League leaders,
whoever they are, will do about equally well.

So, the Yankees excepted, no club would lose any customers because it no longer played some long-time rival.
Instead, they would gain. The attendance drawn by the
natural rivalries created by the regional leagues would be
eye-popping. In 1955, for example, the New York Giants
drew 25 percent of the Brooklyn Dodgers' home attendance.
The Dodgers produced 42 percent of the Giants' home gate.
It is not unreasonable to predict that such regional natural
rivals as the Dodgers and the Angels or the White Sox and
the Cubs, to name but two of many, would do as well. The
probabilities are that they would do even better—and with
no travel expense. It would be lunacy if teams like the
Angels and White Sox were to deny themselves such a

source of revenue simply to retain the Yankees on their schedules.

That regional league teams would have drastically reduced travel expenses is easily shown:

	Present total miles to league cities	*Realigned total miles*	*Reduction*
CUBS	11,629	1,906	83.6%
DODGERS	21,447	3,766	82.4%
YANKEES	16,320	1,596	90.2%

The actual percentage of decrease would, of course, depend on a team's schedule. Let's then compare a 1983 Yankee West Coast road trip from New York and back with the *longest* trip they would have in the Northeast League, assuming Washington were the eighth team. From August 26 through September 4 the Yankees played in Anaheim, Oakland, and Seattle in that order. They traveled 13,769 miles. If instead they had gone to Montreal, Washington, and Toronto, they would have traveled 1,902 miles. Assuming two such West Coast swings (27,538 miles) and three Northeast treks (5,706 miles), the reduction in miles traveled would be 79.3 percent. More logical Northeast scheduling—Washington, Baltimore, Philadelphia (360 miles) —would produce a three-trip total of 1,080 miles, a reduction of 96.1 percent.

Both players and fans would benefit from compact regional schedules. There would be virtually no travel wear-and-tear on the players. No longer would teams have to span the country for their next game. No more red-eye specials. Careers could be lengthened since tired players are more susceptible to injury. The fans would also benefit, for no longer would they pay good money to see a physically drained team.

A further advantage to the fan is that with only seven

other teams to consider—each of which he could see eleven times—he would again know all the players in the league. Visiting players would again become the enemy. They would no longer be occasional visitors who were virtual strangers. Their quirks would be well known. Familiarity would breed contempt for the visiting teams—otherwise known as a healthy rooting interest in the hometown boys.

As a result, major league television rights (which all teams would share equally) would become more valuable. Audiences would be larger because each region would receive telecasts of only its league's games. The viewers would know the players. No longer would viewers be saddled with meaningless games of teams in other leagues. Each game would have a bearing on the pennant race about which the viewer was concerned. And the games would be televised at reasonable times: no longer would the West Coast have to watch games in midmornings, nor the East Coast watch games that ended at two A.M. or later. The greatest time difference between cities in any league would be one hour. An added benefit would be better press coverage: One's morning paper would carry a full story on the previous night's game.

Television would pay more for the All-Star Game since it would be regarded as Connie Mack viewed that of 1933. Each league would go all out to win, for victory in any interleague competition would figure to put more customers in that league's stands. There would be three All-Star Games, but only two dates would be needed. Since two All-Star Games were played in 1959-62, there's precedent for this. Initial pairings would rotate since weather is not a factor in midsummer. The championship game would go to the league that had not most recently hosted it.

Compact regional leagues with their natural rivalries would create new fans. Real fans. When postseason (and, to a lesser degree, All Star) play began, casual fans—and even non-fans, to whom the National and American Leagues now mean nothing—would take notice. It would be their city's team (or their region's) against the world. Interest in baseball would reach new peaks. Television audiences would set records. Inevitably some of these people would become interested enough to pay their way into future games. They would become real fans.

The structural changes required by realignment would, for the most part, only repeat what had been done on occasion before. Those that were novel would be easily handled by any experienced lawyer. Whatever the legal costs, these would be recouped many times over in a short period.

Realignment and expansion would propel baseball into the most prosperous era the game has ever seen. The long-range planning committee should act quickly to bring it about.

The Relief Pitcher's ERA Advantage

Bill James

It has become increasingly common in recent years to hear that a relief pitcher's ERA is unnaturally low, by about 50 points or a full run. A relief pitcher undoubtedly has an ERA advantage over a starting pitcher, created by the fact that he often begins his work with one or two men out in the inning. If three pitchers pitch one inning, with each pitcher giving up two walks and then getting an out, the first (starting) pitcher will be charged with two runs, the second with one run, the third with none. A relief pitcher has an advantage because his share of the inning most often comes at the end of it, while the men who score the runs come at the beginning.

But how large is the advantage? Who says it is a run or a half a run? Since every announcer in baseball seems determined to say that, shouldn't somebody check and see if it is true? This study, then, is an attempt to measure precisely the relief pitcher's ERA advantage.

I began by compiling a list of every pitcher who pitched at least 40 games or at least 100 innings for any major

BILL JAMES is the author of the annual *Bill James Baseball Abstract*.

league team between 1956 and 1970, and who made at least 90 percent of his appearances either as a starter or a reliever. There are 1006 such pitchers, 512 starters and 494 relievers. For each of these pitchers, three items of information were computed and/or recorded: the number of hits allowed per nine innings (HPG), the number of walks allowed per nine innings (WPG), and the ERA.

The pitchers were then coded to indicate the number of HPG and WPG they allowed. A pitcher who allowed 5.50 to 5.99 HPG was coded "A," 6.00 to 6.49 "B," 6.50 to 6.99 "C," etc. through the letter "J," representing 10.00 to 10.49 HPG. A pitcher who allowed 1.00 to 1.49 WPG was coded "Q," 1.50 to 1.99 "R," etc. through "Z," which indicates 5.50 to 5.99 WPG. There were 40 pitchers who had such extremely high or low ratios of HPG or WPG that they were excluded, but the remaining 956 were thus divided into 100 "cells" of approximately equal pitchers. For example, the code "FT" indicates that the pitcher allowed 8.00 to 8.49 HPG and 2.50 to 2.99 WPG. There are 35 pitchers, 20 starters and 15 relievers, in cell FT. Thus for every starter, we have a field of comparable relief pitchers, and for every reliever, a field of comparable starters.

The earned run averages of the starters and relievers in each cell were then compiled. The complete contents of one of the smaller cells, cell GW, are given for illustrations:

Year	Name		HPG	WPG	ERA
56S	Parnell		8.87	4.05	3.78
58R	Klippstein		8.61	4.24	4.10
66R	Knowles		8.82	4.14	3.06
66S	Cloninger		8.83	4.05	4.12
69S	Kirby		8.50	4.17	3.79
70S	Lockwood		8.95	4.09	4.29
STARTERS		(4)	8.79	4.09	3.99
RELIEVERS		(2)	8.71	4.19	3.58

Once this was done, the information in each cell was weighted and grouped with the information from the nearby cells to improve the reliability of the data. Thus the data listed for cell GW is not identical to the content of that cell alone. An explanation of precisely how the data were grouped, as well as detailed notes of the experiment, can be obtained from the author.

Thus for every range of HPG and WPG, we devise an estimate of the ERA which is typical of starters and relievers in that range, and so have a basis for comparison of essentially equivalent pitchers.

The information from the "border" cells, cells coded A, J, Q, and Z and representing the highest and lowest ranges of HPG and WPG, was not sufficient to establish reliable comparisons in those ranges. The typical ERAs derived from all other cells are presented below (asterisks indicate unreliable data):

STARTERS

		R	S	T	U	V	W	X	Y
		1.50–	2.00–	2.50–	3.00–	3.50–	4.00–	4.50–	5.00–
		1.99	2.49	2.99	3.49	3.99	4.49	4.49	5.49
		WPG	WPG	WPG	WPG	WPG	WPG	WPG	WPG
B	(6.00-6.49 HPG)	2.04*	2.14*	2.40	2.56	2.64*	2.82*	2.82*	3.11*
C	(6.50-6.99 HPG)	2.32	2.41	2.62	2.72	2.92	2.98	3.18	3.38*
D	(7.00-7.49 HPG)	2.54	2.68	2.82	3.00	3.13	3.28	3.37	3.60*
E	(7.50-7.99 HPG)	2.82	2.91	3.06	3.23	3.36	3.47	3.65	3.64*
F	(8.00-8.49 HPG)	2.98	3.14	3.28	3.43	3.57	3.71	3.80	4.05*
G	(8.50-8.99) HPG)	3.28	3.37	3.54	3.66	3.78	3.89	4.13*	4.31*
H	(9.00-9.49 HPG)	3.48	3.62	3.76	3.89	3.98	4.15	4.26*	4.60*
I	(9.50-9.99 HPG)	3.77	3.86	4.03	4.15	4.31	4.49*	—	—

RELIEVERS

	R	S	T	U	V	W	X	Y
B	2.23*	2.18	2.29	2.29	2.35	2.52	2.61*	2.60*
C	2.17	2.36	2.46	2.52	2.63	2.83	3.00	3.01*

	R	S	T	U	V	W	X	Y
D	2.41	2.45	2.63	2.77	2.86	2.99	3.22	3.29*
E	2.49	2.70	2.89	2.99	3.09	3.17	3.31	3.56
F	2.79	3.00	3.15	3.28	3.28	3.36	3.58	3.62
G	3.06	3.19	3.39	3.47	3.62	3.74	3.90	4.04
H	3.43	3.46	3.59	3.77	3.87	4.07	4.35	4.57*
I	3.77*	3.69	3.82	3.90	4.04	4.30	4.83	4.97*

By subtracting the relief ERAs from the starting ERAs (using reliable data only), we then have 45 estimates of the relief pitcher's ERA advantage. These are:

	R	S	T	U	V	W	X	Y	Total	Avg.
B			.11	.27					.38	.19
C	.15	.05	.16	.20	.29	.15			1.00	.17
D	.13	.23	.19	.23	.27	.29	.15		1.49	.21
E	.33	.21	.17	.24	.27	.30	.34		1.86	.27
F	.19	.14	.13	.15	.29	.35	.22		1.47	.21
G	.22	.18	.15	.19	.16	.15			1.05	.17
H	.05	.06	.17	.12	.11	.08			.09	.11
I		.17	.21	.25	.27				.90	.22
TOTALS	1.07	1.14	1.29	1.65	1.66	1.32	.71		8.84	.20
Avg.	.18	.16	.16	.21	.24	.22	.24			.20

1. There is no doubt whatsoever that a relief pitcher does enjoy an advantage in compiling his ERA. There are 45 cells giving reliable information, and in all 45 relief pitchers have better ERAs than starters of comparable ability, as measured by statistics not affected by pitching in relief.

2. The data derived is quite consistent in suggesting an ERA advantage to the relief pitcher in the range of .15 to .25. We may with very little fear of contradiction say that a relief pitcher's ERA should be adjusted upward by .20 for accurate comparison to the ERAs of starting pitchers.

A baseball park as it was meant to be

Bill Veeck Park

Philip H. Bess

In spite of its exorbitant cost and monumental ugliness, the modern-day, multipurpose stadium—with or without a dome—has become the urban icon of our times. This is bad, both for our cities and for our games. It is bad for cities because it perpetuates their division into functional zones, making impossible that concentrated and simultaneous mix of activities that for millennia has been the hallmark of urban life. It is bad for our games because it manages to combine extraordinary lack of character with seating arrangements and playing surfaces that are unsatisfactory for both football and baseball.

Twenty-five years of these mega-buildings have persuaded nearly everyone but those responsible for building them

PHILIP BESS is an architect in Chicago. He would like to thank the School of Architecture at the University of Notre Dame, and its chairman, Robert Amico, for providing workspace; Notre Dame students Jeff Smith, Mauricio Salazar, and David Gester, for their assistance; and SABR members Bob Bluthhardt, Cappy Gagnon, Lloyd Johnson, Cliff Kachline, Philip Lowry, and Philip Bolda for their interest and encouragement.

that they are a blight upon our cities and upon our games. The time has come to abolish these monsters, and to restore the aesthetic, urban, and athletic sanity of the single-purpose sports facility. We need to make both less and more of our baseball parks: they need to be less monumental in scale and intention, and they need to be more suited to baseball and more civic in character, built at a scale that contributes to and promotes the richness and variety of traditional urban life.

To be specific, here are five reasons why the traditional 40,000-seat urban ballpark is good for our cities and good for baseball:

- **1.** Because its size is in part a function of the size of the city block it occupies, it reinforces the traditional urban pattern of streets and squares.
- **2.** Because it is typically near public transit lines, it reduces the amount of automobile traffic generated by ballgames.
- **3.** Because of its relatively modest scale, it is more hospitable to adjacent activities (including residential neighborhoods), and it can be built with standard construction techniques, making it less costly to build.
- **4.** Because of all these factors, the result is ballparks and playing fields with idiosyncrasies and character. This also results in neighborhoods with identities: Wrigley Field and "Wrigleyville," Ebbets Field and Flatbush, Fenway Park and Back Bay.

On the other hand, here are five reasons why the 60,000-seat multi-use stadium is bad for cities and bad for baseball:

- **1.** Because it is unconstrained by the standard unit of urban design (the block), it is typically an island in a sea of parking, mandating exclusive automobile access, and destroying traditional urban spatial patterns.
- **2.** Because of its size and parking requirements, it discourages adjacent development, except for other anti-urban mega-projects of similar scale: convention centers, high-rise hotels, and amusement parks.

- **3.** Because it is conceived as either a dome or as a state-of-the-art technological marvel, it is typically more than twice as costly to build than the traditional park. When it is built to accommodate football as well as baseball, parking requirements (and their costs) increase by as much as 250 percent.
- **4.** Because of its size and the fact that it is not designed for any sport in particular, seating patterns are good for neither football nor baseball, and seats are far removed from the playing field.
- **5.** Finally, the result of all of these factors is stadiums that could be anywhere, and uniform dimension playing fields devoid of idiosyncrasies and character.

Today, more than ever, cherished patterns of urban living and the game of baseball require a disciplined defense against the multipurpose stadium and the violence it does to our cities.

Toward that end I went to work on a proposal for Bill Veeck Park, not as a prototype that could be plopped down anywhere (and certainly—though the point may now be academic—not as an alternative to either Comiskey Park or Wrigley Field), but as a site-specific project intended as a model for how urban ballparks and their environs should be conceived.

The site for this project is a parcel of land on the near South Side of Chicago, which has already been designated by the city for development as a multi-use stadium. The city chose the site in part because of its proximity to both public transportation lines and major expressway connections. Right now, it is the site mostly of abandoned railyards, although a few live railway lines remain as constraints upon the use of the site. None of the adjacent buildings illustrated in my drawings exists; they are part of my proposal.

Bill Veeck Park is a 44,000-seat, natural-grass, baseball-only facility that takes its form in part from existing constraints: The Chicago Transit Authority tracks beyond right field; the St. Charles Airline, a freight line, that runs below the bleachers in left field; the Chicago River beyond the third-base line. The obtuse angle in centerfield implied by the adjacent tracks dictates that left field and left-center field be deeper than right field; and the necessity of entering through the center-field tower entry at about 40 feet above grade provides the opportunity to create loge-like box seating atop the right field wall, some 35 feet above the playing field.

In addition to the center-field tower (which would contain team offices, some executive suites, and a scoreboard), fans enter from the right-field corner and from behind home plate. On the south side of the park—replete with a statue of Bill Veeck—is Bill Veeck Square, the point of arrival by both CTA train and taxi service. On the north side of the park is the grand stair and ramp, which brings pedestrians and fans who use the north parking lot up over the railroad tracks and into the park. I am proposing to relocate Claes Oldenberg's Bat Column to one of the mid-level terraces. In the event of pennants clinched or World Series won (admittedly an uncommon phenomenon here in Chicago), the square and the terrace would lend themselves to spontaneous but manageable civic celebrations.

How does this proposal differ from older traditional urban ballparks? Mainly, it has to take automobile access into account. Bill Veeck Park is accessible by city and regional transit lines, as well as by water taxi from the Loop. Nevertheless, if adjacent neighborhoods are to be protected from the traffic that the ballpark will inevitably generate, it is necessary to provide parking facilities at a ratio of about one space per seven seats. But instead of the typical modern solution of the stadium as an island in an ocean of parking, my design calls for linear parking to the north and to the east. (The parking to the east could also double as overflow parking for Bears games held in nearby Soldier Field.)

How about the economics of a modern, traditional ballpark? Robert Baade, professor of economics at Lake Forest College and a specialist in sports stadium financing, documents impressive evidence that the construction of large-scale mega-stadiums is motivated by reasons that have little to do with economic sanity. He puts it rather succinctly:

"The history of recent stadium construction is written in red ink." He makes a persuasive argument that stadium development *per se* is not profitable, but that a smaller-scale ballpark done as part of a larger adjacent development—like the one I'm proposing—might be not only an aesthetic and urban improvement, but economically feasible as well. My plan calls for a combination of low-rise high-density housing and commercial and office space, as well as civic and institutional buildings and public open space. Most of the buildings range from three and one-half to six stories; a few are as tall as twelve stories. You can get a good idea of the proposal from the diagram of the master plan drawing.

The people who are currently responsible for the planning, financing, and construction of professional athletic facilities seem to have a mental picture of modern stadiums beneath which are captions like "state-of-the-art technology" or "world-class facility." But America is becoming saturated with virtually identical world-class facilities. It is no small irony that almost any one of the more modest ballparks of the early twentieth century contributed more to the uniqueness of its city, to its city's sense of place and identity, than any of the new superstadiums. I know of no one who is enamored of these newer stadiums, except for planners, developers, politicians, and architects.

This architect hopes that this demonstration project can help to change current thinking. I believe that Bill Veeck Park illustrates a reasoned and reasonable alternative to current practice. It has always been, and will always be, necessary for ballpark design to satisfy pragmatic and economic criteria. But the current paradigm is wrong. Bill Veeck Park is right. It is right economically. It is right for our cities. And it is right for baseball.

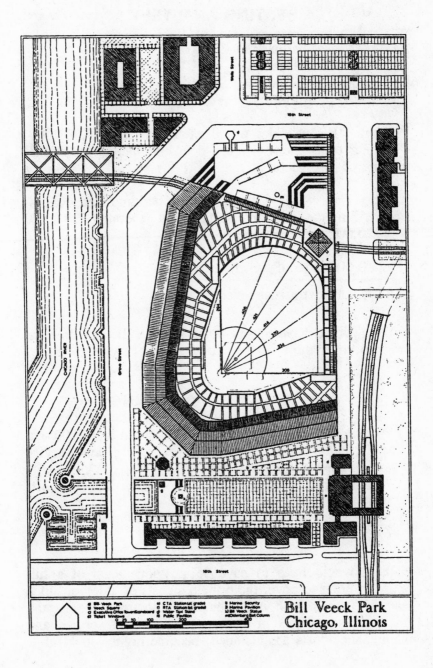

Bill Veeck Park
Chicago, Illinois

SEATING ANALYSIS

A) 44,000-seat ballpark @ $1500/seat
   = $66 million
B) 50,000-seat ballpark @ $1500/seat
   = $75 million

Ballpark "B" provides 6,000 extra seats for $9,000,000. (Building costs *alone*—figure does not include additional parking costs or debt service.)

If every fan spends $20 on tickets, parking, and concessions, filling the additional seats would generate 6000 x $20 = $120,000/game.

$$\frac{\$9,000,000 \text{ (cost of construction)}}{\$120,000 \text{ (extra seat revenue)}} = 75$$

Team would have to sell out Ballpark "B" 75 times in order to cover the *principal* building costs alone.

DOME COST ANALYSIS

1) Assume that a dome built in 1987 would add $700/seat to building construction costs (excluding debt service and dome maintenance).
2) Assume that revenue lost for a weather-induced postponement = $20/seat.
3) $\dfrac{\$700}{\$20} = 35$

Team would have to have 35 postponements of a full house in order to cover the principal costs of a dome. Since teams in a bad year will suffer 2-3 rainouts at home, the financial advantages of a dome (when debt service and maintenance costs are included) become highly doubtful.

COMPARATIVE COST ANALYSES

Costs for 80,000-seat multi-use stadium:

Land costs	$25,000,000
Infrastructure improvements	68,000,000
80,000 seat stadium at $2019/seat	161,520,000
Parking on 60 acres (21,000 spaces required): for 8,700 cars @ $1500/car *surface parking*	13,050,000
for 12,300 cars @ $6000/car *structure parking*	73,800,000
TOTAL	$341,370,000

Costs for 44,000-seat baseball park:

Land costs	$25,000,000
Infrastructure improvements	68,000,000
44,000 seat ballpark @ $1500/seat	66,000,000
Parking on 54 acres (6500 cars required): for 6,500 cars @ $2000/car surface parking	13,000,000
TOTAL	$172,000,000

Figures based upon the following assumptions:
(1) Cost of domed multi-use stadium at $2019/seat (4th quarter, 1984)
(2) Cost of single-use open-air ballpark at $1500/seat
(3) 70 acres of land at $25,000,000
(4) Infrastructure improvements at $68,000,000
(5) Parking requirements of 1 space/4 seats (football) 1 space/7 seats (baseball)
(6) Parking costs of $1500-2000/space (surface) $6000/space (structured)

Forget batting average—this is a better index

On-Base Average

Pete Palmer

There are two main objectives for the hitter. The first is to not make an out and the second is to hit for distance. Long-ball hitting is normally measured by slugging average. Not making an out can be expressed in terms of on-base average (OBA), where:

$$OBA = \frac{Hits + Walks + Hit\text{-}by\text{-}Pitch}{At\ Bats + Walks + Hit\text{-}by\text{-}Pitch}$$

For example, if we were figuring out Frank Robinson's career on-base average, it would be compiled like this: 2943 hits + 1420 walks + 198 hit-by-pitch (4561), divided by 10006 at bats + 1420 walks + 198 HBP (11624). His OBA is .392, which happens to be one of the higher figures of recent years, but does not compare very well with players of the past. Sacrifice hits are ignored in this calculation.

On-base average can be quite different from batting aver-

PETE PALMER is co-author of *The Kidder Game of Baseball* and chairman of SABR's statistical analysis committee.

age. Take for example Joe DiMaggio and Roy Cullenbine, once outfield teammates for the Yankees. DiMag had a lifetime batting average of .325 and Cullenbine .276. But Roy was walked much more frequently than Joe and made fewer outs; he had an OBA of .408, compared to .398 for the Yankee Clipper.

In calculating OBA, the Macmillan Baseball Encyclopedia was used for hits, at bats, and bases on balls. Hit-by-pitch data are from official averages back to 1920 in the AL and 1917 in the NL. Figures back to 1909 have been compiled by Alex Haas from newspaper box scores. Some data before then comes from Haas, John Tattersall, and Bob Davids. Additional information is available in some of the old newspapers, but has not yet been compiled. Players with incomplete totals are credited with HBP at the known rate from available data for those unknown appearances. In the NL prior to 1887, a batter was not awarded first base when hit by a pitch. In the American Association, HBP was started in 1884.

Who is the all-time leader in on-base average? It is Ted Williams with a spectacular .483 mark. Not surprisingly, Babe Ruth is second with .474. It is no secret that Williams and Ruth were both exceptionally good hitters as well as being among the most frequent walk receivers. It was not unusual for them to get on base 300 times a season. Ranking third on the all-time list is John McGraw, who was elected to the Hall of Fame as a manager, but who also was a fine hitter. In addition, he was adept at getting on base by walks and HBP. He holds the all-time NL record for OBA both lifetime and season. Billy Hamilton, the stolen-base king, and Lou Gehrig are next in line, followed by such big names as Rogers Hornsby, Ty Cobb, Jimmie Foxx, and Tris Speaker. Rounding out the top ten is Ferris Fain, former first baseman of the A's, who quietly attained a very high OBA to go with his two batting titles.

Some players who many fans might not think to be among the leaders in OBA are Max Bishop, second baseman of the A's last super teams of 1929-31, Clarence "Cupid" Childs, Cleveland second sacker in the 1890's,

Roy Thomas, Phil center fielder at the turn of the century, and Joe Cunningham, who played with the Cardinals and White Sox just a few years ago. On the other hand, some of the famous hitters of baseball are not included in the accompanying list of players with lifetime on-base averages of .400 or better. Missing are such stars as Willie Keeler, Bill Terry, George Sisler, Nap Lajoie, Al Simmons, Hans Wagner, Cap Anson, Joe DiMaggio, and Roberto Clemente.

Since most of the players in the .400 list are either outfielders or first basemen, an additional table is shown that provides data on the top ten players at each position. Many unheralded players are high in the OBA figures, such as Wally Schang, who played for many AL clubs in the teens and twenties and is second among catchers, and Elmer Valo, another Connie Mack product, who ranks sixth in right field.

There are only two active players with OBAs of .400 or better, and only a few among the leaders by position. The level of OBA in the majors is presently quite low. This could be attributed to many factors, such as improved pitching (bigger and stronger pitchers throwing from the unchanged distance of 60 feet 6 inches, more use of relief pitchers, and the widespread use of the slider as an extra pitch), larger ballparks, and increased emphasis on hitting home runs.

The surprise leader among players active in 1984 is Mike Hargrove of the Indians, who annually receives a high total of bases on balls. His OBA percentage is .401, a few points ahead of Rod Carew of the Angels. Another surprise among the leaders is Gene Tenace, whose career batting average is only .242, but he gets almost as many walks as he does hits. The top ten among players active in 1984 with at least 1000 career games include:

Mike Hargrove	.401	Ken Singleton	.391
Rod Carew	.397	Mike Schmidt	.388
Joe Morgan	.395	Greg Gross	.379
Keith Hernandez	.394	Pete Rose	.377
Gene Tenace	.391	Bobby Grich	.375

Gary Mathews was the season leader in 1984 with a .417 mark. Eddie Murray led in the AL with a .415 figure. These season averages are far below the top season marks of the past, which are dominated by Ted Williams and Ruth. Here is the list of top season OBA performers with averages of .500 or more.

Ted Williams, 1941	.551	Babe Ruth, 1926	.516
John McGraw, 1899	.546	Mickey Mantle, 1957	.515
Babe Ruth, 1923	.545	Babe Ruth, 1924	.513
Babe Ruth, 1920	.530	Babe Ruth, 1921	.512
Ted Williams, 1957	.528	Rogers Hornsby, 1924	.508
Billy Hamilton, 1894	.521	Joe Kelley, 1894	.502
Ted Williams, 1954	.516	Hugh Duffy, 1894	.501

Ted Williams led the league in OBA every year he qualified except for his rookie season, and he had a higher OBA than the leader in three of his four seasons shortened by injury. Those leading the league most often in OBA are:

AL			NL		
	Ted Williams	12		Rogers Hornsby	8
	Babe Ruth	10		Stan Musial	6
	Ty Cobb	6		Billy Hamilton	5
	Lou Gehrig	5		Joe Morgan	5
	Carl Yastrzemski	5		Richie Ashburn	4
	Rod Carew	4		Mel Ott	4
				Honus Wagner	4

It is important to remember that OBA is only one component of hitting, and that slugging is equally valuable. Of course, the best long-ball hitters usually rank high in both departments because they are generally walked more frequently. One thing the OBA does is give percentage recognition to the players' ability to get on via the walk and the HBP as well as the hit. He has saved his team an out and he is in a good position to score a run.

ON-BASE AVERAGE LEADERS
1000 games minimum—through 1984

Player	Years	AB	BH	BB	HBP	OBA
Ted Williams	1939-1960	7706	2654	2018	39	.483
Babe Ruth	1914-1935	8399	2873	2056	42	.474
John McGraw	1891-1906	3924	1309	836	116	.464
Billy Hamilton	1888-1901	6268	2158	1187	93+	.456
Lou Gehrig	1923-1939	8001	2721	1508	45	.447
Rogers Hornsby	1915-1937	8173	2930	1038	48	.434
Ty Cobb	1905-1928	11437	4192	1249	92	.433
Jimmie Foxx	1926-1945	8134	2646	1452	13	.430
Tris Speaker	1907-1928	10205	3514	1381	101	.427
Ferris Fain	1947-1955	3930	1139	903	18	.425
Eddie Collins	1906-1930	9949	3310	1503	77	.424
Joe Jackson	1908-1920	4981	1774	519	59	.423
Max Bishop	1924-1935	4494	1216	1153	31	.423
Mickey Mantle	1951-1968	8102	2415	1734	13	.423
Dan Brouthers	1879-1904	6711	2296	840	105	.423
Mickey Cochrane	1925-1937	5169	1652	857	29	.419
Stan Musial	1941-1963	10972	3630	1599	53	.418
Clarence Childs	1890-1901	5615	1720	990	66	.416
Jesse Burkett	1890-1905	8421	2850	1029	70+	.415
Melvin Ott	1926-1947	9456	2876	1708	64	.414
Ed Delahanty	1888-1903	7505	2597	741	95+	.412
Hank Greenberg	1930-1947	5193	1628	852	16	.412
Roy Thomas	1899-1911	5296	1537	1042	42	.411
Charlie Keller	1939-1952	3790	1085	784	10	.410
Harry Heilmann	1914-1932	7787	2660	856	40	.410
Jackie Robinson	1947-1956	4877	1518	740	72	.410
Eddie Stanky	1943-1953	4301	1154	996	34	.410
Roy Cullenbine	1938-1947	3879	1072	852	11	.408

Player	Years	AB	BH	BB	HBP	OBA
Joe Cunningham	1954-1966	3362	980	599	49	.406
Riggs Stephenson	1921-1934	4508	1515	494	40	.406
Denny Lyons	1885-1897	4294	1333	621	70+	.406
Arky Vaughan	1932-1948	6622	2103	937	46	.406
Paul Waner	1926-1945	9459	3152	1091	38	.404
Chas. Gehringer	1924-1942	8858	2839	1185	51	.404
Joe Kelley	1891-1908	6977	2213	910	86+	.402
Lu Blue	1921-1933	5904	1696	1092	43	.402
Pete Browning	1882-1894	4820	1646	466	24+	.402
Mike Hargrove	1974-1984	5280	1533	926	53	.401

+ Hit by pitch estimated from partial career totals

ON-BASE AVERAGE LIFETIME LEADERS BY POSITION
1000 games minimum—at least 500 games at position

Catcher

.419 Mickey Cochrane
.393 Wally Schang
.389 Gene Tenace
.384 Roger Bresnahan
.382 Bill Dickey
.378 Rick Ferrell
.371 Joe Torre
.370 Gabby Hartnett
.369 Virgil Davis
.353 Ted Simmons

First base

.447 Lou Gehrig
.430 Jimmie Foxx
.425 Ferris Fain
.423 Dan Brouthers
.418 Stan Musial
.412 Hank Greenberg
.406 Joe Cunningham
.402 Lu Blue
.401 Mike Hargrove
.397 Johnny Mize
.397 Roger Connor

Second base

.434 Rogers Hornsby
.424 Eddie Collins
.423 Max Bishop
.416 Clarence Childs

.410 Eddie Stanky
.410 Jackie Robinson
.404 Charlie Gehringer
.397 Rod Carew
.395 Joe Morgan
.392 George Grantham

Third base

.464 John McGraw
.406 Denny Lyons
.394 Eddie Yost
.394 Stan Hack
.390 Harlond Clift
.388 Mike Schmidt
.387 Al Rosen
.381 Richie Allen
.379 Harmon Killebrew
.377 Pete Rose

Shortstop

.406 Arky Vaughan
.399 Luke Appling
.394 Johnny Pesky
.391 Joe Sewell
.390 Honus Wagner
.390 Joe Cronin
.380 Hughie Jennings
.380 Lou Boudreau
.370 Cecil Travis
.368 Peewee Reese

Left field

.483 Ted Williams
.423 Joe Jackson

.418 Stan Musial
.415 Jesse Burkett
.412 Ed Delahanty
.410 Charlie Keller
.406 Riggs Stephenson
.402 Joe Kelley
.398 Ralph Kiner
.397 Elmer E. Smith

Center field

.456 Billy Hamilton
.433 Ty Cobb
.427 Tris Speaker
.423 Mickey Mantle
.411 Roy Thomas
.402 Pete Browning
.398 Joe DiMaggio
.397 Richie Ashburn
.397 Earle Combs
.395 Hack Wilson
.395 Earl Averill

Right field

.474 Babe Ruth
.414 Mel Ott
.410 Harry Heilmann
.408 Roy Cullenbine
.404 Paul Waner
.399 Elmer Valo
.399 Ross Youngs
.392 Frank Robinson
.392 Mike Tiernan
.391 Ken Singleton

June 14, 1870—still the greatest game ever played?

The Day the Reds Lost

George Bulkley

Tuesday, June 14, 1870, was fair and warm in New York City. The mercury on this pleasant day climbed slowly and steadily until the thermometer at Hudnut's popular pharmacy at the corner of Broadway and Ann Street registered 86 degrees at 3 P.M.

Up the Hudson a few miles, at West Point, relatives and friends of the 1870 Class were grateful that the planning committee, in arranging for tomorrow's graduation ceremony, had selected a shady, grassy plot rather than the customary treeless parade ground. Today the cadets would stage their last drill.

But for most Manhattanites, those who were sportsminded at least, the doings up the Hudson were of little moment. The big story for them was the battle scheduled to take place in the city across the East River, sleepy old Brooklyn.

It was a glorious day for a game of ball and Patrolman Wilson, of the 28th Precinct, was unquestionably the only

GEORGE BULKLEY wrote some 30 articles for the old *Baseball Magazine*.

baseball addict in the bustling city of a million and a half souls whose blood didn't race through his veins at the thought of the big doings that lay ahead. Officer Wilson had other thoughts on his mind, for last night, according to James Gordon Bennett's *Herald*, a cowardly sneak thief, entering his bedroom at 111 Prince Street, stole his pants, his shield (NO. 1,530), his fire alarm key (No. 6), and $7 in cash. Wilson, who had intended going to the ballgame (his off-duty day), was destined to spend the morning and most of the afternoon making out reports and attempting to regain his status symbols—along with his trousers.

For the rest of New York's ball fans, there was but one thing to do and that was to make tracks for the Capitoline Grounds in Brooklyn. The Cincinnati Red Stockings—the mighty Reds—were in town and scheduled to cross bats with the once mighty Atlantics.

Nothing like the Red Stockings had ever happened to baseball before. Organized in 1869 as the first avowedly all-professional baseball club, they had proved a remarkable success on the field and become the greatest gate attraction the game had known.

When the English-born Harry Wright sat down with his club directors in the winter of 1868-69, he proposed to get the very best players in the country, many of whom were in the status of what was subsequently called semiprofessional players—those who shared in gate receipts but worked outside baseball for a living—and turn them into outright professionals, drawing regular salaries which would enable them to do nothing all summer except play baseball. But how much would it cost, the directors asked. Harry had it all figured out and, if he could get the players he wanted, he told them the payroll would come to $9300.

Top salary would go to Wright's younger brother George, who in 1868 was playing with the Unions of Morisania, a region of Westchester County then, since absorbed by the Bronx. George would go west for a wage of $1400, and they say he was worth every cent of it, inasmuch as he was the outstanding player of his day. Harry himself would draw $1200 for managing the club and playing the outfield (and managing the club entailed all the duties that are now delegated to the general manager, the manager, and the road secretary, as well as the scheduling of games).

From New Jersey came Doug Allison and Irish-born Andy Leonard; from New Hampshire, Charlie Sweasy, whose name through the years has been misspelled more ways than any other ballplayer's including Carl Yastrzemski. Cal McVey hailed from Montrose County, Iowa, and, except for Cincinnatian Charley Gould, was the only midwesterner on the club. The other four regulars, the Wright brothers, Asa Brainard, and Fred Waterman, came from New York State. The locales of substitutes Hurley, Fowler, Bradford, and Taylor are not known.

Because Gould was the only Cincinnati native on the team there were some critics who insisted on calling it an "eclectic" nine ("all-star," future generations would term it). These critics predicted some terrible things would come of such an arrangement, a team whose motivation was pecuniary rather than civic. (The same dire sentiments have more recently been directed toward George Steinbrenner's "eclectic" nine.)

The Reds swept the baseball scene literally from coast to coast in 1869, defeating all comers and arousing such interest that by the spring of 1870 every city of any size had organized its own team of professionals to beat the Reds when they dared to come to town. From that point on there was no question as to which way baseball was going. Gone was the heyday of the amateur and semi-professional teams, except as feeders for the play-for-pay game.

As the Reds invaded New York in 1870, they were riding a two-year winning streak of 90 games. And only yesterday they'd trounced the Mutuals to make it 91.

The Capitoline, the first enclosed baseball grounds, lay between Nostrand Avenue on the west and Marcy Avenue on the east, and between Putnam Avenue on the north and Halsey Street on the south. It was located on part of a farm leased from the Lefferts family, who had owned the land since Revolutionary days, by Reuben S. Decker's father. Reuben Decker it was who, along with H. A. Weed, built the stands in 1862. (Later, in 1879, the original farm was forced into physical oblivion as Jefferson Avenue and Hancock Street were cut through the ballpark by the city. Today this four-city-block area is part of the Bedford-Stuyvesant section, much in the news in recent years.)

Many years later Decker's daughter recalled the -1870 scene for the writer.

Sheds and stables were located about half the length of the Putnam Avenue side, beginning at Nostrand Avenue. In front of these were permanent buildings housing the restaurant, bandstand, private rooms for the families of the proprietors, sitting rooms for the ladies on the second floor and, on the first floor, lockers and storage rooms for the baseball teams. In addition, bleachers for the accommodation of 5,000 persons were erected along the Nostrand Avenue and Halsey Street sides of the grounds. The entrance was on Nostrand about 200 feet south of Putnam.

The field was known formally as the "Capitoline Skating Lake and Base-Ball Ground." In November the grounds were flooded from a city main at the corner of Halsey and Nostrand and used for skating all winter, as well as baseball matches on ice featuring many of the stars of the field. Come spring, the water was drained off and the grounds turned over first to Phineas T. Barnum for his circus, and then prepared for the baseball season.

If you were a baseball fan in 1870 and lived in Manhattan you crossed the East River to Brooklyn on the ferry. Construction work on the Brooklyn Bridge had just started and wouldn't be finished until 1883; indeed, so little progress had been made that, stare as you might while crossing the river, you could see nothing that indicated a bridge was being built.

In your horsecar, you then followed Fulton Street in a southerly direction through the heart of downtown Brooklyn (population 419,921, 1870 census), and turned eastward for a ramble through the countryside. The total distance from the ferry slip to the ballfield was three and a quarter miles. You left the horsecar at the corner of Fulton and

Nostrand and walked north a few hundred feet to the Capitoline.

One street west of Nostrand is Bedford Avenue, and if you had left the car at the corner and followed Bedford Avenue south exactly one mile you would have found yourself at the future site of another ballpark that figured large in baseball history—Ebbets Field.

On this second day of the Reds' 1870 invasion of the metropolis the fans sensed the possibility of an Atlantic victory. They flowed toward the Capitoline from all directions, starting shortly after noon, until the field was engulfed with humanity. The grounds were jammed to capacity and many hundreds stood on the field itself, along both foul lines and behind the outfielders.

Harper's Weekly estimated the crowd to be between 12,000 and 15,000 shoehorned into a park that could seat at best 5,000. Said the New York *World*: "Hundreds who could or would not produce the necessary fifty-cent stamp for admission [Harry Wright always insisted on that fee although twenty-five cents was the norm of the period] looked on through cracks in the fence or even climbed boldly to the top, while others were perched in the topmost limbs of the trees or on roofs of surrounding houses."

The cause of this wellspring of optimism isn't quite clear. Only the day before, the Red Stockings had mauled the Mutuals, 16 to 3. Yet on their previous visit to New York they had eked out a 4-2 win—an unprecedentedly low score for the time, at this level of play—over these same Mutuals before moving on to clobber the Atlantics by 32-10. On comparative records, then, the visitors appeared likely to overwhelm the Brooklynites.

Add to this the fact that the Atlantics had already suffered defeat three times in 1870, due mostly to trouble within the ranks—trouble so acute that it was freely predicted that Dickey Pearce and other stars would not play in the game with the Reds. Tactless Bob Ferguson, captain of the Atlantics, was in the midst of a feud with the baseball writer of the New York *Herald*. A lively discussion between these worthies had ended with the writer charging the other with running off his best players by his insolence, and Ferguson countering with an offer to do some dental work on the scribe without benefit of a forceps.

As a result, the *Herald* man refused to cover the Atlantics-Cincinnati game, although he had reported the previous day's Mutual match with a thousand-word story. And so, while other papers gave the game of June 14 full coverage, the *Herald* man stayed at home and devoted just 200 words to a critique of the game and the unruly nature of the crowd. And his paper didn't even print a box score of the greatest game of baseball played up until that time.

That the gamblers did not expect a home-team win is shown by what the racing people call the morning line. Before the game, betting was 5-1 on the Red Stockings—and when Cincinnati moved ahead in the early innings 3-0, the odds zoomed to 10-1 with few takers.

The Atlantics, however, had patched up their differences and their strongest team took the field, nattily attired in long dark blue trousers (with a light cord down the outer seams), shirts with the initial letter of the club name embroidered on the chest, and light buff linen caps. The Reds wore their customary knickerbockers and bright red stockings. They had an Old English "C" on their shirt panels. During the day George Zettlein, the hardworking pitcher of the home team, deviated somewhat from the uniform of the day: he worked much of the game stripped to a silk undershirt and his uniform pants.

Every newspaper commented on the boisterous and unruly conduct of the spectators. "As the Red Stockings entered the field," said one paper, "a few of the toughs in the assemblage attempted to hiss them, but at once a round of applause greeted the strangers. . . ." Another reported that "the visitors were annoyed throughout by catcalls, hisses, and jeers, their misplays being applauded, and their finest efforts received in silence."

As the opponents squared off, the batting orders looked like this:

CINCINNATI

George Wright, ss
Charley Gould, 1b
Fred Waterman, 3b
Doug Allison, c
Harry Wright, cf
Andy Leonard, lf
Asa Brainard, p
Charlie Sweasy, 2b
Cal McVey, rf

ATLANTICS

Dickey Pearce, ss
Charles Smith, 3b
Joe Start, 1b
John Chapman, lf
Bob Ferguson, c
George Zettlein, p
George Hall, cf
Lipman Pike, 2b
Dan McDonald, rf

The Reds lost no time once the game got under way, George Wright singling down the left-field line and, after the next two men were retired, scoring on singles by Allison and Harry Wright. On the latter's blow there was an error by McDonald, and Allison also crossed the plate. The Reds increased their lead to 3-0 in the third with hits by George Wright and Waterman proving the decisive blows. Dickey Pearce ended the threat of a big inning by coming up with Allison's sharp grounder and starting a fast double play.

The Atlantics, meanwhile, could do nothing with Brainard's delivery. Pitchers in 1870 worked from a distance of only forty-five feet from home plate but were restricted by the rules to an underhand "pitch." The wrist snap needed to throw curve balls would not be legalized until 1872, so pitchers had to rely on nothing except speed and a change of pace.

Cincinnati was at its defensive best this day. Henry Chadwick, baseball editor of the New York *Clipper,* was fascinated by the style in which the fielders moved about as the different batsmen took their turns. A model display, he thought. "In fact," said Henry, "Harry Wright would at one time be seen playing almost back of second base, while Sweasy would be nearly a first-base fielder, and so they changed about, coming in nearer or going out farther, just as they judged the balls would be sent to the different batters. It is in the lack of judgement like this that our outfielders show their inferiority to the skillfully trained Red Stockings.''

Zettlein, greatest fastballer of his day, was the first line of defense for the Atlantics, who were noted more for their batting prowess than for their fielding finesse. The Reds had never seen Zettlein before, but fastball pitching didn't usually bother them. The previous year, when the Reds clobbered the Atlantics, they pounded Tom Pratt, a fastballer, from pillar to post.

Singles by Pearce, Start, and Ferguson and a two-base overthrow by Waterman gave the home team lads two runs in the fourth. In the sixth, the Atlantics' slashing drives handcuffed Sweasy and Waterman to account for two more, sending them into the lead for the first time.

Cincinnati had not scored in three innings, but as soon as they found themselves trailing they resolutely hammered out a new lead. Brainard, Sweasy, and the irrepressible George Wright pounded out clean hits in the seventh, the younger Wright's hit driving in his fellow Reds.

But the boys in blue weren't licked yet. With one out in the eighth, Smith tripled to deep left field and Start (first player to earn the nickname ''Old Reliable'') clouted viciously down the right-field line. Cal McVey, traveling at top speed, made a brilliant catch and threw quickly to the plate. Smith, holding third until the catch, tried to score but McVey's spectacular throw had him beaten. And then, in this most crucial moment, Allison muffed the ball. The crowd really let loose as Smith crossed the plate with the tying run.

Only three men faced each pitcher in the ninth. Pike closed out the Reds by taking George Wright's hot grounder and converting it into a double play, and Andy Leonard retaliated in the last half with a great catch of Hall's line drive.

Entered at this point the rules book. Several of the Atlantics' directors, reasoning that a tie with the invincible Red Stockings was better than a probable loss, even an extra-inning one, instructed Captain Ferguson to take his team off the field. Exactly opposite reasons prompted Cincinnati to play it out; Harry Wright was so ordered by president Aaron B. Champion.

As the Brooklyn players began to "stack bats" preparatory to leaving the field, the crowd, uproarious all afternoon, swarmed over the field. President Champion clambered onto a bench and announced that the Reds would claim the game by forfeiture if Brooklyn refused to continue. He pointed to Rule 5, which plainly stated that in case of a tie score at the end of nine innings the game should be continued "unless it be mutually agreed upon by the captains of the two nines to consider the game as drawn."

And now Father Chadwick got into the action. Henry was the supreme expert on the rules and the author of several of them. Year after year he served on the rules committee, where his voice was the most respected of all. "How about it, Henry?" asked Harry Wright, and Chadwick agreed that the visitors were right. It was the first time the Reds had been forced into extra innings.

Some of the Atlantics had already reached the clubhouse but they were hastily recalled, the field was cleared with some difficulty, and the game resumed.

Cincinnati was easy in the tenth and the Atlantics were turned back once more by George Wright. With one out McDonald and Pearce singled in succession. Smith lifted a high fly to shortstop; Wright, playing the ball so as to catch it close to the ground, intentionally dropped it, thus forcing the runners to leave their bases. This, of course, was the play whose abuse in later days led to the adoption of the infield fly rule to protect the helpless baserunners. At that time, there being no infield-fly rule, Wright scooped up the ball and started an easy double play.

Years later Albert G. Spalding, writing the first large-scale baseball history, jumped to the conclusion that this was the origin of the trapped-ball play, and present-day writers relied upon Spalding for the dope. Spalding, however, was wrong: When the Reds beat the Mutuals in 1869, Fred Waterman, Cincinnati third sacker, pulled an identical play after the New Yorkers had tied the score in the ninth inning, and there's no reason to imagine that this was the first instance of the trapped-ball maneuver.

The Red Stockings cast deep gloom over Flatbush by tallying twice in the eleventh, apparently sewing up the old ballgame. After Leonard was retired, Brainard doubled to right center. Sweasy lifted one in the same direction and Hall was about to make the catch when McDonald, cruising over from right field, ran into him. McVey also hit into Hall's territory, but this time his mates gave him plenty of room and he grabbed it, Brainard scoring easily from third after the catch. The poisonous George Wright then singled to score the second run of the inning, making the score 7-5.

Charley Smith, who had batted into the spectacular double play to end the tenth inning, led off for the home team in its last chance at bat. If that sounds a bit peculiar, take a look at the 1870 rules. Rule Three, Section 2, specified that: "Players must strike in regular rotation, and, after the first inning is played, the turn commences with the player who stands on the list next to the one who was the third player out."

Now, while Smith had hit into the double play in the tenth he had not been put out: McDonald and Pearce were the victims of Wright's skullduggery. Pearce was the third player put out, and Smith followed Pearce in the batting order. An odd consequence of this rule was that Pearce, the Atlantics' leadoff man, batted only five times while the next three men—Smith, Start, and Chapman—each batted six times.

Smith opened the eleventh by punching a sharp single toward left field. He went all the way to third on a wild pitch. The crowd really came alive when Joe Start slammed a drive to deep right field that landed in the fringe of the crowd. McVey was on the ball in an instant, but as he bent to pick it up a spectator leaped on his back. By the time McVey could fight his way clear and hurl the ball to the infield, Start, representing the tying run, was on third and the complexion of the game had changed.

Now, that's the way the story has always been told.

Everyone who has attempted to recount the story of the great game of 1870 has reported the naughty behavior of the Brooklyn crowd and every sportsman-reader has, presumably, responded with "tch! tch!" and rolled his eyes piously heavenward. Not so, said McVey, shortly before he died. Cal told a newsman that he remembered the play very well and that no one climbed his back. He said that he encountered some difficulty in digging the ball out of the crowd, but that no one deliberately interfered with him.

At any rate, Chapman, the next batter, hit hard to third, but Waterman handled the ball well, held Start at third, and threw the batter out.

If the Atlantics had learned anything at all it was that George Wright could do nothing wrong today. And so, with the object of keeping the ball out of Wright's grasp, Ferguson, a righthanded batter, went up to the plate to hit lefthanded. This seems to be the first recorded instance of a batter switching, although the New York *Clipper,* leading sports weekly of the day, suggested it was not the first time he had done so, remarking that Ferguson "can use one hand as well as the other."

That stratagem worked. Ferguson ripped the ball past the second baseman and scored Start with the tying run.

Zettlein kept the rally alive with a torrid smash to Gould's right. The first baseman couldn't handle it, and when he did recover the ball he flung it to second in a desperate attempt to force Ferguson. The ball, however, was in the dirt and Sweasy missed it completely, the sphere scooting into the outfield. As Ferguson stretched his legs and raced for home base all Brooklyn went mad.

The impossible had happened! Cincinnati had lost!

Joe Nuxhall, Mel Ott, Wee Willie McGill, and more...

The Youngest Major League Players

L. Robert Davids

The public accent on youth in recent years has had little effect on the age of major league players. In fact, while the voting age has been reduced from 21 to 18, the age for entry into the major leagues is generally higher than a generation ago. Clubs have been restricted from signing young stars until they are out of high school, and this reduces the ranks of fuzzy-faced youngsters on big league rosters. The youngest player in 1972, for example, was Rowland Office, outfielder for Atlanta, who played in two games about 2½ months before his 20th birthday on October 25. This was enough to make Joe Nuxhall turn cartwheels in his broadcast booth. Nuxhall, you may recall, was only 15 when he made his debut with the Reds in 1944.

The contribution of teenagers to major league baseball has been somewhat limited over the years, although there have been more than 25 who made their playing debuts at 17, and about 10 who broke in at 16. That doesn't mean that they really took hold at that age, however. Robin Yount of

L. ROBERT DAVIDS is the founder of SABR and a long-time baseball researcher and writer.

the Brewers became a regular at 18 and he was one of the rare exceptions.

The question comes up, for example, was there a hurler who won 20 games in a season prior to his 20th birthday? We have a recent example of Wally Bunker winning 19 for Baltimore in 1964 when he was 19. And Bob Feller won 17 for the Indians in 1939 when he was 19, but no teenager has won 20 games in a season in this century.

Going back before 1900, there were a number of outstanding young hurlers who carried a man-sized load prior to their 20th birthday. Hard-throwing Amos Rusie made his debut with Indianapolis of the NL in 1889 when he was still 17, and the next year when he was 18-19 years old, he won 29 games for the Giants. Hall of Famer Monte Ward started off big in 1878 with Providence when he won 22 games as an 18-year-old. The next year he pitched Providence to the pennant with 47 victories, and by the time he celebrated his 21st birthday, he had won 107 major league games. Of course, his arm was then about shot and he soon had to shift to the infield.

The youngest of the young hurlers in the 19th century was probably Wee Willie McGill, a gifted lefthander picked off the Chicago sandlots by Cleveland of the Players League in 1890. Although his precise age was not publicized at the time, he was only 16 years and six months when he started a game against Buffalo at Cleveland on May 8. He was not only very young, but very short, about 5½ feet tall, and his prospects did not look very good. But this is what the writer of the Buffalo *Express* had to say:

> A young man named McGill, a regular Davy Force sort of ballplayer (very short), was in the box for Cleveland. He is like the little girl's definition of a sugar plumb, round and rosy and sweet all over, and he throws barrel hoops and corkscrews at the plate. Once in a while he varies these with a swift, straight ball that is as full of starch as though it had just come from the laundry.

McGill, backed by such Cleveland stars as Ed Delahanty and Pete Browning, defeated Buffalo 14-5 in a complete game victory. He gave up 7 hits and 7 walks, but fanned 10. He had little trouble with the Buffalo squad, which included such stars as Dummy Hoy, Connie Mack, and Deacon White, who, at 42, was the oldest player then active in the majors. McGill collected a single himself, and knocked in a run.

The young hurler, called Kid or Baby, did not travel with the Brotherhood team at first, but when Buffalo came back to Cleveland on June 6, he beat them again 14-4. He had them biting at his curve ball, but the Buffalo writer this time said: "He was wild enough to lose 9 out of 10 ordinary games. Only the hard hitting of his mates saved him." McGill contributed to the attack himself with a single, double, 1 run scored, and 2 RBIs.

On June 9, Cleveland brought the youngster (accompanied by his father) along to Buffalo. Although he walked 7, McGill beat them again, 14-7. He was getting the reputation as a Buffalo beater, the only team he had faced thus far. But his team could not give him 14 runs on each outing, and on July 9 he lost his first game. He had good stuff, but he was wild, and this showed up on his season record of 11 wins and 9 losses.

With the Players League closed out after the 1890 season, McGill pitched for St. Louis of the American Association in 1891. On June 3 he shut out Baltimore 11-0 for the first whitewash of his career. He was only 17½ and probably the youngest to achieve that feat. He was pitching quite well, and in addition, on June 30 he stole his first base, and on July 6 he hit a triple. The pressure might have been getting to him, though, for in August he was fined by President Chris Von der Ahe for drinking too much. He left the club and went to Chicago, but after a week he returned and won a game for Charlie Comiskey's forces on August 12. In September he was traded to Cincinnati. The 17-year-old finished the season with a 20-15 mark. But now the AA folded, and for 1892 McGill pitched only briefly for Cincinnati in the NL. The next year he won 17 for his hometown

Chicago NL team, but he appeared to be about "over the hill" at 20.

Another 16-year-old who made his debut before 1900 was Joe Stanley, a Washington boy who posted scores and did odd jobs for the Senators in 1897 when he wasn't pitching for amateur teams. On September 11, in a game being hopelessly lost to Cincinnati, Stanley was sent in to pitch the eighth inning. He set down the side, but in the ninth he gave up 5 runs in a 19-10 loss. Stanley spent the next few years in the minors but came back up as an outfielder in 1902.

The main influx of very young players in the 20th century came during World War II when the desperate manpower shortage resulted in a need to tap talent that had not reached draft age. Consequently, at various stages of the 1944 season, there appeared in major league box scores one 15-year-old hurler, two 16-year-old infielders, and four 17-year-olds, one of whom was in his second season. This was the year when the aforementioned Joe Nuxhall first dented the pitching rubber at Crosley Field.

The circumstances of this record-book entry at age 15 years, 10 months, and 11 days were somewhat unusual and Nuxhall himself would just as soon not talk about the results of the game. In the spring of 1944 Joe was a big, strong, hurling star for the Hamilton, Ohio, high school team, and looked a couple of years older than he was. The Redlegs, desperately in need of playing talent, signed the youngster for their farm system.

However, in a game with the Cardinals on June 10, an excellent opportunity presented itself to give the teenager a bit of Big Time experience. St. Louis was leading 10-0, so Manager Bill McKechnie of the Reds sent Nuxhall in to pitch the ninth inning against Stan Musial and company. He walked his pitching rival Mort Cooper, which was an ominous sign, but was able to retire the next two hitters. Nervous, and admittedly scared, he then walked four more batters, uncorked a wild pitch, and gave up two singles and a total of five runs before he was rescued by a fifth Cincy hurler. The final score was 18-0.

That was the extent of Nuxhall's major league experience for several years. After finishing high school, he worked his way back up to the Redlegs in 1952 and eventually became one of the most dependable southpaws in the Senior Circuit. He later became a broadcaster for the Reds.

Hurling only ⅔ of an inning in his debut, Nuxhall failed to acquire any significant record-book distinctions for young hurlers. Essentially the same can be said for Carl Scheib, the youngest player ever to take part in an American League game. He made his debut for the Philadelphia A's in the second game of their September 6, 1943, twin bill with the Yankees when he was 16 years and 8 months old. He gave up two hits in ⅔ of an inning, but got the side out. Scheib made five more relief appearances in 1943. He hurled moderately well, although he was charged with one loss. Scheib was a good hitting pitcher and Connie Mack called on him for pinch hitting duties in later years, but in his few chances at bat in 1943 he failed to connect.

The youngest hurler to *start* a game in the majors since 1900 was Jim Derrington, bonus boy for the White Sox. He hurled six innings against Kansas City on the last day of the 1956 season, losing 7-6. He was then 16 years and 10 months old. Another distinction he gained was collecting a single in two trips, the youngest AL player ever to collect a hit. Derrington pitched briefly for the White Sox the next season, but that was the extent of his big league activity.

Most of the important youthful pitching laurels of the modern era belong to Bob Feller, and rightly so. He was 17 years and 8 months old when he broke in, but had enough ability to put his name in the record book. After several relief jobs, the young speed-baller started his first game on August 23, 1936, against the St. Louis Browns. He won 4-1 and fanned 15 Browns in the process. Feller started seven more games that season, winding up with 5 wins and 3 losses. On September 13, he beat the Athletics 5-2 on two hits, and fanned 17 for a new AL strikeout record. At 17 years of age, he had outdone the best strikeout performances of Rube Waddell, Walter Johnson, and Lefty Grove at full maturity. About the only significant performance that Feller failed to achieve that first season was hurling a shutout. Wildness hurt him there.

Other modern hurlers making sparkling beginnings include the Cardinals' flash Von McDaniel, who hurled a brilliant two-hit 2-0 shutout over the Dodgers in his first start on June 21, 1957. He was 18 years and 2 months when he tossed this gem. Later in the 1957 season, the younger McDaniel brother hurled a one-hit shutout, but the next year he faded badly and was shipped to the minors.

Four years later, Lew Krausse, Jr., of Kansas City blanked the Angels 4-0 on 3 hits. Making his debut on June 16, 1961, Krausse was about two weeks younger than McDaniel was when he hurled his first shutout. Joey Jay was slightly younger than both when he pitched an abbreviated six-inning shutout over the Dodgers on September 29, 1953.

While the pitching records for young hurlers are pretty well spread around, most of the modern batting records and fielding records as well belong to one man—or rather, one boy. Tommy Brown of the Dodgers was one of several young infielders who made their first appearances during World War II. However, Brown was younger and played more often than teenagers like Ralph Caballero, Cass Michaels, Eddie Miksis, Granny Hamner, and Eddie Yost.

Brown was 16 years and 8 months when he was called up from the minors and played shortstop in both games of a Dodger double-header with the Cubs on August 3, 1944. He doubled and scored in the first game and also made an error. His first RBI came several games later. He played regularly with the Dodgers the remainder of the 1944 season. However, as he batted only .164 in 46 games, he was sent down to St. Paul the next spring.

On August 3, 1945, exactly one year after his debut, Brown was back in the Dodger lineup. Although now 17, he was still young enough to corner two more NL firsts. On August 20 in a game against the Pirates, Brown belted one of Preacher Roe's tosses into the upper-left field section at Ebbets Field. He thus became the youngest player ever to hit a homer in the majors, and it was a very impressive wallop. He connected again on August 25.

He kept up his long-ball hitting on August 28 in a game against the Phils. He hit a triple off the centerfield wall and then stole home under a high pitch by Rene Monteagudo. While Brown was probably the youngest to achieve a theft of home, he was not the youngest to steal a base or hit a triple.

These early milestones were achieved by a diminutive outfielder from Cuba whom the Washington Senators used sparingly in 1913. Merito Acosta broke in right after his 17th birthday in June but didn't play much at all until near the end of the season. Acosta collected two hits in a 3-0 win over the Athletics on September 30. He stole third base in the fourth inning. The day before he had been thrown out trying to steal, but he didn't lose his nerve. On October 4 he batted leadoff and hit a triple against the Red Sox. This was the last game of the season and turned into quite a farce. While Acosta was 17 years and 4 months, the Washington lineup in the 8th inning included Manager Clark Griffith, 43, pitching, and Coach Jack Ryan, 44, catching.

Hall of Famer Mel Ott, better known for his slugging feats, was also younger than Brown when he stole his first base. Used sparingly by Giants' Manager John McGraw in his rookie year, Ott played five innings of a 17-3 romp over the Braves on September 3, 1926, and was credited with one theft. Ott, then 17 years and 6 months, also went 3-for-3 at the plate, which contributed to a lusty .383 batting average in 35 games. Ironically, Ott did not collect either a homer or triple in his first season.

Jimmie Foxx was another great slugger who played his first games when he was only 17, but he also went homerless in his brief appearances in 1925. The same thing happened to Harmon Killebrew when he broke in at 17 in 1954. In fact, available records indicate that Brown was the only player to hit round-trippers when he was 17, collecting two. The most hit by a teenager were the 24 hit by Tony Conigliaro of the Red Sox in 1964 when he 'was 19.

Brown was not the only youngster on the Dodgers in 1944. They also had Eddie Miksis, 17, infielder Gene Mauch, 18, and pitchers Ralph Branca and Cal McLish, both 18. However, this teenage quintet was balanced by such veterans as Johnny Cooney, 43, and Paul Waner, 41, so there was no opportunity to field a fuzzy-cheeked squad like the Houston Colts did in 1963. In a game against the Mets on September 27, Houston fielded an all-rookie team that had an average age slightly under 20 years. It included pitcher Jay Dahl, 17; catcher Jerry Grote, 20; 1B Rusty Staub, 19; 2B Joe Morgan, 20; 3B Glenn Vaughan, 19; SS Sonny Jackson, 19; and outfielders Brock Davis, 19, Aaron Pointer, 21, and Jim Wynn, 21.

Of course, not all of these players made it in the Big Time. Pitcher Jay Dahl, for example, was killed in an auto accident when he was only 19. However, the appearance of these youngsters in the same box score served as a reminder that youth is no barrier to major league play. In fact, Rusty Staub played in 150 games as a 19-year-old in 1963, the most for a teenager in any one season.

One of the best cumulative records for teenagers was compiled by Robin Yount of the Brewers in 1974-75. He became a regular almost when he broke in at 18. Before he reached his 20th birthday, he had played in 243 games, just passing the mark previously held by Mel Ott. The chart below indicates that it isn't how early you break in but how much you play after getting into the lineup. It is a listing of the players who compiled the best totals in the majors prior to their 20th birthday.

Teenager	Years	G	AB	R	H	2B	3B	HR	RBI	SB	Bat.
Robin Yount	1974-75	243	857	109	223	41	6	11	75	18	.260
Melvin Ott	1926-28	241	658	99	209	35	7	19	100	8	.318
P. Cavarretta	1934-36	221	856	120	234	36	14	14	117	8	.274
Ed Kranepool	1962-64	208	699	69	166	32	6	12	59	4	.237
Al Kaline	1953-54	168	532	51	146	18	3	5	45	10	.274
Cass Michaels	1943-45	158	520	51	121	12	6	2	59	8	.233
Fred Lindstrom	1924-25	156	435	62	122	18	13	4	37	8	.280
Ty Cobb	1905-06	140	508	64	149	21	5	2	49	24	.293
Jim Sheckard	1897-98	118	458	63	135	20	11	7	78	13	.295
T. Conigliaro	1964	111	404	69	117	21	2	24	52	2	.290

Note that none of the above names is the same as those making the earliest debut, listed below. Part of the reason is that pitchers dominate the latter group.

Age	Players and Club	Pos.	Debut Date	Born
15-10	Joe Nuxhall, Cin. NL	P	6-10-44	7-30-28
16-6	Willie McGill, Cle. PL	P	5-8-90	11-10-73
16-6	Joe Stanley, Wash. NL	P	9-11-97	4-2-81
16-8	Tommy Brown, Bkn. NL	SS	8-3-44	12-6-27
16-8	Carl Scheib, Phil. AL	P	9-6-43	1-1-27
16-9	Milton Scott, Chi. NL	1B	9-30-82	1-7-66
16-10	Jim Derrington, Chi. AL	P	9-30-56	11-29-39
16-10	Ralph Caballero, Phil. NL	3B	9-14-44	11-25-27
16-11	Rogers McKee, Phil. NL	P	8-18-43	9-16-26
16-11	Alex George, K.C. AL	SS	9-16-55	9-27-38
17-0	Merito Acosta, Wash. AL	OF	6-5-13	6-2-96

Maybe the Cardinals weren't so dumb after all.

Is Ozzie Smith Worth $2 Million a Season?

David S. Neft

In April 1985, Ozzie Smith signed a contract which called for a base salary of $2,200,000 a year in 1988 and 1989. This probably caused more derisive comment from both press and fans than any other baseball contract. The focus of all this derision was Smith's batting statistics—the fact that his lifetime batting average was only .238 at the end of the 1984 season and that he had hit only seven home runs. But clearly Ozzie Smith's contract was based much more on his fielding talent than on his batting record. So, the scorn that greeted Smith's contract is really a testament to our inability to measure statistically the value of a major league shortstop when a large component of that value is fielding.

This article proposes a way to measure this value. This measure is certainly not perfect (no sport measurement is), but it is useful for comparing lifetime achievements. The

DAVID S. NEFT is co-author of *The Sports Encyclopedia—Baseball* and *The World Series*.

overall rating starts with a Batting Factor, to which a Running Factor and a Fielding Factor are added, with adjustments for conditions in various years. Then the overall rating was calculated for all players with at least five years' experience as a regular major league shortstop and who had a majority of their good years since 1900. Cal Ripken was included in this list even though he had played only four years as a regular shortstop through 1985.

Batting Factor

John Thorn and Pete Palmer in their outstanding book, *The Hidden Game of Baseball*, use "On Base Plus Slugging" (OPS) as a measure of batting achievement. This is the best simple, overall statistic for batting in a given year. It is defined as the On-Base Average (OBA) plus the Slugging Average (SA). Here, a true "average" is needed, so the Batting Factor (BF) is defined as OPS divided by 2 or $\frac{OBA + SA}{2}$. Of course, SA $= \frac{TB}{AB}$ where TB = Total Bases and AB = At Bats. Ideally, OBA should be $\frac{H + BB + HPB + RBE}{AB + BB + HPB + SF}$ where H = Hits, BB = Bases on Balls, HPB = Hit by Pitched Balls, RBE = Reached Base on Error and SF = Sacrifice Flies in those years when they have not been charged as a time at bat. However, RBE is not available in standard baseball statistics so the common version is OBA $= \frac{H + BB + HPB}{AB + BB + HPB + SF}$. For some years HPB was not included in the official statistics, so for those years OBA $= \frac{H + BB}{AB + BB + SF}$. Using these definitions, a player's batting factor for a particular year is defined as $BF_{iy} = \frac{OBA_{iy} + SA_{iy}}{2}$ where "i" stands for a particular individual and "y" is a particular year.

In order to compare players from different periods, an adjustment must be made for the year in which the player performed. Obviously, it was easier to achieve a high BF_{iy} in 1930 than in 1968. The adjustment is based on relating BF_{iy} to the comparable data for all of the league's batters that year. Thus, $BF_{Ly} = \dfrac{OBA_{Ly} + SA_{Ly}}{2}$ where "L" stands for the league and the data includes all non-pitchers. This takes into account the change due to the introduction of the Designated Hitter in the American League in 1973. An arbitrary norm of $BF_L = .375$ has been used. The specific number is arbitrary, but that doesn't matter because the final results are relative comparisons and not absolute numbers. For these years where HPB is not in the official statistics, this decreases BF_{Ly} by an average of .003, so for these years $BF_L = .372$. Therefore, the final $BY_{iy} = \left(\dfrac{OBA_{iy} + SA_{iy}}{2} \right) + \left(BF_L - BF_{Ly} \right)$ where BF_L is either .375 or .372 depending upon whether HPB is included in or excluded from the official statistics.

Running Factor

Speed is a plus factor in many ways in baseball. Unfortunately, the only available statistics are Stolen Bases (SB) and Caught Stealing (CS), and for many years Caught Stealing was not included in the official statistics. So, one must start with what is available. A stolen base is a way of extending a hit. With no one on base, there is no difference between a batter stretching a single into a double and someone hitting a single and stealing second base. However, the former gets two TB in computing SA and the latter gets only one. So net stolen bases (SB − CS) can be viewed as an

LIFETIME SHORTSTOP RATINGS

Rank—Name	Years Included
1—Honus Wagner*	1903-13
2—Dave Bancroft*	1915-23, 25-27
3—Bobby Wallace*	1899-1910
4—Ozzie Smith	1978-85
5—Ray Chapman	1913, 15, 17-20
6—Joe Tinker*	1902-14
7—Rabbit Maranville*	1913-17, 19-23
8—Donie Bush	1909-18
9—Dick Bartell	1929-40
10—Joe Cronin*	1929-35, 37-41
11—Cal Ripken	1982-85
12—Luke Appling*	1932-43, 46-47
13—Lou Boudreau*	1940-49
14—Robin Yount	1974-84
15—Joe Sewell*	1921-28
16—Luis Aparicio*	1956-70
17—Kid Elberfeld	1901-07
18—Art Fletcher	1912-20
19—Garry Templeton	1977-85
20—Arky Vaughan*	1932-41
21—Travis Jackson*	1924-31, 34
22—Ernie Banks*	1954-61
23—Pee Wee Reese*	1940-42, 46-54
24—Rick Burleson	1975-81
25—Dave Concepcion	1971-82
26—Roy Smalley	1976-80, 82-83
27—Johnny Logan	1952-60
28—Eddie Joost	1941-42, 47-52
29—Mickey Doolan	1905-14

Rating	OBA	SA	Batting Factor	Running Factor	Range	Fielding Factor
.614	.402	.483	.484	+.026	5.59	+.099
.538	.358	.367	.377	+.007	6.15	+.144
.527	.327	.365	.388	+.009	5.95	+.120
.516	.317	.306	.329	+.023	5.63	+.174
.498	.358	.385	.401	+.019	5.50	+.098
.495	.307	.355	.370	+.018	5.54	+.093
.494	.317	.349	.358	+.013	5.93	+.124
.482	.355	.298	.369	+.022	5.54	+.091
.471	.351	.396	.369	+.005	5.73	+.087
.470	.395	.467	.423	+.002	5.28	+.035
.470	.353	.493	.433	−.001	4.99	+.068
.468	.401	.405	.396	+.004	5.34	+.048
.461	.385	.422	.413	0	5.26	+.048
.458	.331	.427	.382	+.006	5.10	+.056
.457	.361	.419	.405	+.003	5.37	+.060
.453	.312	.346	.344	+.020	5.10	+.064
.449	.340	.357	.391	+.015	5.63	+.057
.446	.299	.361	.361	+.009	5.63	+.080
.445	.317	.390	.367	+.009	5.25	+.075
.440	.415	.463	.451	+.006	5.29	−.018
.439	.348	.455	.389	+.004	5.83	+.051
.438	.354	.552	.450	0	4.93	−.002
.434	.373	.384	.385	+.011	5.10	+.029
.434	.333	.363	.363	+.001	5.26	+.085
.431	.326	.381	.363	+.014	5.16	+.044
.430	.349	.397	.386	−.001	5.07	+.059
.425	.331	.389	.358	+.001	5.24	+.071
.423	.374	.387	.389	+.002	5.25	+.043
.421	.280	.314	.334	+.010	5.43	+.077

LIFETIME SHORTSTOP RATINGS (cont.)

Rank—Name	Years Included
30—Roger Peckinpaugh	1913-23
31—George McBride	1906, 08-16
32—Maury Wills	1960-66, 69
33—Gene Alley	1965-68, 70-72
34—Mark Belanger	1968-78
35—Phil Rizzuto	1941-42, 46-53
36—Dick Groat	1952, 55-63
37—Ron Hansen	1960-61, 63-65, 67-68
38—Jim Fregosi	1963-70
39—Marty Marion	1940-49
40—Heinie Wagner	1907-10, 12-13
41—Eddie Miller	1939-48
42—Buck Weaver	1912-15, 18
43—Roy McMillan	1952-65
44—Doc Lavan	1915-21
45—Freddie Patek	1969, 71-79
46—Bert Campaneris	1965-77
47—Gene Michael	1969-73
48—Bill Jurges	1932-39, 41-43
49—Charlie Hollocher	1918-22
50—Vern Stephens	1942-50
51—Rico Petrocelli	1965-70
52—Monte Cross	1895-1904
53—Al Bridwell	1906-11, 13-14
54—Freddy Parent	1901-06, 08-09
55—Tony Kubek	1958, 60-61, 63-64
56—Lyn Lary	1930-31, 34-38
57—Alvin Dark	1948-57

Rating	OBA	SA	Batting Factor	Running Factor	Range	Fielding Factor
.419	.332	.337	.364	+.008	5.33	+.051
.419	.276	.268	.315	+.008	5.52	+.096
.416	.336	.332	.349	+.030	4.91	+.046
.416	.315	.362	.356	+.005	5.29	+.070
.415	.307	.286	.316	+.008	5.24	+.085
.415	.354	.363	.362	+.007	5.15	+.046
.413	.336	.379	.360	−.001	5.15	+.055
.412	.325	.365	.362	−.001	5.04	+.065
.410	.345	.409	.402	+.004	4.86	+.014
.407	.324	.349	.351	+.003	5.34	+.053
.405	.312	.326	.368	+.014	5.41	+.043
.401	.291	.357	.338	+.005	5.48	+.058
.401	.285	.338	.350	+.012	5.43	+.064
.394	.315	.320	.321	+.001	5.17	+.058
.393	.290	.318	.334	+.006	5.56	+.067
.392	.309	.319	.334	+.023	5.04	+.034
.391	.314	.347	.355	+.027	4.83	−.006
.390	.299	.290	.317	+.001	5.33	+.096
.388	.325	.343	.346	+.001	5.43	+.036
.387	.369	.395	.400	+.013	5.61	−.001
.385	.360	.473	.428	+.001	4.97	−.038
.385	.332	.448	.411	−.001	4.76	−.005
.380	.308	.314	.329	+.019	5.72	+.032
.380	.348	.297	.363	+.011	5.16	+.016
.379	.310	.346	.374	+.012	5.39	+.001
.378	.298	.361	.337	+.001	5.14	+.064
.377	.373	.381	.355	+.013	5.21	+.024
.373	.332	.421	.375	+.002	4.97	−.004

LIFETIME SHORTSTOP RATINGS (cont.)

Rank—Name	Years Included
58—Don Kessinger	1965-76
59—Tim Foli	1972-82
60—Chris Speier	1971-80
61—Rafael Ramirez	1981-85
62—Billy Rogell	1932-38
63—Toby Harrah	1971-76
64—Buddy Kerr	1944-48, 50
65—Dal Maxvill	1966-72
66—Ed Brinkman	1963-67, 69-74
67—Bud Harrelson	1967-74, 76
68—Leo Cardenas	1962-72
69—Woody English	1927-31
70—Alan Trammell	1978-85
71—Bill Russell	1972-74, 76-83
72—Don Buddin	1956, 58-61
73—Craig Reynolds	1977-81, 84-85
74—Frank Crosetti	1932-40, 43, 45
75—Ivan DeJesus	1977-84
76—Chico Carrasquel	1950-57, 59
77—Zoilo Versalles	1961-68
78—Billy Myers	1935-39
79—Wally Gerber	1919-24, 26-28
80—Everett Scott	1914-24
81—Ivy Olson	1911, 16-21
82—Terry Turner	1904-07, 10
83—Glenn Wright	1924-28, 30, 32
84—Ed Bressoud	1959-60, 62-64, 66

Rating	OBA	SA	Batting Factor	Running Factor	Range	Fielding Factor
.372	.315	.314	.331	+ .001	5.13	+ .030
.372	.286	.331	.314	+ .002	5.18	+ .051
.372	.332	.349	.356	0	5.06	+ .016
.371	.312	.347	.347	+ .003	5.12	+ .046
.370	.366	.387	.358	+ .003	5.28	+ .023
.370	.341	.379	.381	+ .006	4.95	+ .002
.364	.315	.339	.335	+ .004	5.36	+ .045
.362	.300	.265	.302	− .001	5.32	+ .076
.360	.283	.305	.314	− .001	4.98	+ .041
.360	.331	.292	.332	+ .007	4.99	+ .027
.356	.313	.371	.362	− .001	4.82	− .009
.356	.376	.407	.365	+ .004	5.61	+ .012
.355	.350	.396	.382	+ .007	4.69	− .025
.350	.312	.343	.341	+ .006	4.93	− .002
.348	.318	.364	.366	+ .001	4.94	+ .006
.347	.292	.355	.338	+ .002	4.98	+ .022
.345	.342	.346	.337	+ .004	5.09	+ .004
.345	.326	.330	.339	+ .012	4.91	+ .003
.344	.334	.344	.340	0	4.94	+ .008
.344	.294	.376	.350	+ .005	4.74	0
.340	.335	.388	.365	+ .004	5.26	− .004
.339	.325	.318	.310	− .001	5.25	+ .035
.331	.279	.315	.309	+ .002	5.29	+ .015
.330	.293	.325	.344	+ .009	5.45	− .008
.325	.289	.324	.362	+ .013	5.25	− .024
.324	.333	.455	.374	+ .002	5.53	− .037
.323	.327	.421	.378	0	4.70	− .035

LIFETIME SHORTSTOP RATINGS (cont.)

Rank—Name	Years Included
85—Bobby Wine	1962-63, 65, 67, 69-71
86—Alfredo Griffin	1979-85
87—Larry Bowa	1970-84
88—Denis Menke	1964, 66-67, 69-70
89—Leo Durocher	1929-38
90—Bucky Dent	1974-83
91—Heinie Sand	1923-28
92—Harvey Kuenn	1953-57
93—Johnny Lipon	1948-52
94—Skeeter Newsome	1936-37, 43-44, 46-47
95—Granny Hamner	1949-52, 56
96—Bill Knickerbocker	1933-37
97—Cecil Travis	1936-39, 41, 46
98—Joe DeMaestri	1953-59
99—Johnnie LeMaster	1979-84
100—Chick Galloway	1920-26
101—Enzo Hernandez	1971-72, 74-76
102—Larry Brown	1965-69
103—Frank Taveras	1974-81
104—Frank Duffy	1972-77
105—Roger Metzger	1971-76, 78
106—Billy Urbanski	1932-36
107—Tom Veryzer	1975-81
108—Jack Barry	1909-14
109—Chico Fernandez	1957-58, 60-62

*Elected to Baseball Hall of Fame

Rating	OBA	SA	Batting Factor	Running Factor	Range	Fielding Factor
.320	.264	.285	.289	0	5.11	+.042
.317	.283	.331	.314	+.004	4.88	+.014
.314	.300	.321	.324	+.012	4.78	−.047
.314	.366	.412	.402	−.002	4.70	−.061
.312	.295	.316	.302	+.002	5.39	+.008
.311	.296	.323	.324	−.001	4.87	+.003
.310	.342	.344	.335	+.002	5.68	−.006
.308	.350	.410	.386	+.001	4.75	−.054
.306	.355	.335	.341	+.001	4.98	−.011
.306	.291	.299	.300	+.004	5.33	+.027
.302	.297	.373	.335	+.003	4.94	−.010
.296	.327	.382	.341	−.004	5.20	−.016
.292	.376	.429	.384	−.001	4.84	−.072
.289	.277	.331	.312	0	4.91	−.008
.288	.286	.295	.307	+.007	4.95	−.006
.284	.318	.344	.314	+.003	4.97	−.018
.283	.285	.270	.298	+.021	5.00	−.011
.281	.304	.317	.341	0	4.45	−.035
.276	.302	.315	.318	+.022	4.79	−.054
.276	.280	.313	.322	+.004	4.80	−.030
.275	.292	.293	.312	+.005	4.87	−.027
.273	.313	.340	.331	+.002	5.24	−.035
.267	.281	.293	.302	−.002	4.82	−.018
.258	.322	.312	.353	+.015	4.81	−.090
.241	.299	.341	.321	+.008	4.63	−.064

addition to TB in calculating SA. Since $SA = \dfrac{TB}{AB}$, the base stealing adjustment would be $\dfrac{SB - CS}{AB}$. But SA is one of two components of the Batting Factor. The other, OBA, is not affected by base stealing. Because the player's Running Factor (RF) is an increment of the Batting Factor, it should be $RF_{iy} = \dfrac{\dfrac{SB_{iy} - CS_{iy}}{AB_{iy}}}{2} = \dfrac{SB_{iy} - CS_{iy}}{2AB_{iy}}$. However, this running factor has two limitations. The first is that a stolen base affects only the one runner, whereas an extra-base hit can advance other runners. On this basis, the running factor gives too much credit to the player. On the other hand, there is more to running than stealing bases. This formula does not credit a player's speed for:

— taking an extra base on someone else's hit or out;
— putting pressure on the defense, resulting in additional RBE's and errors on stolen base attempts;
— putting pressure on the opposing pitchers by threatening to steal, sometimes disturbing the pitcher's concentration, and often giving the next batter confidence that he can expect more fast balls;
— avoiding grounding into double plays.

Since these factors are hard to quantify, it is assumed here that they justify the extra credit that the running factor gives a base-stealer. If the necessary data could be produced they would probably show that the upward adjustment factors are somewhat greater than the reverse, and that this formula for RF slightly penalizes the great running shortstops.

RF_{iy} could also have been adjusted by the average amount of base stealing in a league year the same way that BF_{iy} was adjusted. However, RF_{iy} is a very small component of the player's total rating, and the adjustment factor would have been tiny (less than one percent of the final rating in every case) so, for convenience and ease of computation, it was not included.

One adjustment was necessary. The years where CS data

were not available had to be included. In these cases an average base-stealing rate of 75 percent was assumed, which is a reasonable historical figure for players who do a lot of running. It overstates the success rate for players who rarely attempt to steal, but in those cases the effect of the over-statement on the running factor is quite small. A 75 percent

rate means $CS = \dfrac{SB}{3}$ and thus $RF_{iy} = \dfrac{SB_{iy} - \dfrac{SB_{iy}}{3}}{2AB_{iy}} =$

$\dfrac{\dfrac{2}{3} SB_{iy}}{2AB_{iy}} = \dfrac{SB_{iy}}{3AB_{iy}}$ for years when CS data are not available.

Fielding Factor

Since the start of major league baseball more than 100 years ago, Fielding Average (FA) has been the usual statistical measure of fielding performance. Unfortunately, FA isn't a good indicator of fielding ability. The positive elements of FA—putouts (PO) and assists (A)—are satisfactory, but the negative element—errors (E)—is only one of two actual negative fielding elements. The second is that a poorer fielder doesn't reach a ball that a better fielder would have reached or doesn't make a throw quickly enough or doesn't field a bad hop that someone with quicker hands might have fielded. These missed opportunities occur far more frequently than do actual errors and, therefore, are more important in evaluating fielding performances. Unfortunately, there is no direct measure of these missed opportunities. In an attempt to measure this indirectly, baseball people for many years have used some form of range factor, usually defined as $\dfrac{PO + A}{G}$, where G is games played, or Total Chances Per Game, $\dfrac{PO + A + E}{G}$. This concept was introduced by Al Wright in 1875. It was revived by Irwin M. Howe, the statistician for the American League, who ranked AL fielders this way in 1914. Subsequently, Branch Rickey and many other baseball executives used these measures to evaluate players. This author used the concept in 1969 in *The Baseball Encyclopedia* and Bill James has used it in his *Baseball Abstracts*.

There are two problems with this way of measuring fielding. The first is that its usefulness varies greatly by position. The principle works quite well for shortstops and third basemen. It is not as good for second basemen because they are more dependent on other players than are shortstops or third basemen. For example, the second baseman more often covers second base on steal attempts and most often is the middleman on double play attempts. For outfielders, this approach is not very good. Putouts by outfielders are significantly affected by the stadium dimensions and by the fact that two outfielders can often reach the same ball so that an outfielder playing alongside a slower teammate will tend to have more putouts than one playing next to a speedy ball hawk. Assists by outfielders are even more unreliable because runners will often not try to advance on the great throwing arms. For first basemen, this way of looking at fielding is a poor measure. The assists-per-game system is interesting, but it varies with the style of the first baseman. Some first basemen prefer to throw to the pitcher covering the bag on nearly every grounder they field, while others prefer to run to the base and these players do not get an assist. Moreover, much of a first baseman's defensive skill is in handling poor throws from the other infielders, and total putouts provide no indication of this skill. For catchers, these measures are useless. Range is simply not a factor. The catcher's percentage of throwing out opposing basestealers provides some indication of his throwing arm, but even this is often more a reflection of the pitcher than the catcher. Most importantly, the catcher's primary defensive skill is handling pitchers, and no one has yet devised a statistical measure for this.

* * *

The second problem with these measures is that they are based on the implicit assumption that all fielders at one position get the same number of opportunities to make a putout or assist per game played. This, of course, isn't true. Even for shortstops and third basemen, the nature of the pitching staff and chance factors will produce some variation in number of opportunities. As a result, these range factors can vary significantly from year to year. However, with the addition of a few modifications discussed later, the range factor does provide a valid measure of a shortstop's lifetime fielding performance.

The Fielding Factor (FF_{iy}) calculation starts with the Fielding Range (FR_{iy}), defined as $FR_{iy} = \dfrac{PO_{iy} + A_{iy}}{G_{iy}}$.

Of course, all data are for games played at shortstop only. To make this as valid as possible G_{iy} should be complete game equivalents, or defensive innings played at shortstop divided by 9. This distinction is inconsequential for Joe Tinker or any of the early twentieth-century players. It is, however, very important for a player like Mark Belanger, who was often pitch-hit for and who sometimes entered the game only as a late-inning defensive replacement. The proper way to calculate G_{iy} would have been to look at every boxscore where more than one shortstop played for a team and estimate the number of innings played by each. This was done for 1984 and 1985, but it was too monumental a task for the entire project, so for all other years G_{iy} was figured by analyzing the final season fielding data for everyone who played shortstop for the team and year in question and estimating the number of complete-game equivalents for each.

One effect of the pitching staff on a shortstop's opportunities can be measured and dealt with. If the pitchers strike out a large number of opposing batters, all the fielders will have somewhat fewer opportunities. For this paper, an adjustment was made if the Pitchers' Strikeouts (PSO) for the team (T) in question exceeded the average for the other teams in the league that year by 0.5 per game or more. It was then assumed that one-sixth of the reduced opportunities would have gone to the shortstop. Thus, where this adjustment was necessary, $FR_{iy} = \left(\dfrac{PO_{iy} + A_{iy}}{G_{iy}}\right) +$

$$\left(\dfrac{PSO_{Ty} - \left[\dfrac{PSO_{Ly} - PSO_{Ty}}{N_{Ly} - 1}\right]}{6G_{Ty}}\right)$$ where N_{Ly} is the number

of teams in the league that year.

The next step was to convert the absolute measure, FR_{iy}, into a Relative Fielding Range (RFR) by comparing the individual data to the league average. Thus, $RFR_{iy} = FR_{iy} - \left(\dfrac{PO_{Ly} + A_{Ly}}{G_{Ly}}\right)$. This also includes the necessary adjustment for conditions in different years. RFR_{iy} is a measure of the number of PO + A per game that this shortstop was able to get compared to the average of his peers in his league for the year in question. This was related to the Batting Factor by simply assuming that each extra putout or assist prevented an opponent's single and, therefore, is the equivalent of a batter's single. Thus, the increment to the player's SA is $\dfrac{(RFR_{iy})\,(G_{iy})}{\left(\dfrac{AB_{Ly}}{9G_{Ly}}\right)(G_{iy})} = \dfrac{(RFR_{iy})\,(9G_{Ly})}{AB_{Ly}}$ where

AB_{Ly} is the total number of At-Bats for the league that year, including pitchers, and the "9" is the number of positions in the batting order. Similarly, the effect on OBA is the same except that Plate Appearances is substituted for At-Bats. Therefore, the Fielding Factor is $FF_{iy} =$

$$\frac{1}{2}\left(\left[\dfrac{(FRF_{iy})(9G_{Ly})}{AB_{Ly}}\right] + \left[\dfrac{(RFR_{iy})(9G_{Ly})}{AB_{Ly}}\right]\left[\dfrac{AB_{Ly}}{AB_{Ly} + BB_{Ly} + HPB_{Ly} + SF_{Ly}}\right]\right)$$

Longevity Factor and Lifetime Rating

In trying to calculate a shortstop's lifetime rating, an important question was—which years should be included? The first and easiest decision was to include only years where the player was the regular shortstop. However, if that had been the only decision, those players who had many years as a regular shortstop and who continued to play regular shortstop even when their performance declined late in their careers would be penalized while those whose performance tailed off even more and who were switched to third base or first base or who lost their regular jobs completely would not be penalized.

This problem was addressed in two ways. First, if a player's yearly rating ($BF_{iy} + RF_{iy} + FF_{iy}$) declined significantly after reaching the age of 35 or after completing ten years or more as a major league regular shortstop, those final declining years of his career were not included. Second, an arbitrary Longevity Factor (LF_i) was awarded based on the number of years actually included in the Lifetime Rating. For each year more than ten, the player was awarded .005 and for each year less than ten .005 was subtracted. Thus, the Lifetime Rating, LR, =

$$\left[\frac{\Sigma_y(BF_{iy} + RF_{iy} + FF_{iy})}{Y}\right] + LF_i \text{ where Y is the num-}$$

ber of years included and Σ_y means the sum of each year's factors.

Results

The Lifetime Ratings and the main components of those ratings are shown in the accompanying table. The results are evident from looking at the table, but a few observations are in order. The first is that anyone who can play five years as a regular major league shortstop is an excellent baseball player, regardless of his ranking on this list. Another thing to note is that several of these players, including Ernie

Banks, Harvey Kuenn, Buck Weaver, and Toby Harrah, spent much of their careers at other positions. The data shown in the table reflect only their years at shortstop.

The most obvious feature of the results is that they support the reputation of Honus Wagner as the greatest shortstop of all time—and by a wide margin. In fact, Wagner is first in Batting Factor, second in Running Factor, and fifth in Fielding Factor—a remarkable all-around player. Behind Wagner are two other Hall of Famers from the game's earlier years, Dave Bancroft and Bobby Wallace. Looking farther down the list, an obvious conclusion is that the Hall of Fame electors have not been as stupid as some of their critics have charged. The 14 shortstops enshrined in Cooperstown are all in the top 19 eligibles on the list. The people who complained about shortstops such as Wallace, Tinker, or Maranville being enshrined were, once again, relying on batting statistics only. Moreover, these data suggest that Ray Chapman, Donie Bush, and Dick Bartell should join them in Cooperstown.

Finally, we return to Ozzie Smith and his contract. Maybe the Cardinals, like the Hall of Fame electors, aren't so dumb after all. How many other active players would rank in the top five on an all-time list at their position? The only other player who would probably make such a list is Mike Schmidt, and he is in the same salary range as Ozzie Smith, even though Schmidt, at age 36, may be in the twilight of his career.

What would Ty Cobb bat today? Wade Boggs in 1910?

Heresy! Players Today Better Than Old-Timers

Bill Deane

Comparisons between old-time baseball players and modern performers are inevitable: Ty Cobb vs. Pete Rose . . . Babe Ruth vs. Hank Aaron . . . Walter Johnson vs. Nolan Ryan. And, in most cases, the supporters of the old-timers have the edge when it comes to raw statistics: Nobody in our lifetime will ever bat .367 lifetime, as did Cobb, or win 511 games, as did Cy Young.

There is no question that, overall, modern athletes are superior to their predecessors. Athletes today are bigger, stronger, and faster. If Johnny Weismuller, on his finest day in the 100-meter freestyle race, had swum through a timewarp into the 1972 Olympics, he would have found himself eight seconds behind Mark Spitz. Jesse Owens would not come within two feet of the longest jump by modern star Carl Lewis. Glenn Cunningham would finish a couple of hundred yards behind Sebastian Coe in the mile run. In this century, most record times and distances have been improved by 15 to 25 percent, and several by much more.

Why, then, is baseball the one major sport in which

BILL DEANE of the National Baseball Library writes on baseball for many publications.

measurable numerical records have endured for many decades? This, I hope to prove, is *not* because today's players are inferior; it is because the game is so different and the level of competition today is so much higher.

Advocates of the modern player list a number of factors that have made the game more difficult, particularly for hitters: Night baseball, relief specialists, the slider, bigger gloves, increased media pressure, cross-country travel and jet lag.

Supporters of the old-timer often cite expansion as a reason for the watering down of talent in the big leagues. "By sheer numbers," wrote one, "one-third of today's (players) wouldn't be in the major leagues if it weren't for expansion . . ."

And that's where we have them. A statement like that fails to consider the impact of the United States population—which has tripled in this century—on baseball's level of competition.

The accompanying graph introduces the "Level of Competition Index" (LCI), which indicates the relative degree of difficulty of a man making it to the major leagues at a given time and, simultaneously, reflects the depth of talent in the majors.

LCI is arrived at by dividing the number of major league baseball players at a given time by the number of pro baseball candidates (in millions) at the same time. The number of players is defined as the number of major-league-level teams in existence (according to *The Baseball Encyclopedia*, Macmillan) times 25, the current standard roster size. (Yes, rosters were smaller in the 1800s and early 1900s.) Pro baseball candidates, for the purpose of this computation, are defined as "United States males aged 20-39 years," for which the data have been supplied by the U.S. Department of Commerce, Bureau of the Census. Since the census is taken only every ten years, population estimates for the intervening years had to be made based on each particular decade's rate of growth.

Therefore, an LCI of 25.0 means that there were 25

major league players per one million "candidates." The *lower* the LCI, the *higher* the level of talent.

Since 1876, the advent of what is usually recognized as major league baseball, the highest LCI ever recorded occurred a century ago. The addition of four teams to the existing American Association in 1884, plus the single-year existence of the eight-team Union Association, gave the big leagues 28 teams and brought the LCI to a whopping 78.9. The lowest LCI ever was the 16.0 mark of 1900, one year before the American League claimed major league status.

With the inception of the current two-league format in 1901—the beginning of the "modern era"—the LCI stood at 31.2. That number shrank slowly but steadily for half a century, dropping to 25.1 in 1910, 23.1 in 1920, 20.5 in 1930, 19.0 in 1940, and 17.5 in 1950, before leveling off to 17.8 in 1960. (While overall population had grown 18.5 percent in the 1950s, the 20-39 age group actually decreased in number due to the low birthrate of the Depression years.)

Table 1
UNITED STATES MALES AGED 20-39 YEARS, 1870-1985

Source: U.S. Department of Commerce,
Bureau of the Census

Year	Total	Year	Total
1870	5,804,616	1930	19,535,426
1880	7,935,892	1940	21,071,933
1890	10,279,912	1950	22,855,322
1900	12,466,309	1960	22,531,151
1910	15,927,583	1970	25,547,049
1920	17,333,099	1980	35,906,643
		1985 (est.)	39,800,000

The 1960s saw the formation of eight new teams—the Los Angeles Angels and the new Washington Senators in 1961 (the old Senators had moved to Minnesota and become the Twins); the Houston Colt .45s and New York Mets in 1962, and the Kansas City Royals, Seattle Pilots, Montreal Expos and San Diego Padres in 1969. (The Colt .45s became the Astros in 1965, the Pilots became the Milwaukee Brewers in 1970, and the Senators became the Texas Rangers in 1972.) With this 50 percent expansion of the big leagues, while the talent pool increased by only 13.4 percent during the decade, the LCI jumped to 23.8, the highest since World War I.

The maturing of the "baby boom" generation, however, swiftly reversed that effect over the next decade. The male 20-39 age group grew by an astonishing 40.6 percent during the 1970s, while the number of major leaguers—with the addition of the Seattle Mariners and Toronto Blue Jays in 1977—increased only 8.3 percent. This set of circumstances brought the LCI back down to 18.1 by 1980, or about the same as the immediate pre-expansion levels. And with the continuing population growth since the last census, the LCI has dropped to about 16.3—which means that the level of talent in the big leagues today is the highest of this century.

Table 2
NUMBER OF MAJOR LEAGUE
BASEBALL TEAMS, 1876-1985

Year	Teams	Year	Teams
1876	8	1892-99	12
1877-78	6	1900	8
1879-81	8	1901-13	16
1882	14	1914-15	24
1883	16	1916-60	16
1884	28	1961	18
1885-89	16	1962-68	20
1890	24	1969-76	24
1891	16	1977-85	26

This, of course, takes into account only factors of population and expansion. There are other bases to touch.

As many people have pointed out, baseball was, for many years, virtually the only sport in which a talented athlete could hope to perform for financial gain. There are at least two counters to that contention.

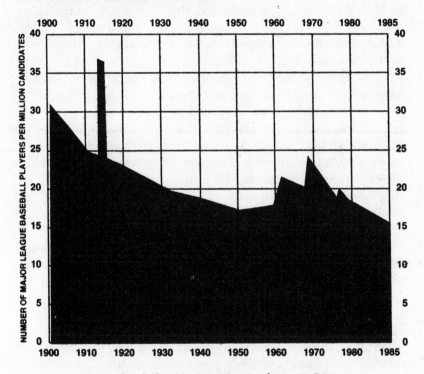

Level of Competition Index (LCI)

Level of Competition Index (LCI)

First, only a select few players really made a decent living playing ball in those days; there were no dreams of multi-million-dollar contracts. For example, a star sandlot player of the 1930s (my father) told me he had to refuse a minor league contract offer because he could not live on $20 a month. The point is, many good athletes couldn't afford to consider a pro sports career, baseball or otherwise.

Second, probably most of the potential baseball players who have opted for other pro sports are either basketball players or skill position football players—and the vast majority of those athletes would not have been *allowed* to play baseball between 1887 and 1947 because they are black. This leads us to the integration factor.

We have already established that, based on population data alone ("sheer numbers"), the number of major leaguers per million candidates has dropped from 31 in 1901 to 16 in 1985. But were those 31 of '01 the best baseball players in existence? No, they were the best *white* players. Meanwhile, of the 16 in 1985, perhaps 11 are white.

So, considering the integration factor on top of the population factor, we can say that only about one-third of the 1901 players would be good enough to make it to the big leagues today. (And with the much-improved overall caliber of the modern athlete, that fraction would be much smaller.) In a normal distribution (bell) curve of baseball ability, the line separating non-players and minor leaguers from major leaguers is moving farther and farther to the right.

What this tells us is that, by today's standards, Cy Young, Walter Johnson, Christy Mathewson, et al, were hurling against lineups of mostly minor-league-level hitters and Ty Cobb, Honus Wagner, Rogers Hornsby and company were batting against mostly minor-league-level pitchers. These Hall of Famers would have excelled in any era, but their individual statistics were embellished by the low levels of talent of the rank-and-file players of their times.

This leaves us only to speculate: What kind of numbers could have been put on the board by the likes of Hank Aaron, Willie Mays, Rod Carew, Pete Rose, Steve Carlton, and Tom Seaver had they played under similar conditions as those old-time heroes?

It boggles the mind.

Bill Deane's thesis is unpalatable to many baseball traditionalists, but alas the logic is inescapable. When I first suggested—in an article in *The Sporting News* in September 1977 marking the fiftieth anniversary of Babe Ruth's 60 homers ("Maybe Babe, Not Rog, Should Have An Asterisk!")—that the population factor has been unfairly protecting the records of the old-timers, the mail poured in. One letter began, "You commie pinko!" and continued in that vein for eight single-spaced typewritten pages. But when I repeated the theme at the annual SABR convention in Providence in 1984, the audience reaction was subdued and thoughtful. (Fellow SABR member Dick Cramer reached a similar conclusion by an entirely different statistical route as explained in his article "Average Batting Skill Through Major League History" in the 1980 *Baseball Research Journal*.)

It would seem the time has at last come when reflective, analytical historians and SABRmetricians can accept what only eight short years ago was unacceptable. I would go a step further: In view of the facts that (a) today's best female athletes have been able to equal the best records compiled in many sports by the best male athletes of 60 years ago and (b) today's best females are not good enough to play major league baseball, ergo the conclusion is stubbornly clear: The best male athletes of the 1920s, including Babe Ruth, just possibly might not fare very well in big league baseball today. Sorry, Gramps, but we gotta tell it like it is.

John B. Holway

They won the first World Series, a century ago.

1884:
Old Hoss Radbourne and the Providence Grays

Frederick Ivor-Campbell

Frank Bancroft, the new manager of the Providence Grays, was having second thoughts. Had he done well to leave Cleveland, where he had been treated kindly and where, the previous season, he had led his club to a respectable fourth-place finish in the National League? In late January 1884, in a letter to Harry Wright, his friend and predecessor as manager of the Grays, Bancroft hinted his distaste for the Rhode Island city, and wondered if he might find himself under too many bosses with the Grays.

Perhaps Bancroft's grumbling was simply new-job jitters. As manager, he would be expected to produce a profitable team—a manager in the 1880s managed his club's scheduling and business matters as well as its players. But Bancroft, although he was not yet thirty-eight years old, was known for his financial genius. In four years of managing National League clubs in Worcester, Detroit, and Cleveland, none had finished a season higher than fourth, but all had turned

FREDERICK IVOR-CAMPBELL of Warren, Rhode Island, is writing a history of Providence baseball.

profits for their owners. Now, with a good team—one that in its six years in the league had never finished lower than third, one that in the two previous seasons had contended strongly for the championship—surely with a team like this he could earn not only money but maybe even a pennant for his new bosses.

Whatever his private fears, Bancroft in public looked toward the 1884 season with optimism. His team was essentially the one that the previous year had finished a strong third, only five games behind the champion Boston Red Stockings. The club had lost its right fielder, John Cassidy, to the Brooklyn club in the rival American Association, but in his place it had signed Paul Revere Radford, a promising young Bostonian who had broken into the majors the previous season with his hometown team, and who could pitch as well as play the outfield.

All the other Grays regulars were club veterans. One, in fact—center fielder Paul Hines—had been with the team since it entered the National League in 1878. In his first three seasons with Providence he led the club in batting (leading the league in 1878), and had been every year among the Grays' two or three best hitters. As a fielder he was known for his fine eye and spectacular catches, especially of low line drives.

Two regulars had joined the Grays the year after Hines: veteran first baseman Joe Start and, late in the season, rookie second baseman Jack Farrell. Start, when he joined the Grays in '79, was already thirty-six. He had played in the old National Association, the first professional league, and before that, as an "amateur" star with Brooklyn's Atlantics and other clubs going back to 1860. Now, in 1884, at age 41 the league's oldest player, Start was still a fine fielder and, next to Hines, the Grays' most consistent hitter. He was the team captain, a responsible position in those days when a nonplaying manager (like Bancroft and, before him, Harry Wright) sat in the grandstand and conveyed through his captain whatever instructions he had for his players. Jack Farrell, after a rocky beginning (he twice led league second basemen in errors), developed into one of the league's surest fielders and led all keystoners in fielding average for 1883.

Three Grays regulars were in their fourth year with the club in 1884. Third baseman Jerry Denny, whose major league career began with the Grays in 1881, had developed into something of a slugger, tying for second in league home runs (with 8) in 1883. But he was better known for his fieldings: Though known to throw the ball away upon occasion, he was splendid at stopping and catching it. Able to field the ball with either hand, he became—and remains today—the all-time leader of major league third basemen in his career averages of 4.2 chances and 1.6 putouts per game.

Also joining the Grays in 1881 were the battery of Charley Radbourne (most sources today omit the final "e," but Old Hoss signed his name "Radbourne") and Barney Gilligan. Gilligan came to the Grays after two years as catcher and outfielder with Cleveland, but Radbourne, though two years older than Gilligan, at age 26, was a virtual rookie. He had played six games in the infield and outfield for Buffalo in 1880, but he never pitched a major league game until he joined Providence. He quickly developed into one of the league's most respected box artists, and in 1883 carried the team's pitching, starting or relieving (four times) in 50 of the Grays' 58 victories. Overall, he pitched 632 innings in 76 games, winning 49 and losing 25.

Manager Bancroft was confident that Radbourne would not be as overworked in 1884, even though the league was expanding its schedule from 98 to 112 games. Charlie Sweeney, a young pitcher/outfielder from San Francisco, was overwhelming batters in California winter ball. Though he had seen limited service with the Grays since joining them in 1882, Bancroft planned to alternate him in the box with Radbourne in 1884.

A second San Franciscan, catcher Vincent (Sandy) Nava, also broke into the majors with Providence in 1882. His heritage has been variously assessed over the years. Harry Wright, who signed him for the Grays, described him as a "Spainard" [sic]; others have called him Portuguese or

Cuban; his death certificate gives his father's birthplace as "America" and his mother's as Mexico; contemporary press accounts hinted that he was black. Whatever his race and ancestry, he caught well, and formed with Sweeney the Grays' "California battery."

The 1882 season saw not only the major league debuts of Sweeney and Nava, but also of left fielder Cliff Carroll, a hunting buddy of Radbourne and, like Radbourne, a resident of Bloomington, Illinois. *Sporting Life* described him as the best man in baseball at beating out a bunt.

The regular team of 1884 was rounded out by shortstop Arthur Irwin, who came to the Grays in 1883 after three years in the league with Worcester. (One of Bancroft's finds, Irwin played shortstop for him at Worcester in 1879, when the team was in a minor league, and the next year, when the team graduated, nearly intact, to the National League.) Irwin was a native of Toronto, but for many years had made his home in Boston. He was a daring though sometimes reckless baserunner, and like Carroll was known for his ability to bunt hit.

In addition to the eleven regulars, Providence had signed two extra catchers—Miah Murray, another Bostonian, and Charlie Bassett, a student at Providence's Brown University—anticipating a "breaking up" of catchers under the new league rule permitting overhand pitching for the first time. Bassett, who would join the Grays after Brown finished its baseball season in June, was also an infielder, and became the Gray's general utility man late in the season when injuries and illness afflicted the team. Murray caught only seven games in 1884, and Bassett none at all, as Gilligan and Nava proved more durable than expected.

Manager Bancroft's confidence in pitcher Sweeney seemed well placed. He pitched well in the month of exhibition games that preceded the opening of the championship season—so well, in fact, that Radbourne must have wondered if he were about to be superseded by the brash twenty-one-year-old as darling of the fans.

Not only Sweeney, but the Grays as a team were impressive in preseason play. After defeating Brown University in

Providence on March 29, the club traveled south to Hampton, Va., and rolled north through April, flattening every minor league and American Association club in its path. The Grays' only preseason loss was a forfeit to Brooklyn on April 21, when Sweeney insisted on throwing overhand although the game was being played according to American Association rules, which forbade deliveries in which the pitcher's arm came higher than the shoulder.

The Grays kept their momentum as the regular season began. After a close opening-day loss to Cleveland on May 1, they won seventeen of their next eighteen games, with winning streaks of five and twelve games. The California battery of Sweeney and Nava worked the opening game and thereafter were generally alternated, as Bancroft had planned, with Radbourne and Gilligan. The pitchers matched won-loss records through May 24 (when both stood at 8-1) before Radbourne began to pull away from Sweeney with a victory on May 26 which Sweeney followed with two losses.

On May 22 the Grays had for the first time moved into the league lead ahead of Boston. Though the two successive losses dropped them back into second place for a day, Radbourne's two victories (morning and afternoon) on Memorial Day, and the third day after, brought the Grays to the end of May in first place by a few percentage points. Boston regained the lead three days later.

Providence and Boston were by geographical proximity natural rivals, and their struggle for first place intensified the rivalry. The teams did not play each other the first month of the season. By the time they met in Providence on June 6, Boston was a game ahead of the Grays, but would slip into second place in percentage if they should lose the game. Excitement ran high, and the crowd of nearly 4500 that packed the Grays' Messer Street grounds included from 300-1500 fans (news accounts varied) who had traveled by train from Boston expecting a close and exciting game. They were not to be disappointed.

One Boston writer, recalling the 1884 Providence-Boston games a decade later, called them "the greatest ever played between two clubs in the history of baseball." This first game set the tone for the seventeen the clubs would play that season. In a monumental pitchers' duel, Radbourne and Boston's "Jumbo" Jim Whitney overpowered batters for sixteen innings without giving up an earned run. Darkness ended the game in a 1-1 tie. It turned out to be the league's longest game that year, and was hailed by one writer as "the most memorable in the history of the national sport." Boston still led the league.

The next day the teams played in Boston, but the league lead returned to Providence as the writers revised their judgment about baseball's most memorable game. Whitney unexpectedly was sent in to pitch again, and again permitted no earned runs, striking out 10 men. But Providence's Sweeney was the hero of the game, striking out 19 Boston batsmen for a new record (which stood for over a century, until Roger Clemens fanned 20 Mariners in 1986), as the Grays defeated the Reds 2-1 on unearned runs.

The Grays returned to a jubilant welcome in Providence that evening, complete with a torchlight parade and a banquet. But the jubilation was short-lived: Providence lost its next four games to Boston, falling four games out of first place, before Radbourne pulled out a 4-3 win in the fifteen-inning series finale.

Though they could not know it, the Grays had passed the low point of their season. For all the troubles to come, they would not again be farther than three games behind the league leader. With the fifteen-inning victory over Boston they began another of their winning streaks—this one ten games—which included Radbourne's fourteen-inning 1-0 three-hitter against Detroit.

The game that ended their winning streak—a no-hitter by Larry Corcoran in Chicago on June 27 (the third of his major league career)—seems to have taken the wind out of the Grays' sail. By the time they next played Boston on July 11, though they had pulled to within two games, they were becalmed in a ten-game stretch of .500 ball.

And they played no better against their archrivals, splitting their six games with Boston and ending the series still two games behind. Because Sweeney had developed arm trouble, Radbourne was now pitching nearly every game; against the Reds he pitched the first three games, winning two. A "phenomenal" acquired from the Worcester club, Joseph "Cyclone" Miller, pitched well in the fourth game but lost a close one, 4-3. Radbourne lost the fifth game, on July 16, and that evening was suspended by manager Bancroft for "insubordination" and lackadaisical play. Although Radbourne's overall record to that date was good (24-8), half his losses had come in the previous two weeks.

With Radbourne out, Miller became the starting pitcher for the next two games, winning the first with Sweeney's help in the ninth (to conclude the Boston series), and giving way to Sweeney in the second inning the next day against New York in a game Providence went on to win. Sweeney's arm trouble seemed to have cleared up. It wasn't his arm that would bring him down.

The next day, July 19, Providence introduced its second phenom of the month. Pitcher Ed Conley, a frail amateur up from the Woonsocket, Rhode Island, "OSRC's" (for Orcutt's Sure Rheumatic Cure, which supplied their uniforms), stunned Harry Wright's Phillies with a two-hit 6-1 victory.

Two days later, on Monday, July 21, during an exhibition game in Woonsocket against Conley's old team, Sweeney (who was playing center field) began drinking between innings in the dressing room. When the Grays returned to Providence after the game, he and Nava remained behind, and failed to show up for practice in Providence the next morning before a game with Philadelphia. Sweeney finally appeared at one o'clock and, taking manager Bancroft aside, said to him: "If you want to know why I was not here this morning I will tell you. I was drunk last night and did not get home."

Despite Sweeney's defiant attitude, Bancroft decided to give him his first start in two weeks. But he put Miller in right field to be available for relief if necessary. (Until 1891, substitutes could not be brought off the bench into a game unless one of the starting nine was injured or became ill.)

Sweeney pitched without will or effort, and it was only the Grays' strong fielding that held the Phillies to two runs in the first four innings. At the start of the fifth, Bancroft asked captain Joe Start to have Sweeney and Miller exchange positions, but Sweeney refused, and continued to pitch the next two innings. In the seventh, Bancroft called Sweeney over to the stands and asked him directly to let Miller relieve him. Sweeney refused, said "I guess I'll quit," and left the field.

Providence completed the game with eight men—Miller pitched, and Carroll and Hines covered the outfield. They managed to preserve their 6-2 lead into the ninth, but then balls began to fall between the fielders and two runs scored. The rattled Grays began to commit errors, and by the time the inning was over Philadelphia had scored eight runs. Final score: 10-6 Phillies.

Sweeney was expelled from the team, and the league, that evening. (There is some reason to suppose Sweeney acted deliberately to provoke his dismissal. Once freed from his league contract obligations, he promptly signed with St. Louis of the outlaw Union Association for higher pay; winning 24 games for them in the half-season that remained, he completed 1884 with a combined record of 41-15.)

Although the *New York Times* report of the Sweeney incident suggested that the Grays might have to disband, that option seemed not to have been seriously considered by the club directors. When they expelled Sweeney, they also reinstated Radbourne, revising his contract to pay him extra for pitching Sweeney's games in addition to his own. Radbourne, for his part (as baseball sage Henry Chadwick put it), "settled down to carry out his intention of 'pitching the Providence team into the championship,' and he did it splendidly, his work in the 'box' never before having been equaled."

For the next two months, until the Grays felt they had the pennant well in hand, Radbourne played every game. Most of them he pitched, but in the four games when Miller or Conley was started in the box, Radbourne played in the field to be available for relief. He did relieve Miller once, preserving the Grays' lead with four innings of no-hit pitching.

On August 7, in New York, after losing to the Maroons (also known as the Gothams, soon to be the Giants) 2-1 in 11 innings the day before, Radbourne came back to defeat them and begin the Grays' longest winning streak of the season—twenty games—and begin for himself a major league record eighteen consecutive wins. (Only two pitchers have surpassed Radbourne in the hundred seasons since then: Tim Keefe in 1888 and Rube Marquard in 1912, both with nineteen.)

When the Grays traveled to Boston two days later for the first game of their final series with the Red Stockings, they entered the most crucial period in their race for the pennant. Boston, only a game behind the Grays, knew it could come out of the series with as much as a three-game lead over Providence.

Boston's pitching was impressive. In the first game, Charlie Buffinton faced only twenty-seven men in nine innings—the two Grays who hit safely were promptly retired on a pickoff and a double play. But Radbourne was invincible. He matched Buffinton's pitching in the first game, which the Grays finally won in the eleventh, 1-0. In the second game, two days later, Boston scored a run, but Radbourne pitched his second two-hitter in a row and the Grays scored three runs to win. The next day Radbourne shut out the Reds for the second time in the series (4-0), and after a day's rest (a rainout) he finished them off with a third shutout, 1-0. The Grays' sweep left Boston five games behind.

For a time, Boston kept pace with an eight-game winning streak, but as Providence was now embarked on its twenty-game streak, and would win twenty-eight of twenty-nine games before easing up, the Reds were out of the race.

Radbourne's endurance was as impressive as his effectiveness. In the two months following Sweeney's departure he pitched thirty-five complete games (plus four innings of relief), winning thirty, losing four, and tying one. Two of his losses came at the end of this marathon as he pitched a twenty-first and twenty-second consecutive championship game for the Grays.

Radbourne's endurance and effectiveness are all the more remarkable in light of his agony in preparing for each game. Frank Bancroft, although he went on to other triumphs (culminating in a long, distinguished career as business manager for the Cincinnati Reds), never forgot 1884, and never tired of telling the Radbourne story. In an article he wrote for *Baseball Magazine* in 1908 he recalled Radbourne's warmup exercises:

> Morning after morning upon arising he would be unable to raise his arm high enough to use his hair brush. Instead of quitting he stuck all the harder to his task[,] going out to the ball park hours before the rest of the team and beginning to warm up by throwing a few feet and increasing the distance until he could finally throw the ball from the outfield to the home plate. The players, all eagerness to win, would watch "Rad," and when he would succeed in making his customary long distance throw they would look at each other and say the "Old Hoss" is ready and we can't be beat, and this proved to be the case nine times out of ten.

The Grays' schedule called for them to play the final month of the season away from home. As the day approached for their departure they were variously honored by their fans. Before the game of September 2, for example, Radbourne and his catcher Gilligan were presented "life-size portraits of themselves, in crayon, handsomely mounted in heavy gilded frames." A week and a half later, "Radbourne was given a great bunch of flowers, in which was a valuable envelope, while Farrell received a magnificent crayon portrait of himself, and a gold watch, chain and charm, the latter articles being valued at $185."

The Grays rewarded their fans, too, with their splendid play. Their loss on September 9 which ended their twenty-game winning streak was doubtless a disappointment, especially as poor umpiring seems to have contributed to Buffalo's two runs. But on the whole the Grays were awesome. On September 5, third baseman Denny hit "the best home run hit yet made on the Messer Street grounds. The ball went far above the roofs of the houses beyond the left field fence, and ere it had dropped Farrell was home and Denny nearly to second base. This won the game."

When the team left for Cleveland in mid-September, Conley and Murray were brought along as the change battery. Miller and Nava were loaned for the remainder of the season to a military team at Ft. Monroe, Virginia.

On September 25, in Chicago, Radbourne missed his first game as pitcher or fielder since returning from his suspension on July 23. He pitched only five of the Grays' twelve remaining games. With his two consecutive losses in late September, the whole team slacked off, winning only half of their final fourteen games. Nevertheless, they clinched the pennant two weeks before the end of the season when Boston, weakened by injuries, lost its third game of the week to last-place Detroit.

On October 15 the Grays' championship season came to an end with a makeup game in Philadelphia. Radbourne pitched and won easily, 8-0, his eleventh shutout of the year. He started 73 games as pitcher and completed them all, winning 59, losing 12 and tying 2. Twice he came in from right field to relieve the starting pitcher and preserve his team's lead; by today's scoring guidelines he would be credited with two saves. (Saves, of course, were not calculated in 1884, and neither were pitching wins and losses. Radbourne, had he been asked, would simply have said he had pitched in 61 Providence victories. The 60-win figure that appears in baseball encyclopedias and record books was arrived at in the early years of this century by crediting one of his relief appearances as a victory in addition to his 59 complete-game wins.)

It was pitching and fielding that carried Providence to its .750 record of 84 wins against only 28 losses. In batting and slugging, the Grays ranked only fifth among the league's eight teams. Their .241 batting average was six points below the league average, and a full forty points below league-leading Chicago's .281. Paul Hines led the Grays in batting with .302. Sweeney in his half season hit .298, and Start batted .276. Denny led the club in home runs with 6.

In fielding the Grays were much more impressive, their fielding average of .918 second only to Boston's .922. Two Grays were at the top of the league in their positions: Joe Start led first basemen with .980, nine points ahead of his nearest rival; second baseman Jack Farrell ended the season in a virtual tie with Boston's Jack Burdock at .922.

Most impressive, of course, were the Grays' pitching statistics. In earned run average (estimated in modern times), Providence pitchers led the league: Radbourne was first (1.38) and Sweeney second (1.55). The team's 1.59 was just over half the league average (2.98), and nearly a run less per game than second-ranked Boston (2.47). Sweeney gave up the fewest hits per nine innings of anyone in the league (6.23); Radbourne was second (with 7.00). Radbourne led the league in strikeouts with 441.

On their return to Providence October 17, the Grays were once again paraded and banqueted. With Sweeney, the hero of the previous celebration, gone, Radbourne was king. He rewarded his fans' adulation by pitching a one-hitter the next day in an exhibition game against Cincinnati of the American Association—his final appearance of the year in Providence.

For Radbourne and the Grays there was one more triumph. Late in July Jim Mutrie, manager of New York's Metropolitans, who were headed for the American Association championship, began to talk about how his team could beat any team in the older National League. When Providence players heard this, they persuaded Bancroft to challenge the Mets to a postseason series to settle the question of league superiority. Mutrie accepted the challenge and, after much negotiation, a three-game series was scheduled for New York's Polo Grounds, then located just north of Central Park, for October 23-25 (six months to the day after the Grays—without pitching Hoss—had defeated the Mets in three preseason games).

This October series looms in importance through the mist

of a hundred years as the forerunner and prototype of America's premier sporting event. But in 1884, even though some papers described it as a series to determine the championship of the world, the public remained unimpressed.

American Association teams were regularly defeated in exhibition games by National League clubs—although this pattern reversed itself in the next two years—and the Association champion Mets, before meeting Providence, had done no better than tie the Maroons, fourth place in the NL, in a series for the city championship. Furthermore, the weather turned windy and cold suddenly, dropping into the low fifties on the afternoon of the first game from a summer-like 76° the day before. Only 2500 spectators saw Radbourne shut out the Mets 6-0. Even that number dropped the next day, along with the temperature, as only 1000 fans saw Grays' third baseman Denny win for Radbourne the second and deciding game, 3-1, with a home run over the center-field fence.

As the outcome of the series had been decided and the weather remained cold, fewer than 500 fans showed up for the final game. The Grays, who were to split with the Mets the profits of the final two games, saw no profit in this small crowd and wanted to go home. When at last they were persuaded to take the field after being given the choice of umpire, they were given the game as well by the Mets' sloppy fielding. Scorers lost count, but when darkness mercifully halted the game after six innings, Radbourne and the Grays were once again victorious, by a score of 11—or perhaps 12—to 2.

Henry Chadwick, reflecting on Radbourne's success while pitching nearly every game, argued his example as a paradigm for all those pitchers who claimed to need rest every other day. But even Radbourne couldn't maintain his 1884 pace beyond that season. The next year he pitched only two-thirds as many games as he had in 1884. And though he often pitched well thereafter, not once in his seven remaining major league seasons did he win even half the number of games he had won in his miracle year.

As for the Providence Grays, in 1885 they slipped below

.500 and into fourth place for the first time in their history. Their fans deserted them, and at the end of the season the club was disbanded. Frank Bancroft, just a year after his greatest triumph, had for the first time managed a failure.

Van Lingle Mungo: An Elegiac Ode

b. June 8, 1911, Pageland, S.C.
d. Feb. 12, 1985, Pageland, S.C.

W	120
L	115
ERA	3.47

Honor now, Van Lingle Mungo
Pound the plate and hoist a fungo
Flaming fastball, fiery nature
Famous for his nomenclature
Hero of that long ago
When players played for keeps, not dough
Lived it up, day/nocturnal
Never read the *Wall Street Journal*
Skippers in those stormy times
Included Carey, Stengel, Grimes
But Van so needed elbow room
It's hard to say who managed whom.
He railed at teammates, cursed the Gods
Who saddled him with fearful odds.
Now, standing on the pitcher's mound
Van draws a breath and looks around
No doubt, a trembling of the knees
To know his fate depends on these:

Fresco Thompson, Whitey Ock
Buster Mills and Lonnie Frey
Jimmy Jordan, Lindsay Brown
Packy Rogers—wanna cry?
Vincent Sherlock, Ernie Koy
Paul Chervinko, Franki Skaff
Danny Taylor, Sid Gautreaux
(Dry your eyes, it's worth a laugh)

And among the others chosen
For his teammates, Goody Rosen
Curly Onis, Gordon Slade

Small wonder that he oft displayed
The passion of a man betrayed.

—it's over, Van; rest easy.

PAUL L. PARKER

Who was buried in Grant's Tomb? The Mets!

A Ballparks Quiz

Bob Bluthardt

1. Who were the two Cincinnati pitchers who took a rowboat across the outfield wall of a flooded Crosley Field in 1937?

2. Where did the 1914 Boston Braves and the 1915-1916 Boston Red Sox play their home World Series games?

3. In several World Series, all the games were played in one park; name the years and parks.

4. What major league park hosted the first night game?

5. Wrigley Field came within months of having lights in 1942. What happened?

6. Where is Navin Field today, and who was Navin?

7. Fenway Park's left-field wall or Connie Mack Stadium's right-field wall: which was higher?

8. In what park did a goat assist the groundskeeper in trimming the outfield grass?

9-14. In what parks would you find these places:

BOB BLUTHARDT works at the Fort Concho Museum in San Angelo, Texas, and chairs SABR's ballparks committee.

171

9. Ashburn's Ridge   12. Ruthville
10. Duffy's Cliff   13. The Jury Box
11. The Crow's Nest   14. Kiner's Korner

15. In what park was umpire George Magerkurth attacked by a fan?

16. First called Weeghman Park, it is still in use today. What is the present name, and who was Weeghman?

17. Who first cleared the right-field roof at Forbes Field with a towering home run?

18. Thirty years ago, a friend says, "Meet me under the tree." What park will you be visiting?

19. What famous event took place at Ebbets Field at its first night game in 1938?

20. Mickey Mantle victimized what pitcher at what park for his famous 565-foot home run?

21. Where did Babe Ruth "call" a World Series homer?

22. The first All-Star Game graced what park?

23. Walter Johnson pitched only one no-hitter in his career; where?

24-33. Match the streets with the parks they bordered:

24. Gaffney Street   Wrigley Field
25. Montgomery Street   Sportsman's Park
26. Waveland Avenue   Shibe Park
27. Trumbull Avenue   Ebbets Field
28. Sennott Street   Tiger Stadium
29. Georgia Avenue   Polo Grounds
30. York Street   Crosley Field
31. Dodier Street   Forbes Field
32. Somerset Street   Braves Field
33. East 155th Street   Griffith Stadium

34. Few hitters ever reached the center-field bleachers at the Polo Grounds; name the first three.

35. Which team can claim the oldest park in operation today in the majors?

36. Who was Abe Stark?

37. It is September 21, 1961; what park is closing and what is unusual about the game?

38. Cite the outfield distances at Yankee Stadium in its last year before remodeling.

39. Where did a groundskeeper live in the ballpark?

40. Which park never hosted a no-hit game?

41. To the distress and embarrassment of all, what park opened without a press box?

42. In what park did a public address system first appear?

43. In the World Series, there has been one unassisted triple play; where did it occur?

44. The home team has just hit a home run; a bird on the scoreboard celebrates the event; where are you?

45. It held fewer than 20,000 seats and its right-field wall loomed a scant 280 feet from home plate. A marvel when it opened in 1887, it was a joke when it closed in 1938. What park?

46. Name the five hitters who have cleared the center-field wall in Fenway Park to the right of the flag pole.

47. Who are the famous Yankees honored by the tablets that used to reside in the center field of Yankee Stadium?

48. What former park now sits in the backyard of a baseball fan?

49. Where did the longest game in the majors take place?

50. You are watching a game at the Polo Grounds, but the Giants are the visiting team! Explain.

Answers on page 174.

ANSWERS TO QUIZ

1. Lee Grissom and Gene Schott. **2.** The Braves used Fenway Park as their new park wasn't ready. Returning the favor, they let the Sox use Braves Field a year later. **3.** In 1921 and 1922 the Yankees and Giants battled at the Polo Grounds; in 1944, the Browns and Cardinals played at Sportsman's Park. **4.** Cincinnati's Crosley Field on May 24, 1935. President Roosevelt threw the lights on from a switch in the White House. **5.** The lights were ready to be installed, but World War II came, and Phil Wrigley donated them to a nearby shipyard to help the war effort. **6.** Tiger Stadium in Detroit. Frank Navin was president of the Tigers from 1911 to 1935. **7.** Fenway's "Green Monster" has stayed at 37-plus feet for over 40 years; from 1934 to 1956 Connie Mack's right-field wall checked in at 50 feet. **8.** In Sportsman's Park in St. Louis in the 1930s. **9.** In Philadelphia's Connie Mack Stadium (Shibe Park). It was a doctored area of the third-base line to assist his bunting. **10.** In Fenway Park, the famed sloped left field that Duffy Lewis played so well. **11.** In Pittsburgh at Forbes Field. This extra deck of seats was added in 1938 in anticipation of a Pirate pennant that didn't happen. **12.** In Yankee Stadium, the right-field bleachers, a favorite target of Babe Ruth. This area was also known as Gehrigsville. **13.** In Braves Field, the detached, box-like bleacher section in right field. **14.** In Forbes Field, the shortened left-field corner feasted upon by Ralph Kiner. Once Kiner left the club, the distance was restored. **15.** In Ebbets Field after a game in 1939. **16.** Today, Weeghman Park is Wrigley Field. Charles Weeghman owned the Chicago Whales of the short-lived Federal League. Built in 1914, the park was taken over by the Cubs in 1916. **17.** Babe Ruth, when he played with the Boston Braves in 1935, his last season. His last of three homers that May 25th cleared the roof. **18.** Griffith Stadium in Washington, D.C. The tree was just outside the center-field wall. **19.** Johnny Vander Meer pitched his second straight no-hitter for Cincinnati. **20.** Senators' pitcher Chuck Stobbs at Griffith Stadium in 1953. **21.** Wrigley Field. **22.** Chicago's Comiskey Park in 1933. **23.** Fenway Park. **24.** Braves Field. **25.** Ebbets Field. **26.** Wrigley Field. **27.** Tiger Stadium. **28.** Forbes Field. **29.** Griffith Stadium. **30.** Crosley Field. **31.** Sportsman's Park. **32.** Shibe Park/Connie Mack Stadium **33.** Polo Grounds. **34.** The Braves' Joe Adcock was first in 1953; later came Lou Brock and Hank Aaron. **35.** The White Sox at Comiskey Park—first game on July 1, 1910. **36.** A Brooklyn businessman whose sign on Ebbets Field's right-field wall offered a free suit for any hitter striking it. **37.** It is the last game at Griffith Stadium and the expansion Washington Senators are playing the old Senator team now called the Minnesota Twins. **38.** Left field, 301 feet; center field, 461 feet; right field, 296 feet. **39.** In the Polo Grounds, head groundskeeper Matty Schwab lived under section 31 in left field. Horace Stoneham had lured him from Ebbets Field, and he built an apartment for Schwab and his family under the stands. **40.** Forbes Field. **41.** Brooklyn's Ebbets Field in 1913. **42.** Polo Grounds, 1929; a microphone was attached to the mask of the home-plate umpire. **43.** At League Park in Cleveland in the 1920 Indians-Dodgers contest. Bill Wambsganss pulled it off in game 5. **44.** Busch Stadium in St. Louis. **45.** Philadelphia's Baker Bowl. **46.** Hank Greenberg, 1937; Jimmie Foxx, 1937; Bill Skowron, 1957; Carl Yastrzemski, 1970; Bobby Mitchell, 1973; Jim Rice, 1975. **47.** Miller Huggins, Babe Ruth, Lou Gehrig, Jake Ruppert. **48.** Crosley Field, at least many pieces of it, now endures in the large yard of a super fan in Kentucky. **49.** At Braves Field: Boston against Brooklyn, 26 innings of 1-1 baseball in 1920. **50.** It is 1962 or 1963 and the Giants, now in San Francisco, are meeting the New York Mets; or it is the World Series of 1921 or 1922 (see question 3).

If baseball crosswords seem easy, try this!

Acrostic Puzzle

Jeff Neuman

ACROSTIC PUZZLE

1R	2T	3F	4D		5R	6D	7A	8E	9N	10B	11T	12K		13J	14H
28R	29C		30O	31L	32S	33H		34W	35S	36O	37I		38L	39U	40R
54B	55G	56S	57K	58M	59E	60U		61D	62I	63Q	64W	65R	66P		67M
80R	81A	82F		83N	84K	85H	86W	87C		88R	89G	90D	91S	92Q	93B
106T		107U	108I	109B	110W		111K	112F	113E	114O	115V		116F	117Q	118O
130Q	131A		132O	133K	134D	135B	136L	137F	138H	139U		140L	141F	142B
157N		158R	159O		160V	161N	162K	163U	164J	165A	166L	167T		168P	169J
	183P	184V	185E	186K		187N	188V	189R	190Q	191D	192L	193P		194O	195I

Fill in the words defined below, one letter over each numbered dash.
Then transfer each letter to the box which is numbered correspondingly
in the acrostic diagram. Black boxes indicate word endings; note that
words may spill over at the right, from one line to the next. When

JEFFREY NEUMAN is an editor at Macmillan, where he edits, among
other things, *The Baseball Encyclopedia*.

JEFFREY NEUMAN

15A	16P	17R	18L	19D	20O	■	21P	22K	■	23G	24F	25M	26B	27I
41G	42K	43V	44A	45T	46J	47I	■	48⊖	49F	50P	■	51Q	52V	53F
68L	■	69N	70J	71B	72I	73G	■	74K	75E	■	76X	77U	78C	79T
94K	95I	■	96R	97F	■	98K	99C	100X	101V	102F	■	103U	104F	105L
119T	120K	■	121J	122U	■	123U	124L	125P	126S	■	127U	128Q	129K	■
143T	144L	145V	146B	147R	148E	149A	150G	■	151M	152H	153F	154W	155P	156E
170T	171B	172G	173W	174A	175X	■	176Q	177T	178U	■	179K	180M	181O	182J
■	196P	197T	198M	199G	■	200K	■	201G	202C	203S	204Q	205D	206F	207R

completed, the diagram will yield a quotation from a celebrate
baseball book; its author and title will be revealed by reading the first
letters of the guessed words below.

Answer on page 186.

CLUES

A. Asks for a song

B. " 'The time has come,' the walrus said,/ 'To talk of many things/ _____ ships and sealing wax. . . .' "
(Lewis Carroll; 3 words)

C. Erstwhile homer champ Cravath

D. Abandon the site of a disaster

E. 67 doubles, 257 hits, 75 complete games, et al.

F. Mythical rotation mate of Spahn, Sain (4 words)

G. Dozed (2 words)

H. Goslin and Gossage

I. Hops aboard a Pullman

J. A faded skill, like the fair-foul hit (2 words)

K. Time for the home stretch (colloq., 4 words)

L. Yardstick for long taters (2 words)

M. Patterns of behavior acquired by frequent repetition

N. His field lay in Flatbush

O. Number six on the field, and number one in St. Louis hearts

P. Like Wambsganss's gem

Q. Stadium where Indians need no reservations

R. Star hurler though down a digit, his middle names were Peter Centennial

S. The branch of philosophy dealing with moral duty and obligation

T. One-time Rookie of the Year, before he was Dick

U. _____ hit (classic assessment of most utility infielders; 3 words)

V. On target

W. Gashouse Gang member Johnny Leonard Roosevelt or modern skipper Alfred Manuel

X. Cincinnati standout Roush

SOLUTIONS

A. $\overline{174}$ $\overline{149}$ $\overline{15}$ $\overline{165}$ $\overline{81}$ $\overline{7}$ $\overline{44}$ $\overline{131}$

B. $\overline{146}$ $\overline{54}$ $\overline{135}$ $\overline{26}$ $\overline{109}$ $\overline{93}$ $\overline{71}$ $\overline{10}$ $\overline{171}$ $\overline{142}$

C. $\overline{29}$ $\overline{202}$ $\overline{99}$ $\overline{78}$ $\overline{87}$

D. $\overline{191}$ $\overline{90}$ $\overline{134}$ $\overline{61}$ $\overline{205}$ $\overline{6}$ $\overline{4}$ $\overline{19}$

E. $\overline{113}$ $\overline{8}$ $\overline{185}$ $\overline{59}$ $\overline{75}$ $\overline{148}$ $\overline{156}$

F. $\overline{3}$ $\overline{49}$ $\overline{82}$ $\overline{116}$ $\overline{206}$ $\overline{104}$ $\overline{102}$ $\overline{97}$ $\overline{24}$ $\overline{53}$ $\overline{137}$ $\overline{153}$ $\overline{112}$ $\overline{141}$

G. $\overline{23}$ $\overline{199}$ $\overline{73}$ $\overline{150}$ $\overline{55}$ $\overline{172}$ $\overline{89}$ $\overline{201}$ $\overline{41}$

H. $\overline{152}$ $\overline{14}$ $\overline{138}$ $\overline{33}$ $\overline{85}$

I. $\overline{72}$ $\overline{47}$ $\overline{95}$ $\overline{108}$ $\overline{62}$ $\overline{27}$ $\overline{37}$ $\overline{195}$

J. $\overline{164}$ $\overline{46}$ $\overline{182}$ $\overline{121}$ $\overline{70}$ $\overline{13}$ $\overline{169}$

K. $\overline{12}$ $\overline{200}$ $\overline{22}$ $\overline{57}$ $\overline{74}$ $\overline{111}$ $\overline{179}$ $\overline{120}$ $\overline{133}$ $\overline{162}$ $\overline{98}$ $\overline{84}$ $\overline{42}$ $\overline{94}$ $\overline{129}$ $\overline{186}$

L. $\overline{166}$ $\overline{140}$ $\overline{38}$ $\overline{68}$ $\overline{105}$ $\overline{31}$ $\overline{124}$ $\overline{192}$ $\overline{136}$ $\overline{18}$ $\overline{144}$

M. $\overline{180}$ $\overline{151}$ $\overline{67}$ $\overline{58}$ $\overline{25}$ $\overline{198}$

N. $\overline{83}$ $\overline{161}$ $\overline{9}$ $\overline{69}$ $\overline{157}$ $\overline{187}$

O. $\overline{20}$ $\overline{118}$ $\overline{48}$ $\overline{159}$ $\overline{132}$ $\overline{181}$ $\overline{114}$ $\overline{194}$ $\overline{36}$ $\overline{30}$

P. $\overline{16}$ $\overline{155}$ $\overline{196}$ $\overline{125}$ $\overline{193}$ $\overline{21}$ $\overline{168}$ $\overline{66}$ $\overline{183}$ $\overline{50}$

Q. $\overline{92}$ $\overline{128}$ $\overline{63}$ $\overline{130}$ $\overline{190}$ $\overline{117}$ $\overline{51}$ $\overline{176}$ $\overline{204}$

R. $\overline{88}$ $\overline{65}$ $\overline{147}$ $\overline{80}$ $\overline{207}$ $\overline{189}$ $\overline{158}$ $\overline{17}$ $\overline{5}$ $\overline{40}$ $\overline{96}$ $\overline{1}$ $\overline{28}$

S. $\overline{91}$ $\overline{126}$ $\overline{35}$ $\overline{203}$ $\overline{56}$ $\overline{32}$

T. $\overline{143}$ $\overline{79}$ $\overline{119}$ $\overline{2}$ $\overline{45}$ $\overline{167}$ $\overline{170}$ $\overline{197}$ $\overline{11}$ $\overline{106}$ $\overline{177}$

U. $\overline{103}$ $\overline{163}$ $\overline{122}$ $\overline{139}$ $\overline{107}$ $\overline{77}$ $\overline{39}$ $\overline{123}$ $\overline{178}$ $\overline{60}$ $\overline{127}$

V. $\overline{160}$ $\overline{145}$ $\overline{43}$ $\overline{188}$ $\overline{101}$ $\overline{184}$ $\overline{115}$ $\overline{52}$

W. $\overline{110}$ $\overline{173}$ $\overline{86}$ $\overline{34}$ $\overline{154}$ $\overline{64}$

X. $\overline{100}$ $\overline{76}$ $\overline{175}$

The head of the Elias Sports Bureau spotlights a new hero.

Newly Discovered RBI Records

Seymour Siwoff

Runs batted in, now one of the most important measures of batting performance, were slow to be recognized by the major leagues. There were no official RBI records until 1920, and they were not carried in many box scores until ten years after that. It is not surprising then that a record such as "Most Consecutive Games, One or More Runs Batted In," would be hard to pin down and might vary based on the latest research.

At one time Lou Gehrig was credited with an American League record of ten consecutive RBI games, which he achieved twice in 1931 and once in 1934. Then further research showed that Babe Ruth and Al Simmons each had 11-game streaks in 1931. Then it was found that Red Sox playing manager Joe Cronin knocked in runs in 12 straight games in 1939 and that his star outfielder, Ted Williams, also had a 12-game string in 1942. In the National League, Mel Ott for many years was carried as the leader with an 11-game streak made in 1929, but two years ago it was discovered that Paul Waner had achieved a 12-game run in 1927.

The Elias Sports Bureau felt that it was time that this evolving run production drama be brought to a climactic conclusion. We decided to research all the official records of runs batted in since they achieved that status in 1920 to see what "great slugger" had achieved the longest string of RBI games. It took considerable checking and rechecking but we finally came up with a 13-game record-holder in the American League and a surprising 17-game streaker in the National League.

They were two Chicago players of modest reputation— Taft Wright of the 1941 White Sox, and Oscar Ray Grimes of the 1922 Cubs. They were good hitters, with lifetime records well over .300, but they didn't have very long careers and were not regarded as particularly good run producers. Nevertheless, they did have legitimate streaks which are of interest also because of some unusual aspects.

First the 13-game streak of Taft Wright in 1941.

The hefty White Sox outfielder was in his third season and playing his first full game of 1941 when the string was launched modestly on May 4 with an RBI single in four trips against Philadelphia. The streak became even more "modest" in the third, fourth, and fifth games when Wright failed to hit in each contest, yet was credited with an RBI each day. On May 7 he hit a sacrifice fly; on May 10 he was walked twice, once with the bases loaded; and on May 11 a run scored on his infield out. After driving in two runs with two hits on May 13, he had another hitless day on May 14 but drove in a run with an infield out. He knocked in four runs with a homer and a single on May 15 and then had two more hitless games where he moved one runner home with a sacrifice fly and another with a force out. He made up for the hitless days with four hits on May 18, producing four runs. After two more run-producing games, the 13-game streak came to a close in Philadelphia on May 21.

The remarkable achievement was magnified in that in six games he knocked in runs without any hits. In that way he edged out the great AL sluggers like Ruth, Gehrig, Foxx, Simmons, and Ted Williams of an important run-production record. Wright ended the 1941 season with 97 RBIs, the most on the White Sox team, and the best of his nine-year career.

The NL record was established by Ray Grimes, who made it to the majors with the Red Sox in 1920. That was also the debut year of his twin brother Roy. Roy lasted only one year, but Ray went on to the Cubs where he played first base and had a very good season in 1922, hitting .354. That was the year of his streak, which started in the second game of a twinbill with Pittsburgh on June 27. The next day he had lumbago and did not play. He returned to the lineup on June 30 and had at least one RBI through the July 8 twinbill. Ironically, he played only one inning of the second game, but connected for an RBI single before leaving the game with a wrenched back.

The injury was serious and he did not return to first base until July 18 when he celebrated with a homer, double, and two singles to lead the Cubs to a 6-3 victory over the Phils. On July 21 he doubled in the only run of the game to give Grover Alexander a 1-0 thriller over Dutch Ruether of the Dodgers. Grimes continued to hit well, driving out extra-base hits in six straight games. Finally, on July 25, in a game against Boston he failed to produce a run. His big chance came in the fourth inning with two teammates on base, but Grimes was walked to load the bases.

His spectacular 17-game RBI streak was not noted at the time, probably because he was absent from the lineup on two occasions, once for nine days. However, the RBI streak, like a consecutive game hitting streak, is based on the games the individual plays and not necessarily those that the team plays.

Ray Grimes, Cubs, 1922

Date	AB	R	H	RBI	Comment
June 27 (2)	5	1	1	1	
June 30	4	1	2	1	Missed June 28 game

Date	AB	R	H	RBI	Comment
July 1	4	0	2	3	Double
July 2	4	0	1	1	Double
July 3	4	0	1	1	
July 4 (1)	4	0	1	1	
July 4 (2)	3	2	2	1	
July 5	4	2	1	1	Double
July 7	4	2	2	2	Double, triple
July 8 (1)	3	2	2	1	
July 8 (2)	1	0	1	1	Played one inning
July 18	4	1	4	2	Homer, double
July 19	5	0	1	1	Double
July 20	5	2	2	3	Homer
July 21	4	0	1	1	Double for 1-0 win
July 22	5	1	3	4	Double, triple
July 23	3	1	1	2	Homer

Taft Wright, White Sox, 1941

Date	AB	R	H	RBI	Comment
May 4	4	1	1	1	First start of 1941
May 5	5	0	2	1	Double
May 7	4	0	0	1	Sacrifice fly
May 10	2	0	0	1	Walk with bases full
May 11	3	0	0	1	Infield out
May 13	4	0	2	2	
May 14	5	0	0	1	Infield out
May 15	5	2	2	4	Homer
May 16	4	0	0	1	Sacrifice fly
May 17	5	1	0	1	Force out
May 18	5	2	4	4	Double
May 19	4	2	2	2	Triple
May 20	2	1	1	1	Double

A boyhood lesson in aerodynamics.

No Knuckles About It

Barry Gifford

There was a man on our block named Rooney Sullavan who would often come walking down the street while the kids would be playing ball in front of my house or Johnny McLaughlin's house. He would always stop and ask if he'd ever shown us how he used to throw the knuckleball back when he pitched for Kankakee in 1930.

"Plenty of times, Rooney," Billy Cunningham would say. "No knuckles about it, right?" Tommy Ryan would say. "No knuckles about it, right!" Rooney Sullavan would say. "Give it here and I'll show you." One of us would reluctantly toss Rooney the ball and we'd step up so he could demonstrate for the fortieth or fiftieth time how he held the ball by his fingertips only, no knuckles about it.

"Don't know how it ever got the name knuckler," Rooney'd say. "I call mine The Rooneyball." Then he'd tell one of us—usually Billy because he had the catcher's glove, the old fat-heeled kind that didn't bend unless somebody stepped

BARRY GIFFORD of Berkeley, Ca., wrote *The Neighborhood of Baseball*.

on it, a big black mitt that Billy's dad had handed down to him from *his* days at Kankakee or Rock Island or some place—to get sixty feet away so Rooney could see if he could "still make it wrinkle."

Billy would pace off twelve squares of sidewalk, each square being approximately five feet long, the length of one nine-year-old boy stretched head to toe, squat down, and stick his big black glove out in front of his face. With his right hand he'd cover his crotch in case the pitch got away and short-hopped off the cement where he couldn't block it with the mitt. The knuckleball was unpredictable; not even Rooney could tell what would happen to it once he let it go.

"It's the air makes it hop," Rooney claimed. His leather jacket creaked as he bent, wound up, rotated his right arm like nobody'd done since Chief Bender, crossed his runny gray eyes, and released the ball from the tips of his fingers. We watched as it sailed straight up at first then sort of floated on an invisible wave before plunging the last ten feet like a balloon that had been pierced by a dart.

Billy always went down on his knees, the back of his right hand stiffened over his crotch, and stuck out his gloved hand at the slowly whirling Rooneyball. Just before it got to Billy's mitt the ball would give out entirely and sink rapidly, inducing Billy to lean forward in order to catch it—only he couldn't because at the last instant it would make a final, sneaky hop before bouncing surprisingly hard off Billy's unprotected chest.

"*Just* like I told you," Rooney Sullavan would exclaim. "All it takes is plain old air."

Billy would come up with the ball in his upturned glove, his right hand rubbing the spot on his chest where the pitch had hit. "You all right, son?" Rooney would ask, and Billy would nod. "Tough kid," Rooney'd say. "I'd like to stay out with you fellas all day, but I got responsibilities." Rooney would muss up Billy's hair with the hand that held the secret to The Rooneyball and walk away whistling "When Irish Eyes Are Smiling" or "My Wild Irish Rose." Rooney was about forty-five or fifty years old and lived with his mother in a bungalow at the corner. He worked nights for Wanzer Dairy, washing out returned milk bottles.

Tommy Ryan would grab the ball out of Billy's mitt and hold it by the tips of his fingers like Rooney Sullavan did, and Billy would go sit on the stoop in front of the closest house and rub his chest. "No way," Tommy would say, considering the prospect of his ever duplicating Rooney's feat. "There must be something he's not telling us."

ANSWER TO ACROSTIC PUZZLE

"What baseball requires is nothing less than perfection, and perfection cannot be eased or divided. Every movement of every game, from first pitch to last out, is measured and recorded against an absolute standard and thus each success is also a failure."

ROGER ANGELL, *The Summer Game.*

Supervisor, disciplinarian, strategist...and scapegoat.

Baseball's Misbegottens: Expansion-Era Managers

David Voigt

In the 1970s, the very time when players and umpires gained wealth and power, baseball's field managers' status declined as they became wretched scapegoats to be sacrificed to the bloodlust of victory-starved fans. True, sacking the manager was a time-honored ploy; whenever rumblings of fan discontent erupted, a manager was bumped off as virgins in ancient rites were thrown down to appease the volcano god. From the 1880s till 1970, indeed, every passing season was littered with cashiered pilots. But beginning in 1970 this practice was accelerated. From then through 1981, National League managers enjoyed but a 2.4-year tenure on the average, while American League managers stood to last only 1.9 years. Incredibly, Earl Weaver of the Baltimore Orioles was the only manager to survive with the same team thru the '70s, and in 1981 12 of the 26 teams changed managers.

DAVID VOIGT is the author of *American Baseball,* a three-volume major-league history.

Managers have always known that they were hired to be fired. But if any manager in 1946 dared think that his status had sunk so low that it must improve, he was deluded. In the years 1946-66 firings reduced managerial tenure to 2.3 years on the average. Thus, Walter Alston, the most enduring manager of the 1946-1981 era, who served 23 years with the Dodgers, watched about 85 colleagues get walking papers. And from 1968 till now, Weaver, the next hardiest survivor, exchanged lineup cards at home plate with 95 different helmsmen.

Like vulnerable foremen in industry, managers had every right to feel paranoid. On the one hand their bosses expected them to win games with personnel provided by the front office; on the other, they faced the hopeless task of pleasing 25 individualistic players. Worse, the latter gained steadily in power what with multiyear contracts and salaries often exceeding the manager's own. As Dick Williams recently put it: "If a manager who's in the last year of his contract tries to tell a player who's got four or five more years left in *his* contract what to do, the player won't pay attention, because he knows he's going to be there long after the manager is gone."

In the postwar era a few managers still emulated the dictatorial style of the late John McGraw, who regularly called five-hour practices on days of scheduled games and who made both major and minor tactical decisions himself, down to the calling of each pitch. Convinced of his own importance, McGraw was contemptuous of his charges. Once, spotting a player at practice ogling a woman in the stands, he told a nearby rookie: "See that? That cement head is thinking more about that girl than today's game. Remember this, son. One percent of ballplayers are leaders of men. The other 99 percent are followers of women."

For many reasons that kind of vanity became *passé*. Nevertheless, the years after World War II still provided some Little Napoleon managers who wore number 1 on their backs and lorded their rank over the players. In the '40s the archetype of McGraw was Leo Durocher: in the three-way classification of managers served up by pitcher-

writer Jim Brosnan—the "I did it," the "We did it," and
the "They did it"—Leo the Lip was an unreconstructed
"I" type. Managers of this category also included such men
as Charley Dressen, Eddie Stanky, and Gene Mauch.

But increasing pressure from organized players and from
owners was endangering this breed to the point of extinc-
tion, replacing them with "We" and "They" types. Resembling school guidance counselors, the "We's" oozed concern for players and tried to win their cooperation by
downplaying their own roles. According to Brosnan, exam-
ples included Walter Alston, Ralph Houk, and Danny
Murtaugh; one surely must add Tom Lasorda of the Dodgers. Of course, some like Hank Bauer, Fred Hutchinson,
Sparky Anderson, and Weaver mixed into the "We" method
a strong dash of egoistic "I" projections.

Meanwhile a third type spotted by Brosnan, the "They's,"
sought to weld players into tightly knit communities. Insisting
on conformity to team standards, they unloaded trouble-
making players. In general, this posture worked best with
talent-rich teams. Representatives of this type in Brosnan's
judgment included Joe McCarthy, Casey Stengel, Billy
Southworth, and Al Lopez.

The growing number of "We" and "They" types spot-
lighted the tendency of status-deprived managers trying to
adapt to eroding powers. Certainly the importance of field
managers was being questioned. Bill Veeck voiced his
opinion that managerial strategy and tactics were a minor
factor in a game's outcome. Naturally a Durocher or a Paul
Richards disputed this, but not Yogi Berra who, while
managing the 1964 Yankees, told a reporter that he could
hardly invent any new plays!

For openly debasing managers in the 1960s, nobody
matched Charles Finley. After firing a dozen, Finley suggested
that any fan could do the job—even an above-average
monkey. Yet, ironically, to this day only the conservative
owner Phil Wrigley has ever tried to eliminate managers.
Back in the '60s he employed a system of revolving coaches
for a couple of years before returning to the manager
system. Not surprisingly, Wrigley's experiment was derided

by other clubs; still, a general trend was taking shape in the direction of excluding managers from such matters as trade decisions, player discipline, policy-making and—by surrounding them with bevies of coaching specialists—even from strategy, tactics, and training.

Even with clipped wings some managers are avidly courted, especially those reputed to be good strategists and leaders. In 1967 the Mets gave the Senators $100,000 and a pitcher to obtain Gil Hodges as manager, and in 1976 the Pirates paid cash and a good catcher for Chuck Tanner, who currently holds a five-year contract—the longest ever issued to a manager. In the fullness of time each of these acquisitions produced a world championship, thus fueling the mystique of the charismatic manager. Even the cynical Finley was not wholly immune to its siren song as demonstrated by his refusal to let the Yankees sign one of his better prodigals, Dick Williams.

With geniuses in short supply, many managers when sacked were paid off only to be plucked later by another club to fit the same role. Sometimes this game of managerial musical chairs waxed ludicrous, as in the early '50s when three working managers drew double salaries, one for managing their current team and another from the team that had discarded them. Usually this kind of double-dipping was limited, but sacking managers was not. Open season began in earnest in the Eisenhower decade when a record 58 were fired or quit, but that record was erased by the 90 cashiered in the 1960s and by the 95 jettisoned in the '70s.

One must look hard to find the logic behind some managerial dismissals. Incredibly, two were fired during spring training after having given apparent satisfaction over the previous season. The Cubs dumped Phil Cavaretta in March 1954, and shortly before the 1978 season was to open the Padres fired Alvin Dark. In 1969 the Angels' big-spender owner Gene Autry dropped Bill Rigney to save money from Rigney's salary. And that same year Larry Shepard was dismissed as Pirate pilot for winning only 88 games; in 1970 his successor, Danny Murtaugh, went on to become Manager of the Year on the strength of 89 wins!

Such Alice-in-Wonderland owners' antics were accompanied by their growing contempt for managers and their tendency to impose their whims as tacticians and strategists. Most notorious was Finley, whose dreaded phone calls reduced managers to page boys. And late in the 1970s George Steinbrenner's clashes with Billy Martin drew national attention, especially when Steinbrenner laid down a list of commandments aimed at reining in Martin's independence. But Martin hung tough. In times past, his defiance of owners cost him jobs at Minnesota, Detroit, and Texas, and with the Yankees he was twice fired by Steinbrenner. Bloodied but unbowed, Martin surfaced in 1980 at Finley's Oakland *gulag*. Yet the brash Martin, after getting that sorry team off to a flying start with his old-fashioned "Billy Ball," warned Finley to take no credit, saying, "I've dealt with owners like that before. I didn't take it then, and I'm not gonna take it now. If it does happen, it's bye-bye Billy."

Luckily for Martin, Finley sold out to a jeans manufacturer, ending that owner's stormy baseball career during which no manager satisfied. Outfielder Rick Monday, during his five years with the Athletics, saw six skippers come and go, including hard-nosed "I" type Williams, "We" type Al Dark, and "They" type Bob Kennedy.

As if meddling owners were not enough of a plague, managerial authority was challenged by the new breed of players. While admitting that expansion players were able, older managers generally viewed them as less dedicated and tougher to discipline than players of the '50s. Now shielded by a strong Association, a generation of better-educated, better-paid players resisted dogmatic authority. They challenged training programs, demanding the right to use regimens of their own design. Nor did they passively accept strategical and tactical decisions: sidelined players protested lineup decisions hotly, and in 1980 pitcher Luis Tiant, when taken out of a game by Dick Howser, angrily threw the ball to the ground and later tossed his glove into the stands. Humiliated by this public tantrum, Howser could only level a $500 fine; to do more would have brought Player Association counteraction.

In the 1970s all managers faced this problem of lese majesty and eroding credibility. From their retirement haunts, former hard-line managers like Jimmy Dykes and Billy Herman wondered how modern managers survived. Dykes blasted opinionated players, interfering wives, and pampered specialists. And after being fired by the 1966 Red Sox, Herman accused modern players of placing personal glory ahead of the team. In 1977 Sparky Anderson groused that only rookies responded to discipline, and after three seasons they too were prima donnas.

Billy Martin blamed the salary revolution for eroding his authority: in 1972 he urged owners to adopt pro football's policy of paying coaches higher salaries than players and giving them long-term contract security. Managers also complained of affluent players being distracted by their outside business investments. But reforming the new pluto-crats was touchy—push a star too hard and a manager was likely to be the loser. It was a lesson Martin learned from Reggie Jackson. Comparative beggars amid affluence, to survive some managers evoked ethereal ideals like team loyalty and "family" spirit. A favorite ploy of "We" types, making it work took great patience and huge dollops of praise. When it worked, according to Jim Bouton, the style produced nondescript managers like Houk, Ed Kasko, Ken Aspromonte, Tom Lasorda, Bill Virdon, and Whitey Herzog. But even if a sunny optimist like Lasorda managed to make a theology of Dodger blue and Great Dodgers in the Sky, glory was fleeting at best: by 1980 he presided over a divided team and admitted that most players nursed griev-ances against him.

Besides having to fight off interfering owners and hostile players, managers had to contend with their ancient enemies the sportswriters, who often sided with the players in their reporting of confrontations. In Billy Martin's Yankee ordeal, writers seized on every rumble involving that embattled manager: when Martin blew off steam, writers captured his words and printed them, thus hastening his ouster. (When Bob Lemon succeeded Martin, a providential New York newspaper strike blacked out baseball news for the second half of the campaign. Thus in blissful silence, Lemon regrouped the team and drove it to a miracle victory.) But even phlegmatics like Danny Ozark of the Phils suffered at the hands of the scribes: a year-long campaign mounted by *Inquirer* writers ended with Ozark's dismissal in 1979. And in 1972 Durocher was cut loose as persistent Chicago writers eventually wore down Phil Wrigley's stubborn refusal to let any "reporter S.O.B. . . . run my ballclub."

In what must be the most unkindest cut of all, even umpires now lorded it over managers. Long the whipping boys, umpires turned tartars behind their Association, which won them job security and relief from harassing managers. In times past a manager could confront an ump, blame him for a defeat or a boner, and blast him in postseason evaluations, but by the mid-'70s the tables were turned. Now arbiters like Tom Gorman wrote taunting books, citing ump-baiters like Hutchinson, Durocher, Stanky, Mauch, Anderson, and Weaver. And Gorman's best line might have been his description of his visit to Durocher's bedside: he came, he told the ailing Durocher, "to see if you were dying."

By the 1980s it was abundantly clear that with the possible exception of super managers like Weaver, any semblance of job security was a thing of the past: even winning was no assurance of continued employment. Although the divisional system adopted in 1969 provided four winners in place of two, in the minds of owners a division victory was not enough, a lesson learned by Whitey Herzog and Danny Ozark. Each won three consecutive division titles in the '70s, but for failure to do more both were canned in 1979, and before the axe fell, each was booed by fans, scorned by players and pilloried by scribes.

It was the same with Don Zimmer, who managed Boston to more than 90 victories in 1978 and 1979, yet was sacked in 1980. His Red Sox had taken the 1978 Eastern race to a playoff game with a valiant final-week win streak; the following season he was so cruelly booed at Fenway that his wife quit going to games.

To be fired or laid off from one's job is a major trauma.

Like bereavement or divorce, it is linked with suicide. Yet managers, whose firings are so flagrantly public, seem to suffer surprisingly little stigma. Indeed, firings are usually gentlemanly affairs, with damnation speedily followed by redemption. And often the fallen wretch is replaced with a previous victim, which makes for a lively market in used managers (Bucky Harris setting the record by being rehired seven times.) Still, the public airing of one's failures is devastating upon one's family; according to Frank Lucchesi, after a firing his school-aged son came home crying, saying, "Dad . . . do we have to go through that again?" To escape the stigma of being fired some "resigned," but Harris sneered at that dodge, saying that departing managers are always fired.

Once dismissed, decorum prescribed a quiet exit. Yogi Berra showed how when dumped by the Mets in 1975: questioned by reporters, he badmouthed no one and even promised to pray for the Mets, who needed supernatural intervention. Only a cut below this in style were performances by Frank Robinson and Preston Gomez. When fired by Cleveland, Robinson—the first black manager—told reporters that some players took advantage of him, but added that he learned much and would go home and live on his severance. When Gomez was fired by the Padres, he took it philosophically, saying that the club needed a fresh face to hype attendance.

But some did not go gentle into the night. At Baltimore, tough Hank Bauer raged at the new breed of players, saying he'd manage no more. To the GM who pink-slipped him, Bauer warned that the severance payments better not be late. Mayo Smith, when told, quickly downed a drink and summed up his experience with the judgment that "Detroit fans don't know the difference between a ballplayer and a Japanese aviator."

Among the cashiered were weepers, drinkers, and solitary brooders. But few outdid Bill Norman. Fired by the Tigers in 1959 after winning two of 17 games, he stripped to his shorts in the clubhouse, downed two cases of beer, and was finally led out "in a maudlin state," according to *Sports Illustrated*.

Next to the ordeal by public firing, loss of effective control over players ranked high on the list of woes. In 1971 rebellious Astros destroyed Harry Walker's tough disciplinary code. A good teacher of hitting and fundamentals, Walker fined players for tactical mistakes and sought to curb boozing and wenching. But the Astros mocked Walker's "horseshit" lectures, protested his fines, and openly parodied his moral stance by loudly singing a satirical ditty with this refrain:

> Now Harry Walker is the one that manages this crew;
> He doesn't like it when we drink and fight and smoke and screw:
> But when we win our game each day,
> Then what the fuck can Harry say?
> It makes a fellow proud to be an Astro.

One year afterward, Walker walked the plank, but his was no isolated fate. At Philadelphia and other stopovers Richie Allen's refusal to meet deadlines undercut managers. Alex Johnson bounced around not only because he refused to hustle, but also because he persisted in calling teammates and managers alike "shitheads." And Minnesota pitcher Jim Kaat protested manager Sam Mele's firing of pitching coach John Sain by festooning his locker with heroic poses of Sain.

Not only were managers routinely undercut, but at times they were uppercut. In 1977 the luckless Lucchesi was punched and kicked into unconsciousness by Lenny Randle, who was embittered at being benched. Lucchesi's injuries required plastic surgery and dental work, but humiliation hurt him more. Randle was fined $10,000 and dispatched to another team, but Lucchesi was fired soon after. Although retained by the club, Lucchesi still sued for $200,000 to preserve "the integrity of baseball."

Protesting fans could undercut managers, too, and their protests were often orchestrated by the press. Indeed, columnist Milt Richman once told Frank Robinson that his chief managerial task was to please writers. Some managers, like Stengel and Murtaugh, were great with reporters. And those who were not, like Durocher, Ozark, and Zimmer, had their stays shortened by massive press criticisms.

Managers were likely to feel pressure from above, in the form of meddlesome owners and general managers, and also from below, in the form of their coaches. Usually these were cronies of the manager, but they also represented a labor pool of potential replacements. Realizing this, some managers rid themselves of underlings who became too popular. Thus Sain was cut loose on at least three occasions for his close rapport with pitchers. And for his personal zeal as Dodger batting coach, Jim Lefebvre was first barred from filming Dodger batters and later fired by Manager Lasorda. In the stormy aftermath to that firing, Lefebvre decked Lasorda. If such outcomes were rare, the plenitude of coaches threatened all managers by 1980. Some teams counted as many as eight coaches, plus auxiliaries that included trainers, physicians, and occasional psychologists and priests. If managers might otherwise be lulled into thinking they were prime movers, the presence of so many experts sent a message that perhaps a single manager was no longer up to the job.

The role of the modern manager is that of supervisor, disciplinarian, and strategist. As supervisors, managers now delegate authority to coaches who conduct practices and instruct players; each coach contributes his bit of expertise and the manager is charged with coordinating these activities. As a disciplinarian, the manager retains enough authority to compel players to follow rules and do their duty. Indeed, some managerial discipline codes yet resemble those of closed institutions like police forces and mental asylums. At Philadelphia in 1980, Dallas Green's rules were formally printed and issued to each man. The code established a curfew, set dress standards, limited drinking and card playing, imposed rigorous rules of conduct at practices, and banned players' children from the dugout during practice sessions. As strategist, which is still the essence of the managerial mystique, pilots still rely on time-honored devices such as flashing signals to third-base coaches, devising defensive alignments to thwart hitters, and most important, setting a pitching rotation and knowing when to change pitchers.

In the final analysis, however, it may be that the manager's main function is to serve as scapegoat and thus preserve the jobs of others. Like the legendary *lamed vov*, whose task was to shoulder the collective grief of his downtrodden Jewish brethren, the manager is answerable for a multitude of sins, few of his direct commission. Lest one doubt this continuing function, consider that during last year's (1981) grotesque split season, which canceled more than a third of the games, six managers were jettisoned, and over the winter another six.

And with an owner like Steinbrenner intervening incessantly, going so far as to order special fundamental drills, one can only expect continuing pressure on managers. Indeed, the best relief for these besieged foremen seems to have been hit upon by Whitey Herzog. By functioning both as manager and GM, he seems to be pointing the way toward a protective adaptation for an otherwise highly endangered species. And if he can find a way to *buy* his club—well, how do you think Connie Mack lasted 50 years?

The devil didn't make them do it.

The Year the Yankees Lost the Pennant

Mark Gallagher

Everyone, both those who cheered the Bronx Bombers and those who muttered, "Damn Yankees," expected the pinstriped powerhouse to win the pennant again. It was a great time to be a Yankee fan. It was 1959.

New York had won the American League pennant every year of the decade but 1954, and that was a lightning bolt season in which New York won 103 games—the most ever by Stengel's men—only to finish eight games behind Cleveland. And the Yanks would capture the first five pennants of the 1960s.

But what about 1959? That season the imperial Yankees crawled home in disheveled disgrace with a record of 79-75, a distant fifteen games out of first place. What went wrong? Everything. But 1959 wasn't just the year the Yankees lost the pennant; the first-place Chicago White Sox, with 94 wins, won two more games than the champion Yankees of

MARK GALLAGHER has chronicled Yankee triumphs and tragedies in several books, including *The Yankee Encyclopedia*.

1958. Given their wealth of woes, the wonder is that the Yankees finished as high as third place. It was, despite a brief run at the pennant in June and a first-division finish, a disastrous season—at least by the unforgiving standards of the Yankees and their fans.

Still fresh was the image of Casey Stengel stepping off an airplane in New York following the 1958 World Series, his rugged countenance sporting the burnt-cork dollar signs Whitey Ford applied during a victory-celebrating flight. Casey's charges had courageously overcome a three-games-to-one deficit, won three straight games, and wrested the World Championship back from the Milwaukee Braves, the team of Aaron and Mathews, Spahn and Burdette. Now Stengel was basking in the glory of a dramatic World Series victory. He was at the pinnacle of his immense fame.

The Yankees of 1958 quickly had blown open the American League race, sprinting to a 25-6 record and all but locking up the flag by Memorial Day. New York's lead reached 17 games in early August, and then, perhaps because the games no longer mattered, or more likely because a string of injuries began to take its toll, the Yankees sleepwalked home with a 25-28 record. But the last two months of the season, the harbinger of the season to come, were paid scant heed as the Yanks still won the flag by a healthy ten games and went on to dethrone the Braves—and probably saved Stengel's job.

Yankee co-owners Dan Topping and Del Webb reportedly were not happy about having Stengel back as their manager in 1959, despite his record of nine pennants in ten years. The Ol' Perfesser would be sixty-nine in July of '59, and was showing signs of losing his grip. But the owners' hands were tied by the 1958 Series comeback; they couldn't fire Casey in his greatest hour. When Stengel signed a two-year contract in February 1959, Topping fully intended that this would be Casey's final pact with the Yankees. There was an uneasiness in the once strong relationship between Topping, Stengel, and General Manager George Weiss, whom Topping was also preparing to release. The normal lines of communication were strained as the Yankees broke spring training camp in 1959. Although troubled by Topping's aloofness, a robustly confident Stengel boasted, "I'll tell you what I think of our prospects. I think we've got the world by the ears, and we're not letting go."

But Stengel was bedazzled by the World Series, and was himself becoming aloof—if not downright irascible—to his players. Several key Yankees of past years crumbled in '59. Don Larsen and Tom Sturdivant had arm miseries. Larsen didn't win a game after mid-June, and it was a winless Sturdivant who was traded to Kansas City late in the spring. Gil McDougald, a World Series hero the previous October, was hit on the hands by a pitched ball and missed two weeks. He also was hindered by a bad back. McDougald hit .251 in 127 games in 1959, one point higher than his batting average of 1958—but his home runs dropped from 14 to 4, and his RBIs from 65 to 34. He was shuffled between second base, shortstop, and third, as a hole-plugging Stengel took advantage of Gil's versatility. But Casey may have weakened one of his most important bats in the process. McDougald had been an All-Star at all three positions—but not in the same season.

Like McDougald, first baseman Bill "Moose" Skowron, one of the league's premier sluggers, began the year with a serious back ailment. Wearing a back brace and gritting his teeth, Skowron was truly murdering the ball when he was able to play—but he would play in fewer than half the team's games.

Stengel's patience had worn thin with third baseman Andy Carey. Stengel wanted Carey to chop down on the ball and hit for a higher batting average—to "butcher boy." Andy, who hit .302 in 1954, ignored Stengel's advice and swung for the fences. But he just wasn't a power hitter, and now he wasn't hitting for average, either. Defensively, he was good on bunts, but his range was limited. Still, his biggest handicap in 1959 was bad luck. He had an early-season hand infection and after playing in only 41 games, developed an illness that sidelined him for the season.

The 1959 Yankees were bothered most of all by the physical problems of Mickey Mantle. For some time leg problems had taxed the Mick's play, but now a shoulder injury, the result of a collision with Red Schoendienst in the 1957 World Series, was even more hampering. Pain shot through his damaged right shoulder whenever the switch-hitting Mantle swung lefthanded and missed. Mantle had a much smoother and more level swing as a righthanded hitter in 1958 and 1959.

Early in the 1959 campaign, Mantle reinjured his shoulder in making a throw from center field. His woes gathered in early May when he was hit by a pitch in batting practice and suffered a chipped bone in his right index finger. Then Mickey became one of several Yankees to come down with the Asian flu. And it wasn't even summer yet.

On May 20 the Yankees, owning a 12-19 record, tumbled into the American League cellar for the first time in nineteen years. Mantle, insisting on playing in pain, hit a two-run homer in a losing cause and was booed unmercifully by unfeeling Yankee Stadium fans as he circled the bases. But Mickey on this day was beginning a 20-for-42 streak (with 12 walks) and by May 31 the Yankees were out of last place. The Bronx Bombers were, in fact, commencing a great run at the league leaders, a surge that corresponded with Mantle's hot bat.

George Weiss, meantime, made a deal that helped the Yankees both in the short term and over the long haul. On May 26 Weiss sent the sore-armed Sturdivant, pitcher Johnny Kucks, and infielder Jerry Lumpe to Kansas City for Ralph Terry and Hector Lopez. Terry, a righthander who was originally in the Yankee farm chain and who was considered an excellent pitching prospect, was still maturing as a pitcher in 1959 and would go 3-7 with New York. However, he did flash a few spectacular outings that hinted at his 16-3 season in 1961 and his 23-win year in 1962. Lopez, on the other hand, paid immediate dividends. Stengel put him at third base, and although Hector wasn't much with the glove, he was a first-class hitter. In his first 32 Yankee games, the native of Panama had 26 RBIs, and for his full season with the A's and Yanks, Lopez had 93 RBIs; no other Yankee of 1959 could match that figure. Led by

Lopez, Mantle, and Skowron, Yankee bats came alive in June.

Relief pitcher Ryne Duren led a resurgence in New York's pitching. From late April through mid-July, Duren pitched 36 consecutive scoreless innings over 18 appearances. The intimidating, flamethrowing Duren, the Goose Gossage of his era, posted a full-season ERA of 1.88, but at the point the Yankees were eliminated from pennant contention, his ERA was well under 1.00.

Yet Duren won only 3 games and saved only 14. The problem was that his great efforts were often wasted; the Yankees weren't scoring runs in the late innings, and didn't have many leads in need of protection. For years the Yankees excelled at keeping a game close and pulling it out in the late going, but the '59 Yanks were no five o'clock wonders, as their record stood around .500 for both extra-inning and one-run games.

Emancipated from the basement, the Yankees stormed through their June schedule, winning 17 of 23 games at one point and racing to within 1½ games of first-place Cleveland. But their momentum was halted in late June when the White Sox licked them in three of four games at Comiskey Park. Chicago was 13-9 against New York in 1959, the first year since 1925 that the Yankees lost their season series with the Chisox.

A few days later, Mantle hurt his right ankle; he would go on to hit only two home runs in July. He should have rested, but with the Yankees struggling to remain in the race, he limped through the summer. As Mantle slumped, to an unprecedented chorus of boos, the Yanks fell back, going 12-16 in July. Mantle was an unselfish player who realized his importance to the club and, pressing to turn the team's fortunes around, lost his rhythm. His impatience at the plate widened the strike zone and he swung at bad pitches rather than accept a walk. Mantle wound up striking out 127 times, the most in his career, while drawing only 94 walks, his only dip below 100 between 1954 and 1962. He ended the season with 31 homers, 75 RBIs, a .285 batting average, and a .514 slugging percentage, numbers that were considered, overall, his worst since 1951, his rookie year. Yet there were some positive numbers, too. That he had a career-high 21 stolen bases (in only 24 attempts) may say more about the team's punch than about his baserunning.

Through midsummer, Weiss and Stengel believed the Yankees would rally again. For good or bad, neither would panic; Weiss would make no wholesale roster changes and Stengel would not play his kids. If Casey was going to bite the dust, it would be with his veterans. But Boston dealt a damaging blow in mid-July. As the Fenway faithful roared their approval, New York dropped five consecutive games and fell seven and a half games off the pace.

More injuries followed. Gil McDougald and Tony Kubek collided in chasing a pop-up and both suffered lingering aches. Yankee fans were finding themselves in the unaccustomed position of using the loser's lament—bad luck—for the tribulations of 1959. Then, on July 25, Moose Skowron reached for an errant throw, stepping into the first-base line, and was struck by Detroit's Coot Veal. The result: Skowron's arm was broken in two places and his season was over. So, most definitely, was the Yanks' season. "If you had him," said Stengel, "you could even think about winning it." But not without him.

Skowron finished 1959 at .298 and with 15 homers in 74 games. At the time of his broken arm, he was second in the league in RBIs with 59. Marv Throneberry, the famous beer commercial star, was Skowron's part-time replacement; Marvelous Marv's batting average was a lite .240.

The Yankees played out the string in August and September, and then everyone went home. Everyone, that is, except Stengel, who covered the World Series for *Life* magazine.

Bob Turley's poor year was the single most puzzling aspect of 1959. "Bullet Bob" had won the Cy Young Award with a 21-7 record in 1958 and had rescued the Yankees in the World Series with two wins and a save in the final three games. But in 1959 he had no pop in his once blazing fastball, and he dropped to 8-11 with a fat ERA of 4.32.

Turley in his prime was one of the game's most awesome power pitchers, relying almost exclusively on heat. Then he learned to throw a slow curveball and fell in love with the pitch. When hitters began to sit on the curve, Bob went back to his fastball, only to discover that the old zip wasn't there. Writing of Turley and 1959, Stengel in his autobiography (*Casey at the Bat*, 1962) observed that there "was nothing wrong with his arm or his willingness to work. He just couldn't win." Casey complained that Turley wasn't throwing hard and "it looked like he was experimenting on all the hitters with slow stuff and junk."

Turley's 1959 decline was a critical jolt to a starting crew that was without a stopper, although Duke Maas (14-8) and Art Ditmar (13-9) were adequate and Bobby Shantz and Jim Coates pitched well out of the pen in support of Duren. Whitey Ford followed his 14-7 record in 1958 with a fine 16-10 mark, but his ERA was up by more than one run per game and he allowed more hits and walks while pitching in fewer innings than he did the year before. (Ford was far from finished, of course. In 1961 under rookie manager Ralph Houk, Ford began working every fourth day in a regular rotation for a change, posted a 25-4 record, and won the Cy Young Award.)

The Yankee lineups of the 1950s were characterized by the tremendous back-to-back punch of Mickey Mantle and Yogi Berra. As the Yankees rolled to four successive pennants from 1955 through 1958 (usually with Mantle batting third and Berra fourth), the twosome averaged a combined 67 home runs per season. They hit only 50 round-trippers in 1959. The aging Berra no longer was putting the big power numbers on the board: He had 19 homers and 69 RBIs. Yogi may have been the league's most valuable player for the 1950s. Not only was he a first-rate defensive catcher, but he hit between 22 and 30 homers and had between 82 and 125 RBIs in every season of the decade until 1959. However, he turned thirty-four in 1959 and some of his power was sapped after years of playing the game's most demanding position.

With Berra aging and Skowron hurting, Elston Howard

was the man most likely to protect Mantle in the batting order, but at age thirty he still didn't have a regular position in the field. Playing first base, catcher, and outfield in 1959, Ellie had 18 homers and 73 RBIs but might have done better still with the predictability of having a permanent, everyday job. Casey liked all-purpose players like McDougald and Howard because they increased his managerial options. "You can substitute but you can rarely replace," Stengel once said. "With Howard, I have a replacement, not a substitute." Stengel handed him the bulk of the catching in 1960, but Howard had his greatest seasons under Houk in the early 1960s.

The Yankees had a problem in right field, where for years Hank Bauer had roamed. Bauer had been a solid, all-round player, who symbolized Stengel's Yankee teams. He did nothing spectacularly but everything well, and he knew how to win. The tough ex-Marine didn't make mistakes and seemed to save his best performances for crucial moments. But his great effort in the 1958 World Series turned out to be his last hurrah. He turned thirty-seven in 1959, a season in which he batted only .238 with 9 homers. The next year would find him in the Yankee's last stop before sundown, otherwise known as Kansas City.

The 1959 Yankees had records of around .500 against righthanded pitching and at home, indicating the club wasn't taking advantage of the short right-field porch at Yankee Stadium. The Bombers should never be vulnerable to righties, and yet in 1959 Frank Lary and Cal McLish (as well as southpaw Don Mossi) each defeated New York five times. Clearly the Yanks needed a new rightfielder, preferably one who batted lefthanded. (Kansas City was to oblige with Roger Maris.)

The Yankees who didn't win the pennant had problems off the field as well as on. When spring training opened in 1959, Mantle and Ford were among the unsigned. Mickey signed for $72,000, a small raise, and other Yankees fell into line. Stengel maintained that the tough negotiating stance of the front office put his players in a bad frame of mind. Casey may have forgotten that his old buddy Weiss was always a tough man to shake a nickel out of, in an age when players had little recourse but to sign on the dotted line. How tough was Weiss? Well, following Mantle's 1959 season, he wanted to cut Mickey's salary by $17,000—yes, they actually cut salaries in those days—and Mantle finally signed for $65,000, a painful cut of $7,000.

Stengel was also bitter over losing his instructional school in 1959 (by act of Dan Topping). Stengel once had been a good teacher and enjoyed working with the organization's young prospects. But by 1959, having grown impatient with the inevitable mistakes of youth, Casey was browbeating and intimidating many of the youngsters. The more the Ol' Perfesser fussed and criticized, the tighter and more erratic the kids played. The cases of Norm Siebern and Jerry Lumpe make the point. Stengel rode both and both struggled; finally they were traded to Kansas City in separate 1959 deals. Lumpe was shifted from third base to second and Siebern was moved from the outfield to first base. Each was better suited to his new position. In 1962 Lumpe hit .301 with 193 hits and Siebern hit .308 with 25 homers and 117 RBIs. They weren't such bad players after all.

Tony Kubek and Bobby Richardson took Stengel's hazing, survived, and developed into stars with New York. Stengel liked Kubek's versatility—Tony played all four infield positions as well as the outfield under Stengel—but Tony, who developed into an excellent shortstop, may have lost a chance to be even better because he wasn't kept at the position from the start. Stengel wasn't a Richardson fan. He kept Bobby in a backup role until 1959, when the sweet fielder finally became the regular second sacker. Richardson hit .301, best of the 1959 Yankees. He and Kubek, who hit a solid .279, formed a dynamic double-play combo, too.

Stengel may have hindered Mantle, whom he didn't always treat warmly. Mantle's batting average peaked at .365 in 1957, and then fell to .304 in 1958 and .285 in 1959, a source of great frustration to Stengel, who always believed Mickey should have been even better than he was. Mantle was helped by two circumstances in the early 1960s. The first was the 1960 arrival of Maris, who became the

new whipping boy of the fans and press, as Mantle finally
became the people's choice. The second was Houk taking
the managerial reins in 1961. Houk boosted Mantle's confidence and the Mick responded with perhaps his greatest
season.

Yankee shake-ups seemed forthcoming after the 1959
disaster. But in the end, Weiss, Stengel, and most of the
players returned in 1960. Pitching coach Jim Turner was
made the scapegoat and after the season was replaced by
Eddie Lopat, the former great Yankee southpaw. As for
Casey, he had one thing going for him; he had a year left on
his contract, and Topping, unlike the management in New
York today, wasn't in the habit of eating big contracts
(Stengel's was for $90,000). Nonetheless, Ralph Houk was
clearly the heir apparent, and Stengel knew it. He didn't like
one bit having Houk looking over his shoulder, but the
players found Houk an antidote to their irascible manager.
Although still the darling of the fans and the media, Casey
had lost the respect of several players and didn't ingratiate
himself with his troops when he allowed management to use
him in a midwinter press conference. This get-together with
the media laid blame for the 1959 failure on the night owls.
Casey, who had always been a nocturnal animal, cracked:
"I got these players who got the bad watches, that they
can't tell midnight from noon."

Weiss typically blamed 1959 on some of his players'
outside business interests. But if George was correct, then
he was the one at fault; with the salaries he was paying, the
players were forced to supplement their incomes. Another
theory held that the Yankees' slowness in signing black and
Latin players had finally caught up with them. It would
catch up with them, but not until 1965.

Wrote Stengel in *Casey at the Bat*: "This bad 1959
season was an emergency to our owners. They thought the
manager was slipping. They thought the coaches were
slipping. They thought the players were slipping. . . . But
maybe those people in the front office didn't have such a
good year themselves." Casey had it right—everyone slipped
in the year the Yankees lost the pennant. The sagging Bronx

Bombers were not defeated by a Joe Hardy—instead they went out and got one, a Roger Maris who would hit 100 home runs in the next two years and restore to the Yankees their accustomed splendor.

Baseball draws the color line, 1887.

Out at Home

Jerry Malloy

Baseball is the very symbol, the outward and visible expression of the drive and push and rush and struggle of the raging, tearing, booming nineteenth century.

MARK TWAIN

...social inequality...means that in all the relations that exist between man and man he is to be measured and taken not according to his natural fitness and qualification, but that blind and relentless rule which accords certain pursuits and certain privileges to origin or birth.

MOSES F. WALKER

It was a dramatic and prophetic performance by Jackie Robinson. The twenty-seven-year-old black second baseman opened the 1946 International League season by leading the Montreal Royals to a 14-1 victory over Jersey City. In five

JERRY MALLOY is an expert on black baseball before Jackie Robinson. This was his first published article.

209

trips to the plate, he had four hits (including a home run) and four RBIs; he scored four runs, stole two bases, and rattled a pitcher into balking him home with a taunting *danse macabre* off third. Branch Rickey's protégé had punched a hole through Organized Baseball's color barrier with the flair and talent that would eventually take him into the Hall of Fame. The color line that Jackie Robinson shattered, though unwritten, was very real indeed. Baseball's exclusion of the black man was so unremittingly thorough for such a long time that most of the press and public then, as now, thought that Robinson was making the first appearance of a man of his race in the history of Organized Baseball.

Actually, he represented a return of the Negro ballplayer, not merely to Organized Baseball, but to the International League as well. At least eight elderly citizens would have been aware of this. Frederick Ely, Jud Smith, James Fields, Tom Lynch, Frank Olin, "Chief" Zimmer, Pat Gillman, and George Bausewine may have noted with interest Robinson's initiation, for all of these men had been active players on teams that opened another International League season, that of 1887. And in that year they played with or against eight black players on six different teams.

The 1887 season was not the first in which Negroes played in the International League, nor would it be the last. But until Jackie Robinson stepped up to the plate on April 18, 1946, it was the most significant. For 1887 was a watershed year for both the International League and Organized Baseball, as it marked the origin of the color line. As the season opened, the black player had plenty of reasons to hope that he would be able to ply his trade in an atmosphere of relative tolerance; by the middle of the season, however, he would watch helplessly as the IL drew up a written color ban designed to deprive him of his livelihood; and by the time the league held its offseason meetings, it became obvious that Jim Crow was closing in on a total victory.

Yet before baseball became the victim of its own prejudice, there was a period of uncertainty and fluidity, however brief, during which it seemed by no means inevitable that men would be denied access to Organized Baseball due solely to skin pigmentation. It was not an interlude of total racial harmony, but a degree of toleration obtained that would become unimaginable in just a few short years. This is the story of a handful of black baseball players who, in the span of a single season, playing in a prestigious league, witnessed the abrupt conversion of hope and optimism into defeat and despair. These men, in the most direct and personal manner, would realize that the black American baseball player soon would be ruled "out at home."

I

The International League is the oldest minor league in Organized Baseball. Founded in 1884 as the "Eastern" League, it would be realigned and renamed frequently during its early period. The IL was not immune to the shifting sands of financial support that plagued both minor and major leagues (not to mention individual franchises) during the nineteenth century. In 1887 the league took the risk of adding Newark and Jersey City to a circuit that was otherwise clustered in upstate New York and southern Ontario. This arrangement proved to be financially unworkable. Transportation costs alone would doom the experiment after one season. The New Jersey franchises were simply too far away from Binghamton, Buffalo, Oswego, Rochester, Syracuse, and Utica in New York, and Hamilton and Toronto in Ontario.

But, of course, no one knew this when the 1887 season opened. Fans in Newark were particularly excited, because their "Little Giants" were a new team and an instant contender. A large measure of their eager anticipation was due to the unprecedented "colored battery" signed by the team. The pitcher was George Stovey and the catcher was Moses Fleetwood Walker.

"Fleet" Walker was born in Mt. Pleasant, Ohio, on the route of the Underground Railroad, on October 7, 1857. The son of a physician, he was raised in nearby Steubenville.

At the age of twenty he entered the college preparatory program of Oberlin College, the first school in the United States to adopt an official admissions policy of nondiscrimination by sex, race, or creed. He was enrolled as a freshman in 1878, and attended Oberlin for the next three years. He was a good but not outstanding student in a rigorous liberal arts program. Walker also attended the University of Michigan for two years, although probably more for his athletic than his scholastic attainments. He did not obtain a degree from either institution, but his educational background was extremely sophisticated for a nineteenth-century professional baseball player of whatever ethnic origin.

While at Oberlin, Walker attracted the attention of William Voltz, former sportswriter for the Cleveland *Plain Dealer,* who had been enlisted to form a professional baseball team to be based in Toledo. Walker was the second player signed by the team, which entered the Northwestern League in 1883. Toledo captured the league championship in its first year.

The following year Toledo was invited to join the American Association, a major league rival of the more established National League. Walker was one of the few players to be retained as Toledo made the jump to the big league. Thus did Moses Fleetwood Walker become the first black to play major league baseball, sixty-four years before Jackie Robinson. Walker played in 42 games that season, batting .263 in 152 at-bats. His brother, Welday Wilberforce Walker, who was two years younger than Fleet, also played outfield in five games, filling in for injured players. Welday was 4-for-18 at the plate.

While at Toledo, Fleet Walker was the batterymate of Hank O'Day, who later became a famous umpire, and Tony Mullane, who could pitch with either hand and became the winningest pitcher, with 285 victories, outside the Hall of Fame. G. L. Mercereau, the team's batboy, many years later recalled the sight of Walker catching barehanded, as was common in those days, with his fingers split open and bleeding. Catchers would welcome swelling in their hands to provide a cushion against the pain.

The color of Walker's skin occasionally provoked another, more lasting, kind of pain. The Toledo *Blade,* on May 5, 1884, reported that Walker was "hissed . . . and insulted . . . because he was colored," causing him to commit five errors in a game in Louisville. Late in the season the team traveled to Richmond, Virginia, where manager Charley Morton received a letter threatening bloodshed, according to Lee Allen, by "75 determined men [who] have sworn to mob Walker if he comes on the ground in a suit." The letter, which Morton released to the press, was signed by four men who were "determined" not to sign their real names. Confrontation was avoided, for Walker had been released by the team due to his injuries before the trip to Richmond.

Such incidents, however, stand out because they were so exceptional. Robert Peterson, in *Only the Ball Was White,* points out that Walker was favorably received in cities such as Baltimore and Washington. As was the case throughout the catcher's career, the press was supportive of him and consistently reported his popularity among fans. Upon his release, the *Blade* described him as "a conscientious player [who] was very popular with Toledo audiences," and *Sporting Life's* Toledo correspondent stated that "by his fine, gentlemanly deportment, he made hosts of friends who will regret to learn that he is no longer a member of the club."

Walker started the 1885 season with Cleveland in the Western League, but the league folded in June. He played the remainder of 1885 and all of 1886 for the Waterbury, Connecticut, team in the Eastern League. While at Waterbury, he was referred to as "the people's choice," and was briefly managed by Charley Hackett, who later moved on to Newark. When Newark was accepted into the International League in 1887, Hackett signed Walker to play for him.

So in 1887 Walker was beginning his fifth season in integrated professional baseball. Tall, lean, and handsome, the thirty-year-old catcher was an established veteran noted for his steady, dependable play and admired, literally, as a gentleman and a scholar. Later in the season, when the Hamilton *Spectator* printed a disparaging item about "the coon catcher of the Newarks," *The Sporting News* ran a typical response in defense of Walker: "It is a pretty small paper that will publish a paragraph of that kind about a member of a visiting club, and the man who wrote it is without doubt Walker's inferior in education, refinement, and manliness."

One of the reasons that Charley Hackett was so pleased to have signed Walker was that his catcher would assist in the development of one of his new pitchers, a Negro named George Washington Stovey. A 165-pound southpaw, Stovey had pitched for Jersey City in the Eastern League in 1886. Sol White, in his *History of Colored Base Ball,* stated that Stovey "struck out twenty-two of the Bridgeport [Connecticut] Eastern League team in 1886 and lost his game." *The Sporting News* that year called Stovey "a good one, and if the team would support him they would make a far better showing. His manner of covering first from the box is wonderful."

A dispute arose between the Jersey City and Newark clubs prior to the 1887 season concerning the rights to sign Stovey. One of the directors of the Jersey City team tried to use his leverage as the owner of Newark's Wright Street grounds to force Newark into surrendering Stovey. But, as the *Sporting Life* Newark correspondent wrote, ". . . on sober second thought I presume he came to the conclusion that it was far better that the [Jersey City] club should lose Stovey than that he should lose the rent of the grounds."

A new rule for 1887, which would exist only that one season, provided that walks were to be counted as hits. One of the criticisms of the rule was that, in an era in which one of the pitching statistics kept was the opposition's batting average, a pitcher might be tempted to hit a batter rather than be charged with a "hit" by walking him. George Stovey, with his blazing fastball, his volatile temper, and his inability to keep either under strict control, was the type of pitcher these skeptics had in mind. He brought to the mound a wicked glare that intimidated hitters.

During the preseason contract dispute, Jersey City's manager, Pat Powers, acknowledged Stovey's talents, yet added:

Personally, I do not care for Stovey. I consider him one of the greatest pitchers in the country, but in many respects I think I have more desirable men. He is head-strong and obstinate, and, consequently, hard to manage. Were I alone concerned I would probably let Newark have him, but the directors of the Jersey City Club are not so peaceably disposed.

Newark planned to mute Stovey's "head-strong obstinance" with the easygoing stability of Fleet Walker. That the strategy did not always work is indicated by an account in the Newark *Daily Journal* of a July game against Hamilton:

That Newark won the game [14-10] is a wonder, for Stovey was very wild at times, [and] Walker had several passed balls. . . . Whether it was that he did not think he was being properly supported, or did not like the umpire's decisions on balls and strikes, the deponent saith not, but Stovey several times displayed his temper in the box and fired the ball at the plate regardless of what was to become of everything that stood before him. Walker got tired of the business after awhile, and showed it plainly by his manner. Stovey should remember that the spectators do not like to see such exhibitions of temper, and it is hoped that he will not offend again.

Either despite or because of his surly disposition, George Stovey had a great season in 1887. His 35 wins is a single-season record that still stands in the International League. George Stovey was well on his way to establishing his reputation as the greatest Negro pitcher of the nineteenth century.

The promotional value of having the only all-Negro battery in Organized Baseball was not lost upon the press. Newspapers employed various euphemisms of the day for "Negro" to refer to Newark's "colored," "Cuban,"

"Spanish," "mulatto," "African," and even "Arabian" battery. *Sporting Life* wrote:

> There is not a club in the country who tries so hard to cater to all nationalities as does the Newark Club. There is the great African battery, Stovey and Walker; the Irish battery, Hughes and Derby; and the German battery, Miller and Cantz.

The Newark correspondent for *Sporting Life* asked, "By the way, what do you think of our 'storm battery,' Stovey and Walker? Verily they are dark horses, and ought to be a drawing card. No rainchecks given when they play." Later he wrote that "Our 'Spanish beauties,' Stovey and Walker, will make the biggest kind of drawing card." Drawing card they may have been, but Stovey and Walker were signed by Newark not for promotional gimmickry, but because they were talented athletes who could help their team win.

Nor were other teams reluctant to improve themselves by hiring black players. In Oswego, manager Wesley Curry made a widely publicized, though unsuccessful, attempt to sign second baseman George Williams, captain of the Cuban Giants. Had Curry succeeded, Williams would not have been the first, nor the best, black second baseman in the league. For Buffalo had retained the services of Frank Grant, the greatest black baseball player of the nineteenth century.

Frank Grant was beginning the second of a record three consecutive years on the same integrated baseball team. Born in 1867, he began his career in his hometown of Pittsfield, Massachusetts, then moved on to Plattsburg, New York. In 1886 he entered Organized Baseball, playing for Meriden, Connecticut, in the Eastern League until the team folded in July. Thereupon he and two white teammates signed with the Buffalo Bisons, where he led the team in hitting. By the age of twenty Grant was already known as "the Black Dunlap," a singularly flattering sobriquet referring to Fred "Sure Shot" Dunlap, the first player to sign for $10,000 a season, and acknowledged as the greatest second baseman of his era. Sol White called Frank Grant simply "the greatest ball player of his age," without reference to race.

In 1887, Grant would lead the International League in hitting with a .366 average. Press accounts abound with comments about his fielding skill, especially his extraordinary range. After a series of preseason exhibition games against Pittsburgh's National League team, "Hustling Horace" Phillips, the Pittsburgh manager, complained about Buffalo's use of Grant as a "star." The Rochester *Union* quoted Phillips as saying that "This accounts for the amount of ground [Grant] is allowed to cover . . . and no attention is paid to such a thing as running all over another man's territory." Criticizing an infielder for his excessive range smacks of praising with faint damns. Grant's talent and flamboyance made him popular not only in Buffalo, but also throughout the IL.

In 1890 Grant would play his last season on an integrated team for Harrisburg, Pennsylvania, of the Eastern Interstate League. His arrival was delayed by several weeks due to a court battle with another team over the rights to his services. The Harrisburg *Patriot* described Grant's long awaited appearance:

> Long before it was time for the game to begin, it was whispered around the crowd that Grant would arrive on the 3:20 train and play third base. Everybody was anxious to see him come and there was a general stretch of necks toward the new bridge, all being eager to get a sight at the most famous colored ball player in the business. At 3:45 o'clock an open carriage was seen coming over the bridge with two men in it. Jim Russ' famous trotter was drawing it at a 2:20 speed and as it approached nearer, the face of Grant was recognized as being one of the men. "There he comes," went through the crowd like magnetism and three cheers went up. Grant was soon in the players' dressing room and in five minutes he

appeared on the diamond in a Harrisburg uniform.
A great shout went up from the immense crowd to
receive him, in recognition of which he politely
raised his cap.

Fred Dunlap should have been proud had he ever been
called "the White Grant." Yet Grant in his later years
passed into such obscurity that no one knew where or when
he died (last year an obituary in the New York *Age* was
located, revealing that Grant had died in New York on June
5, 1937).

Meanwhile, in Binghamton, Bud Fowler, who had spent
the winter working in a local barbershop, was preparing for
the 1887 season. At age 33, Fowler was the elder statesman
of Negro ballplayers. In 1872, only one year after the
founding of the first professional baseball league, Bud
Fowler was playing professionally for a white team in New
Castle, Pennsylvania. Lee Allen, while historian of baseball's Hall of Fame, discovered that Fowler, whose real
name was John Jackson, was born in Cooperstown, New
York, in about 1854, the son of itinerant hops-pickers.
Thus, Fowler was the greatest baseball player to be born at
the future site of the Hall of Fame.

As was the case with many minor league players of his
time, Fowler's career took him hopscotching across the
country. In 1884 and 1885 he played for teams in Stillwater,
Minnesota; Keokuk, Iowa; and Pueblo, Colorado. He played
the entire 1886 season in Topeka, Kansas, in the Western
League, where he hit .309. A Negro newspaper in Chicago,
the *Observer,* proudly described Fowler as "the best second
baseman in the Western League."

Binghamton signed Fowler for 1887. *The Sportsman's
Referee* wrote that Fowler "...has two joints where an
ordinary person has one. Fowler is a great ball player."
According to *Sporting Life*'s Binghamton correspondent:

Fowler is a dandy in every respect. Some say that
Fowler is a colored man, but we account for his
dark complexion by the fact that...in chasing

after balls [he] has become tanned from constant and careless exposure to the sun. This theory has the essential features of a chestnut, as it bears resemblance to Buffalo's claim that Grant is of Spanish descent.

Fowler's career in the International League would be brief. The financially troubled Bings would release him in July to cut their payroll. But during this half-season, a friendly rivalry existed between Fowler and Grant. Not so friendly were some of the tactics used by opposing base-runners and pitchers. In 1889, an unidentified International League player told *The Sporting News*:

> While I myself am prejudiced against playing in a team with a colored player, still I could not help pitying some of the poor black fellows that played in the International League. Fowler used to play second base with the lower part of his legs en-cased in wooden guards. He knew that about every player that came down to second base on a steal had it in for him and would, if possible, throw the spikes into him. He was a good player, but left the base every time there was a close play in order to get away from the spikes.
>
> I have seen him muff balls intentionally, so that he would not have to try to touch runners, fearing that they might injure him. Grant was the same way. Why, the runners chased him off second base. They went down so often trying to break his legs or injure them that he gave up his infield position the latter part of last season [i.e., 1888] and played right field. This is not all.
>
> About half the pitchers try their best to hit these colored players when [they are] at the bat . . . One of the International League pitchers pitched for Grant's head all the time. He never put a ball over the plate but sent them in straight and true right at Grant. Do what he would he could not hit the

Buffalo man, and he [Grant] trotted down to first
on called balls all the time.

Fowler's ambitions in baseball extended beyond his career as a player. As early as 1885, while in between teams,
he considered playing for and managing the Orions, a Negro
team in Philadelphia. Early in July 1887, just prior to his
being released by Binghamton, the sporting press reported
that Fowler planned to organize a team of blacks who would
tour the South and Far West during the winter between 1887
and 1888. "The strongest colored team that has ever appeared
in the field," according to *Sporting Life*, would consist of
Stovey and Walker of Newark; Grant of Buffalo; five
members of the Cuban Giants; and Fowler, who would play
and manage. This tour, however, never materialized.

But this was not the only capitalistic venture for Fowler in
1887. The entrepreneurial drive that would lead White to
describe him as "the celebrated promoter of colored ball
clubs, and the sage of base ball" led him to investigate
another ill-fated venture: The National Colored Base Ball
League.

II

In 1886 an attempt had been made to form the Southern
League of Colored Base Ballists, centered in Jacksonville,
Florida. Little is known about this circuit, since it was so
short-lived and received no national and very little local
press coverage. Late in 1886, though, Walter S. Brown of
Pittsburgh announced his plan of forming the National
Colored Base Ball League. It, too, would have a brief
existence. But unlike its Southern predecessor, Brown's
Colored League received wide publicity.

The November 18, 1886, issue of *Sporting Life* announced that Brown already had lined up five teams. Despite the decision of the Cuban Giants not to join the league,
Brown called an organizational meeting at Eureka Hall in
Pittsburgh on December 9, 1886. Delegates from Boston,

Philadelphia, Washington, Baltimore, Pittsburgh, and Louisville attended. Representatives from Chicago and Cincinnati also were present as prospective investors, Cincinnati being represented by Bud Fowler.

Final details were ironed out at a meeting at the Douglass Institute in Baltimore in March 1887. The seven-team league consisted of the Keystones of Pittsburgh, Browns of Cincinnati, Capitol Citys of Washington, Resolutes of Boston, Falls City of Louisville, Lord Baltimores of Baltimore, Gorhams of New York, and Pythians of Philadelphia. (The Pythians had been the first black nine to play a white team in history, beating the City Items 27-17 on September 18, 1869.) Reach Sporting Goods agreed to provide gold medals for batting and fielding leaders in exchange for the league's use of the Reach ball. Players' salaries would range from $10 to $75 per month. In recognition of its questionable financial position, the league set up an "experimental" season, with a short schedule and many open dates.

"Experimental" or not, the Colored League received the protection of the National Agreement, which was the structure of Organized Baseball law that divided up markets and gave teams the exclusive right to players' contracts. *Sporting Life* doubted that the league would benefit from this protection "as there is little probability of a wholesale raid upon its ranks even should it live the season out—a highly improbable contingency." Participation in the National Agreement was more a matter of prestige than of practical benefit. Under the headline "Do They Need Protection?" *Sporting Life* wrote:

> The progress of the Colored League will be watched with considerable interest. There have been prominent colored base ball clubs throughout the country for many years past, but this is their initiative year in launching forth on a league scale by forming a league . . . representing . . . leading cities of the country. The League will attempt to secure the protection of the National Agreement. This can only be done with the consent of all the

National Agreement clubs in whose territories the colored clubs are located. This consent should be obtainable, as these clubs can in no sense be considered rivals to the white clubs nor are they likely to hurt the latter in the least financially. Still the League can get along without protection. The value of the latter to the white clubs lies in that it guarantees a club undisturbed possession of its players. There is not likely to be much of a scramble for colored players. Only two [sic] such players are now employed in professional white clubs, and the number is not likely to be ever materially increased owing to the high standard of play required and to the popular prejudice against any considerable mixture of races.

Despite the gloomy—and accurate—forecasts, the Colored League opened its season with much fanfare at Recreation Park in Pittsburgh on May 6, 1887. Following "a grand street parade and a brass band concert," about 1200 spectators watched the visiting Gorhams of New York defeat the Keystones, 11-8.

Although Walter Brown did not officially acknowledge the demise of the Colored League for three more weeks, it was obvious within a matter of days that the circuit was in deep trouble. The Resolutes of Boston traveled to Louisville to play the Falls City club on May 8. While in Louisville, the Boston franchise collapsed, stranding its players. The league quickly dwindled to three teams, then expired. Weeks later, Boston's players were still marooned in Louisville. "At last accounts," reported *The Sporting News*, "most of the Colored Leaguers were working their way home doing little turns in barbershops and waiting on table in hotels." One of the vagabonds was Sol White, then nineteen years old, who had played for the Keystones of Pittsburgh. He made his way to Wheeling, West Virginia, where he completed the season playing for that city's entry in the Ohio State League. (Three other blacks in that league besides White were Welday Walker, catcher N. Higgins, and an-

other catcher, Richard Johnson.) Twenty years later he
wrote:

> The [Colored] League, on the whole, was without
> substantial backing and consequently did not last
> a week. But the short time of its existence served
> to bring out the fact that colored ball players of
> ability were numerous.

Although independent black teams would enjoy varying
degrees of success throughout the years, thirty-three seasons
would pass before Andrew "Rube" Foster would achieve
Walter Brown's ambitious dream of 1887: a stable all-Negro
professional baseball league.

III

The International League season was getting under way.
In preseason exhibitions against major league teams, Grant's
play was frequently described as "brilliant." *Sporting Life*
cited the "brilliant work of Grant," his "number of difficult
one-handed catches," and his "special fielding displays" in
successive games in April. Even in an 18-4 loss to Philadelphia, "Grant, the colored second baseman, was the lion of
the afternoon. His exhibition was unusually brilliant."
Stovey got off to a shaky start, as Newark lost to
Brooklyn 12-4 in the team's exhibition opener. "Walker
was clever—exceedingly clever behind the bat," wrote the
Newark *Daily Journal*, "yet threw wildly several times." A
few days later, though, Newark's "colored battery" performed
magnificently in a 3-2 loss at the Polo Grounds to the New
York Giants, the favorite National League team of the
Newark fans (hence the nickname "Little Giants"). Stovey
was "remarkably effective," and Walker threw out the
Giants' John Montgomery Ward at second base, "something
that but few catchers have been able to accomplish." The
play of Stovey and Walker impressed the New York sportswriters, as well as New York Giants' Captain Ward and

manager Jim Mutrie who, according to White, "made an offer to buy the release of the 'Spanish Battery,' but [Newark] Manager Hackett informed him they were not on sale."

Stovey and Walker were becoming very popular. The Binghamton *Leader* had this to say about the big southpaw:

> Well, they put Stovey in the box again yesterday. You recollect Stovey, of course—the brunette fellow with the sinister fin and the demonic delivery. Well, he pitched yesterday, and, as of yore, he teased the Bingos. He has such a knack of tossing up balls that appear as large as an alderman's opinion of himself, but you cannot hit 'em with a cellar door. There's no use in talking, but that Stovey can do funny things with a ball. Once, we noticed, he aimed a ball right at a Bing's commissary department, and when the Bingo spilled himself on the glebe to give that ball the right of way, it just turned a sharp corner and careened over the dish to the tune of "one strike." What's the use of bucking against a fellow that can throw at the flag-staff and make it curve into the water pail?

Walker, too, impressed fans and writers with his defensive skill and baserunning. In a game against Buffalo, "Walker was like a fence behind the home-plate . . . [T]here might have been a river ten feet behind him and not a ball would have gone into it." Waxing poetic, one scribe wrote:

> There is a catcher named Walker
> Who behind the bat is a corker,
> He throws to a base
> With ease and with grace,
> And steals 'round the bags like a stalker.

Who were the other black ballplayers in the IL? Oswego, unsuccessful in signing George Williams away from the Cuban Giants, added Randolph Jackson, a second baseman from Ilion, New York, to their roster after a recommendation from Bud Fowler. (Ilion is near Cooperstown; Fowler's real name was John Jackson—coincidence?) He played his first game on May 28. In a 5-4 loss to Newark he "played a remarkable game and hit for a double and a single, besides making the finest catch ever made on the grounds," wrote *Sporting Life*. Jackson played only three more games before the Oswego franchise folded on May 31, 1887.

Binghamton, which already had Bud Fowler, added a black pitcher named Renfroe (whose first name is unknown). Renfroe had pitched for the Memphis team in the Southern League of Colored Base Ballists in 1886, where "he won every game he pitched but one, averaging twelve strikeouts a game for nine games. In his first game against Chattanooga he struck out the first nine men who came to bat," wrote the Memphis *Appeal*; "he has great speed and a very deceptive down-shoot." Renfroe pitched his first game for Binghamton on May 30, a 14-9 victory over Utica, before several thousand fans.

"How far will this mania for engaging colored players go?" asked *Sporting Life*. "At the present rate of progress the International League may ere many moons change its title to 'Colored League.'" During the last few days in May, seven blacks were playing in the league: Walker and Stovey for Newark, Fowler and Renfroe for Binghamton, Grant for Buffalo, Jackson for Oswego, and one player not yet mentioned: Robert Higgins. For his story, we back up and consider the state of the Syracuse Stars.

IV

The 1887 season opened with Syracuse in a state of disarray. Off the field, ownership was reorganized after a lengthy and costly court battle in which the Stars were held liable for injuries suffered by a fan, John A. Cole, when he fell from a grandstand in 1886. Another fall that disturbed management was that of its team's standing, from first in 1885 to a dismal sixth in 1886. Determined to infuse new talent into the club, Syracuse signed seven players from the defunct Southern League after the 1886 season. Although these players were talented, the move appeared to be back-firing when, even before the season began, reports began circulating that the Southern League men had formed a "clique" to foist their opinions on management. The directors wanted to sign as manager Charley Hackett, who, as we have seen, subsequently signed with Newark. But the clique insisted that they would play for Syracuse only if Jim Gifford, who had hired them, was named manager. The directors felt that Gifford was too lax, yet acquiesced to the players' demand.

By the end of April, the Toronto *World* was reporting:

> Already we hear talk of "cliqueism" in the Syracuse Club, and if there be any truth to the bushel of statement that team is certain to be doomed before the season is well under way. Their ability to play a winning game is unquestioned, but if the clique exists the club will lose when losing is the policy of the party element.

Another offseason acquisition for the Stars was a catcher named Dick Male, from Zanesville, Ohio. Soon after he was signed in November 1886, rumors surfaced that "Male" was actually a black named Dick Johnson. Male mounted his own public relations campaign to quell these rumors. The Syracuse correspondent to *Sporting Life* wrote:

> Much has been said of late about Male, one of our catchers, being a colored man, whose correct name is said to be Johnson. I have seen a photo of Male, and he is not a colored man by a large majority. If he is he has sent some other fellow's picture.

The Sporting News' Syracuse writer informed his readers that "Male . . . writes that the man calling him a negro is himself a black liar."

Male's performance proved less than satisfactory and he was released by Syracuse shortly after a 20-3 drubbing at the hands of Pittsburgh in a preseason game, in which Male played right field, caught, and allowed three passed balls. Early in May he signed with Zanesville of the Ohio State League, where he once again became a black catcher named Johnson.

As the season began, the alarming specter of selective support by the Southern League players became increasingly apparent. They would do their best for deaf-mute pitcher Ed Dundon, who was a fellow refugee, but would go through the motions when Doug Crothers or Con Murphy pitched for the Stars. Jim Gifford, the Stars' manager, not equal to the task of controlling his team, resigned on May 17. He was replaced by "Ice Water" Joe Simmons, who had managed Walker at Waterbury in 1886.

Simmons began his regime at Syracuse by signing a nineteen-year-old lefthanded black pitcher named Robert Higgins. Like Renfroe, Higgins was from Memphis, and it was reported that manager Sneed of Memphis "would have signed him long ago ... but for the prejudice down there against colored men." Besides his talents as a pitcher Higgins was so fast on the basepaths that *Sporting Life* claimed that he had even greater speed than Mike Slattery of Toronto, who himself was fast enough to steal 112 bases in 1887, an International League record to this day.

On May 23, two days after he signed with the Stars, Higgins pitched well in an exhibition game at Lockport, New York, winning 16-5. On May 25 the Stars made their first trip of the season to Toronto, where in the presence of 1,000 fans, Higgins pitched in his first International League game. The Toronto *World* accurately summed up the game with its simple headline: "DISGRACEFUL BASEBALL." The Star team "distinguished itself by a most disgusting exhibition." In a blatant attempt to make Higgins look bad, the Stars lost 28-8. "Marr, Bittman, and Beard ... seemed to want the Toronto team to knock Higgins out of the box, and time and again they fielded so badly that the home team were enabled to secure many hits after the side should have been retired.

In several instances these players carried out their plans in the most glaring manner. Fumbles and muffs of easy fly balls were frequent occurrences, but Higgins retained control of his temper and smiled at every move of the clique . . . Marr, Bittman, Beard and Jantzen played like schoolboys." Of Toronto's 28 runs, 21 were unearned. Higgins' catcher, Jantzen, had three passed balls, three wild throws, and three strikeouts, incurring his manager's wrath to the degree that he was fined $50 and suspended. (On June 3 Jantzen was reinstated, only to be released on July 7.) *The Sporting News* reported the game prominently under the headlines: "THE SYRACUSE PLOTTERS; The Star Team Broken Up by a Multitude of Cliques; The Southern Boys Refuse to Support the Colored Pitcher." The group of Southern League players was called the "Ku-Klux coterie" by the Syracuse correspondent, who hoped that player Harry Jacoby would dissociate himself from the group. "If it is true that he is a member of the Star Ku-Klux-Klan to kill off Higgins, the negro, he has made a mistake. His friends did not expect it. . . ."

According to the Newark *Daily Journal*, "Members of the Syracuse team make no secret of their boycott against Higgins. . . . They succeeded in running Male out of the club and they will do the same with Higgins." Yet when the club returned to Syracuse, Higgins pitched his first game at Star Park on May 31, beating Oswego 11-4. *Sporting Life* assured its readers that "the Syracuse Stars supported [Higgins] in fine style."

But Bob Higgins had not yet forded the troubled waters of integrated baseball. On the afternoon of Saturday, June 4, in a game featuring opposing Negro pitchers, Syracuse and Higgins defeated Binghamton and Renfroe 10-4 before 1,500 fans at Star Park. Syracuse pilot Joe Simmons instructed his players to report the next morning to P. S. Ryder's gallery to have the team portrait taken. Two players did not comply, left fielder Henry Simon and pitcher Doug Crothers. The Syracuse correspondent for *The Sporting News* reported:

The manager surmised at once that there was "a
nigger in the fence" and that those players had
not reported because the colored pitcher, Higgins,
was to be included in the club portrait. He went
over to see Crothers and found that he was right.
Crothers would not sit in a group for his picture
with Higgins.

After an angry exchange, Simmons informed Crothers
that he would be suspended for the remainder of the season.
The volatile Crothers accused Simmons of leaving debts in
every city he had managed, then punched him. The manager
and his pitcher were quickly separated.

There may have been an economic motive that fanned the
flames of Crothers' temper, which was explosive even under
the best of circumstances: he was having a disappointing
season when Simmons hired a rival and potential replacement for him. According to *The Sporting News'* man in
Syracuse, Crothers was not above contriving to hinder the
performance of another pitcher, Dundon, by getting him
liquored-up on the night before he was scheduled to pitch.

Crothers, who was from St. Louis, later explained his
refusal to sit in the team portrait:

I don't know as people in the North can appreci-
ate my feelings on the subject. I am a Southerner
by birth, and I tell you I would have my heart cut
out before I would consent to have my picture in
the group. I could tell you a very sad story of
injuries done my family, but it is personal history.
My father would have kicked me out of the house
had I allowed my picture to be taken in that
group.

Crothers' suspension lasted only until June 18, when he
apologized to his manager and was reinstated. In the meantime he had earned $25 per game pitching for "amateur"
clubs. On July 2, he was released by Syracuse. Before the

season ended, he played for Hamilton of the International League, and in Eau Claire, Wisconsin, all the while threatening to sue the Syracuse directors for $125.

Harry Simon, a native of Utica, New York, was not punished in any way for his failure to appear for the team portrait; of course, he did not compound his insubordination by punching his manager. The Toronto *World* was cynical, yet plausible, in commenting that Simon "is such a valuable player, his offense [against Higgins] seems to have been overlooked." The sporting press emphasized that Crothers was punished for his failure to pose with Higgins more than his fisticuffs with Simmons.

Thus in a period of ten days did Bob Higgins become the unwilling focus of attention in the national press, as the International League grappled with the question of race. Neither of these incidents—the attempt to discredit him with intentionally bad play nor the reluctance of white players to be photographed with a black teammate—was unprecedented. The day before the Stars' appointment with the photographer, the Toronto *World* reported that in 1886 the Buffalo players refused to have their team photographed because of the presence of Frank Grant, which made it seem unlikely that the Bisons would have a team portrait taken in 1887 (nonetheless, they did). That Canadian paper, ever vigilant lest the presence of black ballplayers besmirch the game, also reported, ominously, that "The recent trouble among the Buffalo players originated from their dislike to [sic] Grant, the colored player. It is said that the latter's effective use of a club alone saved him from a drubbing at the hands of other members of the team."

Binghamton did not make a smooth, serene transition into integrated baseball. Renfroe took a tough 7-6 eleven-inning loss at the hands of Syracuse on June 2, eight days after Higgins' 28-8 loss to Toronto. "The Bings did not support Renfroe yesterday," said the Binghamton *Daily Leader*, "and many think the shabby work was intentional."

On July 7, Fowler and Renfroe were released. In recognition of his considerable talent, Fowler was released only upon the condition that he would not sign with any other

team in the International League. Fowler joined the Cuban
Giants briefly, by August was manager of the (Negro)
Gorham Club of New York, and he finished the season
playing in Montpelier, Vermont.

On August 8, the Newark *Daily Journal* reported, "The
players of the Binghamton base ball club were . . . fined $50
each by the directors because six weeks ago they refused to
go on the field unless Fowler, the colored second baseman,
was removed." In view of the fact that two weeks after
these fines were imposed the Binghamton franchise folded,
it may be that the club's investors were motivated less by a
tender regard for social justice than by a desire to cut their
financial losses.

According to the Oswego *Palladium*, even an International
League umpire fanned the flames of prejudice:

> It is said that [Billy] Hoover, the umpire, stated in
> Binghamton that he would always decide against
> a team employing a colored player, on a close
> point. Why not dispense with Mr. Hoover's ser-
> vices if this is true? It would be a good thing for
> Oswego if we had a few players like Fowler and
> Grant.

There were incidents that indicated support for a color-
blind policy in baseball. For example:

> A citizen of Rochester has published a card in the
> *Union and Advertiser* of that city, in which he
> rebukes the Rochester *Sunday Herald* for abusing
> Stovey on account of his color. He says: "The
> young man simply discharged his duty to his club
> in white-washing the Rochesters if he could. Such
> comments certainly do not help the home team;
> neither are they creditable to a paper published in
> a Christian community. So far as I know, Mr.
> Stovey has been a gentleman in his club, and
> should be treated with the same respect as other
> players."

But the accumulation of events both on and off the field drew national attention to the International League's growing controversy over the black players. The forces lining up against the blacks were formidable and determined, and the most vociferous opposition to integrated baseball came from Toronto, where in a game with Buffalo on July 27, "The crowd confined itself to blowing their horns and shouting, 'Kill the nigger'." The Toronto *World*, under the headline "THE COLORED BALL PLAYERS DISTASTEFUL," declared:

> The *World*'s statement of the existence of a clique in the Syracuse team to "boy cott" Higgins, the colored pitcher, is certain to create considerable talk, if it does not amount to more, in baseball circles. A number of colored players are now in the International League, and to put it mildly their presence is distasteful to the other players. . . . So far none of the clubs, with the exception of Syracuse, have openly shown their dislike to play with these men, but the feeling is known to exist and may unexpectedly come to the front. The chief reason given for McGlone's* refusal to sign with Buffalo this season is that he objected to playing with Grant.

A few weeks later the *World* averred, in a statement reprinted in *Sporting Life*:

> There is a feeling, and a rather strong one too, that an effort be made to exclude colored players from the International League. Their presence on the teams has not been productive of satisfactory results, and good players as some of them have shown themselves, it would seem advisable to take action of some kind, looking either to their

---

*John McGlone's scruples in this regard apparently were malleable enough to respond to changes in his career fortunes. In September 1888 he signed with Syracuse, thereby acquiring two black teammates—Fleet Walker and Bob Higgins.

non-engagement or compelling the other element
to play with them.

Action was about to be taken.

V

July 14, 1887, would be a day that Tommy Daly would
never forget. Three thousand fans went to Newark's Wright
Street grounds to watch an exhibition game between the
Little Giants and the most glamorous team in baseball:
Adrian D. (Cap) Anson's Chicago White Stockings. Daly,
who was from Newark, was in his first season with the
White Stockings, forerunners of today's Cubs. Before the
game he was presented with gifts from his admirers in
Newark. George Stovey would remember the day, too. And
for Moses Fleetwood Walker, there may have been a sense
of déjà vu—for Walker had crossed paths with Anson
before.

Anson, who was the first white child born among the
Pottawattomie Indians in Marshalltown, Iowa, played for
Rockford and the Philadelphia Athletics in all five years of
the National Association and twenty-two seasons for Chicago
in the National League, hitting over .300 in all but two. He
also managed the Sox for nineteen years. From 1880 through
1886, Anson's White Stockings finished first five times, and
second once. Outspoken, gruff, truculent, and haughty,
Anson gained the respect, if not the esteem, of his players,
as well as opponents and fans throughout the nation. Cigars
and candy were named after him, and little boys would
treasure their Anson-model baseball bats as their most
prized possessions. He was a brilliant tactician with a flair
for the dramatic. In 1888, for example, he commemorated
the opening of the Republican national convention in Chicago
by suiting up his players in black, swallow-tailed coats.

In addition to becoming the first player to get 3,000 hits,
Anson was the first to write his autobiography. *A Ball
Player's Career*, published in 1900, does not explicitly

delineate Anson's views on race relations. It does, however, devote several pages to his stormy relationship with the White Stockings' mascot, Clarence Duval, who despite Anson's vehement objections was allowed to take part in the round-the-world tour following the 1888 season. Anson referred to Duval as "a little darkey," a "coon," and a "no account nigger."

In 1883, when Walker was playing for Toledo, Anson brought his White Stockings into town for an exhibition. Anson threatened to pull his team off the field unless Walker was removed. But Toledo's manager, Charley Morton, refused to comply with Anson's demand, and Walker was allowed to play (in right field, not as catcher, despite the quote below). Years later *Sporting Life* would write:

> The joke of the affair was that up to the time Anson made his "bluff" the Toledo people had no intention of catching Walker, who was laid up with a sore hand, but when Anson said he wouldn't play with Walker, the Toledo people made up their minds that Walker would catch or there wouldn't be any game.

But by 1887 times had changed, and there was no backing Anson down. The Newark press had publicized that Anson's White Stockings would face Newark's black Stovey. But on the day of the game it was Hughes and Cantz who formed the Little Giants' battery. "Three thousand souls were made glad," glowed the *Daily Journal* after Newark's surprise 9-4 victory, "while nine were made sad." The *Evening News* attributed Stovey's absence to illness, but the Toronto *World* got it right in reporting that "Hackett intended putting Stovey in the box against the Chicagos, but Anson objected to his playing on account of his color."

On the same day that Anson succeeded in removing the "colored battery," the directors of the International League met in Buffalo to transfer the ailing Utica franchise to Wilkes-Barre, Pennsylvania. It must have pleased Anson to read in the next day's Newark *Daily Journal*:

THE COLOR LINE DRAWN IN BASEBALL.

The International League directors held a secret meeting at the Genesee House yesterday, and the question of colored players was freely discussed. Several representatives declared that many of the best players in the league are anxious to leave on account of the colored element, and the board finally directed Secretary White to approve of no more contracts with colored men.

Whether or not there was a direct connection between Anson's opposition to playing against Stovey and Walker and, on the same day, the International League's decision to draw the color line is lost in history. For example, was the league responding to threats by Anson not to play lucrative exhibitions with teams of any league that permitted Negro players? Interestingly, of the six teams which voted to install a color barrier—Binghamton, Hamilton, Jersey City, Rochester, Toronto, and Utica—none had a black player; the four teams voting against it—Buffalo, Oswego, Newark, and Syracuse— each had at least one.

In 1907, Sol White excoriated Anson for possessing "all the venom of a hate which would be worthy of a Tillman or a Vardaman* of the present day...."

Just why Adrian C. Anson...was so strongly opposed to colored players on white teams cannot be explained. His repugnant feeling, shown at every opportunity, toward colored ball players, was a source of comment throughout every league in the country, and his opposition, with his great popularity and power in baseball circles, hastened the exclusion of the black man from the white leagues.

*Sen. Benjamin R. ("Pitchfork Ben") Tillman, of South Carolina, and Gov. James K. Vardaman, of Mississippi, were two of the most prominent white supremacists of their time.

Subsequent historians have followed Sol White's lead and portrayed Anson as the *meistersinger* of a chorus of racism who, virtually unaided, disqualified an entire race from baseball. Scapegoats are convenient, but Robert Peterson undoubtedly is correct:

> Whatever its origin, Anson's animus toward Negroes was strong and obvious. But that he had the power and popularity to force Negroes out of organized baseball almost singlehandedly, as White suggests, is to credit him with more influence than he had, or for that matter, than he needed.

The International League's written color line was not the first one drawn. In 1867 the National Association of Base Ball Players, the loosely organized body which regulated amateur baseball, prohibited its members from accepting blacks. The officers candidly explained their reason:

> If colored clubs were admitted there would be in all probability some division of feeling, whereas, by excluding them no injury could result to anybody and the possibility of any rupture being created on political grounds would be avoided.

This 1867 ban shows that even if blacks were not playing baseball then, there were ample indications that they would be soon. But the NABBP would soon disappear, as baseball's rapidly growing popularity fostered professionalism. Also, its measure was preventative rather than corrective: it was not intended to disqualify players who previously had been sanctioned. And, since it applied only to amateurs, it was not intended to deprive anyone of his livelihood.

Press response to the International League's color line generally was sympathetic to the Negroes—especially in cities with teams who had employed black players. The Newark *Call* wrote:

If anywhere in this world the social barriers are broken down it is on the ball field. There many men of low birth and poor breeding are the idols of the rich and cultured; the best man is he who plays best. Even men of churlish dispositions and coarse hues are tolerated on the field. In view of these facts the objection to colored men is ridiculous. If social distinctions are to be made, half the players in the country will be shut out. Better make character and personal habits the test. Weed out the toughs and intemperate men first, and then it may be in order to draw the color line.

The Rochester *Post-Express* printed a shrewd and sympathetic analysis by an unidentified "old ball player, who happens to be an Irishman and a Democrat":

We will have to stop proceedings of that kind. The fellows who want to proscribe the Negro only want a little encouragement in order to establish class distinctions between people of the white race. The blacks have so much prejudice to overcome that I sympathize with them and believe in frowning down every attempt by a public body to increase the burdens the colored people now carry. It is not possible to combat by law the prejudice against colored men, but it is possible to cultivate a healthy public opinion that will effectively prevent any such manifestation of provincialism as that of the ball association. If a negro can play better ball than a white man, I say let him have credit for his ability. Genuine Democrats must stamp on the color line in order to be consistent.

"We think," wrote the Binghamton *Daily Leader*, "the International League made a monkey of itself when it undertook to draw the color line"; and later the editor wondered "if the International League proposes to exclude

colored people from attendance at the games." Welday
Walker used a similar line of reasoning in March 1888.
Having read an incorrect report that the Tri-State League,
formerly the Ohio State League, of which Welday Walker
was a member, had prohibited the signing of Negroes, he
wrote a letter to league president W. H. McDermitt. De-
nouncing any color line as "a disgrace to the present age,"
he argued that if Negroes were to be barred as players, then
they should also be denied access to the stands.

The sporting press stated its admiration for the talents of
the black players who would be excluded. "Grant, Stovey,
Walker, and Higgins," wrote *Sporting Life*, "all are good
players and behave like gentlemen, and it is a pity that the
line should have been drawn against them." That paper's
Syracuse correspondent wrote "Dod gast the measly rules
that deprives a club of as good a man as Bob Higgins. . . ."
Said the Newark *Daily Journal*, "It is safe to say that
Moses F. Walker is mentally and morally the equal of any
director who voted for the resolution."

Color line or no color line, the season wore on. Buffalo
and Newark remained in contention until late in the season.
Newark fell victim to injuries, including one to Fleet Walker. Grant's play deteriorated, although he finished the year
leading the league in hitting. Toronto, which overcame
internal strife of its own, came from the back of the pack,
winning twenty-two of its last twenty-six games; they may
have been aided by manager Charley Cushman's innovative
device of having his infielders wear gloves on their left
hands. On September 17, Toronto swept a doubleheader
from Newark at home before 8,000 fans to take first place.
One week later they clinched their first International League
title. To commemorate the triumphant season, the Canadian
Pacific Railway shipped a 160-foot tall pine, "the second
tallest in America," across the continent. Atop this pole
would fly the 1887 International League pennant.

Before the season ended there was one further flareup of
racial prejudice that received national attention. On Sunday,
September 11, Chris Von der Ahe, owner of the St. Louis
Browns, canceled an exhibition game that was scheduled for

that day in West Farms, New York, against the Cuban
Giants. Led by its colorful and eccentric owner, and its
multitalented manager-first baseman, Charles Comiskey, the
Browns were the Chicago White Stockings of the American
Association. At ten o'clock in the morning Von der Ahe
notified a crowd of 7,000 disappointed fans that his team
was too crippled by injuries to compete. The real reason,
though, was a letter Von der Ahe had received the night
before, signed by all but two of his players (Comiskey was
one of the two):

> Dear Sir: We, the undersigned members of the St.
> Louis Base Ball Club, do not agree to play
> against negroes tomorrow. We will cheerfully play
> against white people at any time, and think by
> refusing to play, we are only doing what is right,
> taking everything into consideration and the shape
> the team is in at present.

The Cuban Giants played, instead, a team from Danbury,
New York, as Cuban Giant manager Jim Bright angrily
threatened to sue the Browns. Von der Ahe tried to mollify
Bright with a promise to reschedule the exhibition, a promise that would be unfulfilled. The Browns' owner singled out
his star third baseman, Arlie Latham, for a $100 fine. Von
der Ahe did not object to his players' racial prejudice. In
fact, he was critical of them not for their clearly stated
motive for refusing to play, but for their perceived lack of
sincerity in pursuing their objective:

> The failure to play the game with the Cuban
> Giants cost me $1000. If it was a question of
> principle with any of my players, I would not say
> a word, but it isn't. Two or three of them had made
> arrangements to spend Sunday in Philadelphia,
> and this scheme was devised so that they would
> not be disappointed.

VI

There was considerable speculation throughout the offseason that the International League would rescind its color line, or at least modify it to allow each club one Negro. At a meeting at the Rossin House in Toronto on November 16, 1887, the league dissolved itself and reorganized under the title International Association. Buffalo and Syracuse, anxious to retain Grant and Higgins, led the fight to eliminate the color line. Syracuse was particularly forceful in its leadership. The Stars' representatives at the Toronto meeting "received a letter of thanks from the colored citizens of [Syracuse] for their efforts in behalf of the colored players," reported *Sporting Life*. A week earlier, under the headline "Rough on the Colored Players," it had declared:

> At the meeting of the new International Association, the matter of rescinding the rule forbidding the employment of colored players was forgotten. This is unfortunate, as the Syracuse delegation had Buffalo, London, and Hamilton, making four in favor and two [i.e., Rochester and Toronto] against it.

While the subject of the color line was not included in the minutes of the proceedings, the issue apparently was not quite "forgotten." An informal agreement among the owners provided a cautious retreat. By the end of the month, Grant was signed by Buffalo, and Higgins was retained by Syracuse for 1888. Fleet Walker, who was working in a Newark factory crating sewing machines for the export trade, remained uncommitted on an offer by Worcester, as he waited "until he finds whether colored players are wanted in the International League [sic]. He is very much a gentleman and is unwilling to force himself in where he is not wanted." His doubts assuaged, he signed, by the end of November, with Syracuse, where, in 1888 he would once again join a black pitcher. The Syracuse directors had fired manager Joe

Simmons, and replaced him with Charley Hackett. Thus, Walker would be playing for his third team with Hackett as manager. He looked forward to the next season, exercising his throwing arm by tossing a claw hammer in the air and catching it.

After a meeting in Buffalo in January 1888, *Sporting Life* summarized the IA's ambivalent position on the question of black players:

> At the recent International Association meeting there was some informal talk regarding the right of clubs to sign colored players, and the general understanding seemed to be that no city should be allowed more than one colored man. Syracuse has signed two whom she will undoubtedly be allowed to keep. Buffalo has signed Grant, but outside of these men there will probably be no colored men in the league.

Frank Grant would have a typical season in Buffalo in 1888, where he was moved to the outfield to avoid spike wounds. For the third straight year his batting average (.346) was the highest on the team. Bob Higgins, the agent and victim of too much history, would, according to *Sporting Life*, "give up his $200 a month, and return to his barbershop in Memphis, Tennessee," despite compiling a 20-7 record.

Fleet Walker, catching 76 games and stealing 30 bases, became a member of a second championship team, the first since Toledo in 1883. But his season was blighted by a third distasteful encounter with Anson. In an exhibition game at Syracuse on September 27, 1888, Walker was not permitted to play against the White Stockings. Anson's policy of refusing to allow blacks on the same field with him had become so well-known and accepted that the incident was not even reported in the white press. The Indianapolis *World* noted the incident, which by now apparently was of interest only to black readers.

Fowler, Grant, and Stovey played many more seasons,

some with integrated teams, some on all-Negro teams in white leagues in Organized Baseball, some on independent Negro teams. Fowler and Grant stayed one step ahead of the color line as it proceeded westward.

Fleet Walker continued to play for Syracuse in 1889, where he would be the last black in the International League until Jackie Robinson. Walker's career as a professional ballplayer ended in the relative obscurity of Terre Haute, Indiana (1890) and Oconto, Wisconsin (1891).

In the spring of 1891 Walker was accused of murdering a convicted burglar by the name of Patrick Murphy outside a bar in Syracuse. When he was found not guilty "immediately a shout of approval, accompanied by clapping of hands and stamping of feet, rose from the spectators," according to *Sporting Life*. His baseball career over, he returned to Ohio and embarked on various careers. He owned or operated the Cadiz, Ohio, opera house, and several motion picture houses, during which time he claimed several inventions in the motion picture industry. He was also the editor of a newspaper, *The Equator*, with the assistance of his brother Welday.

In 1908 he published a 47-page booklet entitled *Our Home Colony; A Treatise on the Past, Present and Future of the Negro Race in America*. According to the former catcher, "The only practical and permanent solution of the present and future race troubles in the United States is entire separation by emigration of the Negro from America." Following the example of Liberia, "the Negro race can find superior advantages, and better opportunities... among people of their own race, for developing the innate powers of mind and body...." The achievement of racial equality "is contrary to everything in the nature of man, and [it is] almost criminal to attempt to harmonize these two diverse peoples while living under the same government." The past forty years, he wrote, have shown "that instead of improving we are experiencing the development of a real caste spirit in the United States."

Fleet Walker died of pneumonia in Cleveland at age 66 on May 11, 1924, and was buried in Union Cemetery in

Steubenville, Ohio. His brother Welday died in Steubenville thirteen years later at the age of 77.

VII

In *The Strange Career of Jim Crow*, historian C. Vann Woodward identifies the late 1880s as a "twilight zone that lies between living memory and written history," when "for a time old and new rubbed shoulders—and so did black and white—in a manner that differed significantly from Jim Crow of the future or slavery of the past." He continued:

> . . . a great deal of variety and inconsistency prevailed in race relations from state to state and within a state. It was a time of experiment, testing, and uncertainty—quite different from the time of repression and rigid uniformity that was to come toward the end of the century. Alternatives were still open and real choices had to be made.

Sol White and his contemporaries lived through such a transition period, and he identified the turning point at 1887. Twenty years later he noted the deterioration of the black ballplayer's situation. Although White could hope that one day the black would be able to "walk hand-in-hand with the opposite race in the greatest of all American games—base ball," he was not optimistic:

> As it is, the field for the colored professional is limited to a very narrow scope in the base ball world. When he looks into the future he sees no place for him. . . . Consequently he loses interest. He knows that, so far shall I go, and no farther, and, as it is with the profession, so it is with his ability.

The "strange careers" of Moses Walker, George Stovey, Frank Grant, Bud Fowler, Robert Higgins, Sol White, et al., provide a microcosmic view of the development of race relations in the society at large, as outlined by Woodward. The events of 1887 offer further evidence of the old saw that sport does not develop character—it reveals it.

And toss in night ball, gangsters, and a "kidnapping," too.

The Year of the Hitter

William B. Mead

Hitting has been on the rise in baseball the past decade or so, and there is talk that today's ball, the Rawlings Rabbit, has more spring than any hare of seasons past. This is shortsighted history. Let me tell you, Sonny, about a time there was *hitting* in the major leagues.

The 1930 season is remembered for Hack Wilson's 56 home runs and 191 runs batted in, and Bill Terry's .401 batting average. Great as those achievements were, they stand out more in historical perspective than they did in their own day. In 1930, lusty hitting was a democratic activity, shared by all.

In 1984, the American League batted .264 and the National League hit .255. In 1930, the American League batted—including pitcher batting—.288 and the National League came in at .303. If the senior circuit had been a player—Nat League, 6-1, 190, throws right, switch-hits—it

WILLIAM B. MEAD is the author of *Even the Browns* and co-author of *The Ten Worst Years of Baseball*.

would have finished tenth in last season's batting race. In 1983 Lonnie Smith of the Cardinals missed the NL batting championship by only .002; if he had been warped back to 1930 with his .321 average, he would have found himself ranking seventh—not in the league, but *on his own team.* The 1930 Cardinals had twelve .300 hitters, only eight of whom could play at a time.

Wilson, of the Cubs, and Terry, of the Giants, had to hustle to stay on top. Wilson's 56 homers stand as the National League record, but his mark of 191 runs batted in is considered more impressive, and often is listed among baseball's few unbreakable records. It may be, but in 1930 Chuck Klein of the Phillies wasn't far behind, with 170, and Lou Gehrig of the Yankees led the American League with 174. Six major leaguers drove in more than 150 runs each that season, and thirty-two had 100 or more.

For the batting championship, Terry edged Babe Herman of the Dodgers, who hit .393, and Klein, at .386. As any good fan knows, no National Leaguer has batted .400 since Terry. What's more, no National Leaguer has hit .390 since Herman, either, or .386 since Klein.

Klein was the quintessential also-ran that season: second in the league in RBIs, second all-time; second to Terry in hits with 250, tied for third all-time; second to Wilson in slugging with .687, sixth best all-time. As for homers, Klein set the National League record just the year before, with 43, and lost it to Wilson in 1930. Strictly a spear-carrier, that Klein.

We could go on with these statistics. For example, count the .300 hitters: thirty-three in the National League, thirty-two in the American, a record. Trouble is, the figures understate the case, because they include only men who played in 100 games or more. In 1930, lots of .300 hitters couldn't crack the lineup. Some of them were pitchers, like Red Ruffing of the Yankees (.374), Erv Brame of the Pirates (.353), Chad Kimsey of the St. Louis Browns (.343), Red Lucas of the Reds (.336), and Firpo Marberry of the Washington Senators (.329).

The hitters splattered the 1930 season all over the record

books, but it was a remarkable baseball year in other ways, too. It was the first year of the Great Depression, and the first year of Babe Ruth's $80,000 salary. Night baseball began in the minor leagues, was an immediate sensation, and was denounced by major league owners as a blight and a fad. Gabby Hartnett of the Cubs was caught by a photographer while chatting with Al Capone, and Babe Herman twice was caught and passed by teammates on the basepaths. The Yankees traded a star pitcher because of a detective's report, and the Cardinals staged one of the greatest pennant drives in history, the more dramatic because of the disappearance—kidnapping?—of a star pitcher.

Baseball was such the dominant sport back then that its stars, like it or not, had to provide copy for the sports pages during the offseason as well as the summer. None filled the role as well as Ruth, who by then was a public idol of gargantuan proportions. Dour men like Rogers Hornsby made news only with their bats, but Ruth's ebullient personality and hearty living habits enhanced his reputation.

Ruth was holding out for $85,000 that spring, and Jacob Ruppert, the Yankee owner, grumped at the figure. "Ruth has taken more money from the Yankees than I have," he said. One venture fell through, *Ruth's Home Run Candy* running afoul of the thirty-five-year-old copyright on the *Baby Ruth* bar, which had been named after the infant daughter of President and Mrs. Grover Cleveland. But no matter. Without playing another game of baseball or lending his name to another product, Ruth said, he was assured of a comfortable income for life.

But Ruth did not feel comfortable as a holdout, and during spring training he yielded, accepting $80,000 a year for two years. It was a stunning figure, forty times the wage of the average worker, and it brought out the prophet in Edward G. Barrow, business manager of the Yankees. "You will never hear of another ballplayer getting that kind of money," Barrow said. *Never?* he was asked. "I'm sure there will never be another one on *this* ballclub," Barrow replied.

Next to Ruth, other players paled. Lefty O'Doul of the

Phils also held out that spring. O'Doul had led the National League in batting the season before at .398, with 32 homers and 122 runs batted in. He demanded—think of it!—$17,000. Too much, his boss said; O'Doul already was pulling down $8,000, more than any other Phillie, ever. O'Doul, like Ruth, had to compromise.

Edd Roush of the New York Giants would not compromise. A .324 hitter in 1929 and a future member of the Hall of Fame, Roush held out all spring, and all summer, too; he didn't play a game. Al Simmons, the Philadelphia Athletics' slugger, threatened to do the same, and Connie Mack announced that Spence Harris, a minor league lifer with an American League career average of .249, would take Simmons' place. While the Athletics were warming up on opening day, Simmons signed. The fans at Shibe Park roared when he appeared in uniform, and roared again when he came to bat in the first inning, with a man on base, and homered off George Pipgras of the Yanks. So much for the value of spring training.

While Ruth's physical dimensions were fully the match of his accomplishments on the field, Wilson supplied a contrast. With short legs, size 5½ shoes, and a huge torso, Wilson looked dwarfish, almost deformed. He was only 5 feet 6 inches tall, but weighed 190. His arms were large and muscular, his hands small. Even his nicknames were degrading; he was referred to as a gorilla, a sawed-off Babe Ruth, the Hardest-Hitting Hydrant of All Time, the Squatty Outfielder, the Pugnacious Clouter, the Abbreviated One, the Boy with the Mountainous Chin, none of which did much for his ego.

While Ruth went into the 1930 season with the dramatic flourish of his record salary, Wilson carried the humiliation of a dreadful inning during the 1929 World Series. Trailing the Cubs 8-0 in the fourth game, the Athletics scored ten runs in the seventh inning. Wilson, the Cubs' center fielder, lost two balls in the sun, one of them falling for a single and the other for a three-run homer. The A's went on to win that game and the Series, four games to one.

Wilson was said to have been a pathetic figure following

the Series. But he was a cheerful and likable man, and at spring training in 1930 Wilson was the life of the Cubs' camp. Cub players shouted "Wilson!" when fungoes were hit into the sun. Lampooning his own misplays, Wilson pulled the window shade in the hotel dining room, and asked the maitre d' to dim the light so he wouldn't misjudge his soup. Perhaps wishing to share in the fun, Calvin Coolidge visited Catalina Island, California, where the Cubs trained. The former President had little to say, but posed for photographers with a macaw on his shoulder.

From the season's beginning, the hitting in 1930 was extraordinary, and was recognized as such. Not that baseball had been a pitcher's game in the 1920s—far from it; neither league had batted under .280 since 1920, and the number of home runs more than doubled between that decade's first and last years. But in 1930 there was even more of what the club owners obviously considered a good thing, since attendance had increased with hitting.

Rallies were immense, and pitchers absorbed terrible punishment; it was not yet the custom to relieve short of disaster. On May 12, in Chicago, the Giants scored six runs in the second inning and seven in the third, helped by a home run by Mel Ott and two doubles by Fred Lindstrom. Larry Benton, the New York pitcher, carried a 14-0 lead into the fifth inning, and little seemed amiss when Cliff Heathcote homered for the Cubs; 14-1.

In the Cub sixth, Wilson and Gabby Hartnett walked, and Clyde Beck homered; 14-4. In the seventh, Heathcote led off with his second homer, and, after one out, Wilson homered to right. So did Charley Grimm. Les Bell flied out and Hartnett fanned for what would have been the third out, but Shanty Hogan, the Giant catcher, dropped the ball, and then threw it wildly, Hartnett reaching second. Beck homered again; 14-9. At this point John McGraw decided that Benton was weakening. McGraw brought in Joe Heving, who gave up six hits and three runs, but no homers. The Giants won 14-12, the Cubs having run out of time.

In late May, the Yankees and Athletics played three doubleheaders in four days, and the hitters gorged. Ninety-nine runs scored, and there were twenty-four home runs, eight of them by Ruth and three each by Gehrig and Philadelphia's Jimmie Foxx. As if the sluggers were swinging a massive pendulum, all three doubleheaders were swept, and no game was close—15-7 and 4-1 for the A's, 10-1 and 20-13 for the Yankees, 10-6 and 11-1, Yanks again.

In a devastating road swing in July, the Athletics scored ninety-seven runs in eight games, winning all of them while averaging twelve runs and fifteen hits a game. They scored ten runs in one inning at St. Louis, then, the next day, nine runs in the first three innings. In Chicago, Foxx hit a ball clear over the left field stands at Comiskey Park, the first player to do so.

The Senators, who had led the AL on Memorial Day, fell back, and so did the Yanks. Walter Johnson, the Washington manager, was appalled at the slugging and scolded his pitchers. Johnson was forty-four and hadn't pitched for three years, but he thought he could do no worse than the younger men, and said he might pitch relief. Owner Clark Griffith talked him out of it. In truth, the Senators' pitching staff was excellent, compared with others: Washington was the only team in baseball that yielded fewer than four earned runs per game that season.

Ruth was hitting so many home runs that he predicted he'd wind up with about 75. He might have, but on July 2 he jumped for a ball, caught a finger in the outfield screen, and lost the nail. The team doctor said the Babe would be out for a while, but he played the next day, his finger bandaged. Two days later, he hit his 32nd home run, putting him more than twenty games ahead of his pace in 1927, when he hit 60. But Ruth's slugging tailed off; he finished with 49 homers.

The Yanks were managed in 1930 by Bob Shawkey, and were watched surreptitiously by a detective, who was hired by Ruppert and traveled with the team, socializing with the players without letting them know he was snitching on them. Waite Hoyt, a pitcher who enjoyed night life, was traded to Detroit early in the season after the detective reported he was staying out even the night before pitching assignments. The Yankees could have used Hoyt, even with a hangover; their pitching was dreadful, and they finished a distant third.

The Cubs were the pick of the National League, but Hornsby broke his ankle and the race was close. Everyone expected the Brooklyn Dodgers, 70-83 in 1929, to improve in 1930, but not to contend. They did both. These were the Daffiness Boys, the Robins of veteran manager Wilbert Robinson. The Dodgers made errors in horrendous clusters, and, led by Herman, tended to squelch rallies with baserunning blunders.

On May 30 Herman, leading off first base, stood and watched while Del Bissonette's towering fly ball cleared the right-field screen at Ebbets Field. There was no chance that the ball would be caught, but Bissonette thought it might hit the screen and was running hard, as Herman should have been. Bissonette was declared out for passing a runner on the bases; his hit was registered as a single. On September 15 Herman did it again, this time depriving Glenn Wright of a home run.

On June 15, the Cardinals presented the Dodgers with three early runs on an outfield misplay. But the Dodgers fought back with five errors of their own, two of them by second baseman Mickey Finn, who fielded as if he had swallowed his name. Andy High, a Brooklyn castoff who was to haunt his old team all season, followed two of the errors with a triple, and a subsequent error with a home run. Dazzy Vance twice hit Taylor Douthit with pitches, but in the ninth decided to pitch to him, Dodger errors having placed two Cardinals on base. Douthit tripled, and the Cardinals won, 9-4.

Even while excelling, the Dodgers managed to err. At Pittsburgh on June 24, they managed to *conclude* the sixth inning with 10 straight hits, the last one a single to center on which Al Lopez was thrown out at the plate. Never mind; Brooklyn opened the seventh with a double by Wally Gilbert and a homer by Herman. That made twelve straight hits, a record even when done the Dodger way. Perhaps aware that he could depend on the Dodgers to do themselves in, Pirate Manager Jewel Ens stuck through that awful sixth inning with his starter, the pitcher with the rhyming name, Heine Meine, who then departed, having yielded 14 runs and 19 hits, the last 10 of them in a row.

For hitting, no team was the superior of the Phillies, except whomever they were playing. In the nightcap of a doubleheader on July 23, the Phils attacked the Pirates with 27 hits, including two home runs by Don Hurst. Not enough; the Pirates won, 16-15, on a homer by Pie Traynor in the thirteenth inning. The Phils scored 15 runs the next day, too, against the visiting Cubs—who, alas, tallied 19.

An extraordinary number of high-scoring games were played that season on the home grounds of the Phillies, and it was no coincidence. The Phils played in Baker Bowl, a decaying museum of a stadium with a right field wall so close, according to Ray Benge, then a Phillie pitcher, that "standing on the mound it looked like you could reach back there and thump it."

It was 280 feet to the right field corner, 300 feet in the right-center power alley. Today's most inviting wall, the Green Monster in left field at Fenway Park, Boston, is distant by comparison at 315 feet—and short, too, at 37 feet, 2 inches. Baker Bowl was built in 1887, and whoever designed it should have invented the skyscraper instead. The stadium was rimmed with a high wall, and in right field a screen was put on top of that for a total height of 58 feet. Even the clubhouse, in center field, was two stories tall. The Phils dressed on the top floor, with a commanding view of the patchy green surface. "Down on the field it was like a hole," Benge recalls.

Particularly for pitchers. "You just had one way to pitch," according to Benge. "That was to the righthand side of the plate, outside to lefthanders, inside to righthanders. You wanted the righthanders to pull, but a lot of them wouldn't do it. They'd punch the ball to right and ping it off the wall."

One of the best pingers was Pinky Whitney, the Phils' third baseman. "I hit a bunch of pop flies against it,"

Whitney says. He batted .342, including 41 doubles, and batted in 117 runs.

On the Phils, that was good but not exceptional. The team scored an average of 6.13 runs a game, and batted .315. They had two strong lefthanded pull hitters in Klein and O'Doul, and both of them batted over .380. Together, Klein, Whitney, and O'Doul drove in 384 runs and scored 367. What would such a team do to the league?

The Phils' answer, in 1930, was: bring up the rear. They won 52 games, lost 102, and never threatened seventh place. Phillie pitchers allowed a record 6.71 earned runs a game, about two more than a very bad pitching staff yields today, and Phillie fielders led the majors with 239 errors, 50 or so more than the most butterfingered of today's teams.

Between the Phils and their opponents, the overall batting average at Baker Bowl that season was .350. Klein hit .439 at home, .332 away. The tall right-field barrier was made for doubles, both live and by ground rule, the latter coming when balls punched through the rusty metal wall and rattled to the ground behind, lost forever. Klein hit 59 doubles himself, and, playing right field, stymied many an opposing batter by becoming a ricochet artist. He had 44 assists, enough to divide in two and lead the league twice.

The Phils started the 1930 season with high hopes. Les Sweetland and Claude Willoughby had pitched well the season before, and Sweetland pitched a shutout to open the Phillie season. But he soon foundered, and poor Willoughby never got started. "He had pretty good stuff," Whitney recalls, "But when he had to pitch, he couldn't pitch. It was all-day baseball." Indeed, Sweetland and Willoughby held down so much combat duty on the mound that local sportswriters wove their names into a patriotic song:

> My country, 'tis of thee,
> Sweetland and Will-ough-by
> Of thee I sing.

For obvious reasons, sportswriters nicknamed Willoughby "Weeping Willie." He won 4 games that season and lost

17, with a 7.58 ERA. Sweetland was 7-15, 7.71.

Baker Bowl, since torn down, was not the only stadium of that era to favor hitters. In addition, gloves were small and primitive by today's standards, and pitching was less sophisticated. The slider was not in general use, and relief pitching was not used as effectively as it is today. Batting averages were boosted by a rule that counted as a sacrifice any fly ball that moved a runner up, and scoring by a rule that counted as a home run any drive that bounced into the stands.

Although these factors help explain the hitting of that era, they do not account for the extraordinary surge of 1930. Nor can it be said that major league hitters just had a hot year. Batting overwhelmed the minor leagues, too. Joe Hauser of Baltimore hit 63 home runs to establish an International League record that still stands, but it wasn't enough to win him a promotion to the major leagues, or even to earn him recognition as the best first baseman in the league. That honor went to Rip Collins of Rochester, who had only 40 homers but batted .376 with 180 RBIs.

According to survivors, the fuel behind the hitting binge of 1930 was in the ball. The stitches were low, almost countersunk, which kept pitchers from getting a good grip. The insides had been gradually pepped up for a decade, and in 1930 they reached such superball resiliency that Ring Lardner called it "a leather-covered sphere stuffed with dynamite."

Benge, the Phillie pitcher, first noticed that his infielders looked slow. They were, but the 1930 ball darted past even the fastest glovemen. Some were not so lucky. Fred Lindstrom of the Giants, a good enough third baseman to make the Hall of Fame, was knocked unconscious by a batted ball— not a line drive, but a grounder.

Lindstrom, too, noticed a difference early in the season, but from a happier perspective. He was hitting extraordinarily well, and so were his teammates. Indeed, Lindstrom batted .379 that season, far above his norm, and the Giants' team average was .319

Pitchers were intimidated. Joe Tinker, a star infielder for

the Cubs a generation before, noted that many pitchers were not following through. "Pitchers are afraid to get off-balance for fear they'll get killed when the ball comes back at them," Tinker said. "Sakes alive," recalls Benge, "that ball was so lively you'd throw it and look for a mole hole to get in."

The hitting prompted a lively debate. Ruppert, of all people, wanted less of it, although he had benefited greatly from the lively ball as the owner of the Yankees and the employer of Ruth. "I should like to see the spitball restored and the emery ball, too," Ruppert said, adding this scornful comment about a proposal designed to boost hitting even more: "Why, they have suggested someone hitting for the pitchers. Now, isn't that rich?"

John J. McGraw, nearing the end of his long managerial career with the Giants, suggested that the ball be deadened and the pitching distance reduced by a couple of feet. Otherwise, he said, no one would want to pitch. "Youngsters in the amateur ranks and on the sandlots no longer have ambitions to become pitchers," McGraw said. "They want to play some other position in which they can get by without being discouraged."

On the status quo side of things was Joe McCarthy, the Cubs' manager, who noted that the fans seemed to like high-scoring games. McCarthy, of course, had Wilson on his team.

The rabbit ball was not the only subject of controversy. Innovation comes hard to baseball, and in 1930 the major leagues grappled with all sorts of radical ideas. American League teams put numbers on the players' backs, but the National League held out; true fans were supposed to recognize their heroes at a glance.

Broadcasting of baseball games had begun in 1927, but three years later most teams still spurned it, fearing that fans would not buy tickets if they could listen free at home. The St. Louis teams adopted a middle ground: Allow broadcasts, but keep them dull. As the price of admission—it had not yet occurred to club owners that they could charge radio stations for the privilege—St. Louis broadcasters agreed to give a straight play-by-play, with no commentary. "This should be mutually satisfactory to both the fans and the magnates, for there are some announcers prone to wander far from the actual occurrences on the field," reported *The Sporting News*, which little knew how truly it spoke.

The most radical notion of all was night baseball, although it was not really a new idea. An amateur game was played under the lights in 1880, just a year after Edison invented the light bulb, and in 1896 Honus Wagner played a night game as a member of the Paterson, New Jersey, team of the Atlantic League. The exhibition was staged by none other than Ed Barrow, by 1930 the dignified business manager of the Yankees and a staunch opponent of night baseball—a position to which he was still clinging fifteen years later with the same prescience he brought to the subject of baseball salaries.

Legend has it that the first night game in Organized Baseball was played on May 2, 1930, at Des Moines, Iowa. In fact, Des Moines, of the Class A Western League, was beaten to the punch by Independence, Kansas, of the Class C Western Association. On April 28, the illuminated Independence Producers beat Muskogee, 12-2. Four days later, Des Moines played under what a local sportswriter called "33,000 candle power of mellow light," and scored 11 runs in the first inning en route to a 13-6 drubbing of Wichita. The game was attended by Cy Slapnicka, a Cleveland scout, who reported that he "did not see a man flinch from a ball, either batted or thrown."

The fans certainly did not flinch; more than 10,000 attended. The minor leagues, which had resisted night baseball for so long, now rushed to embrace it. By the end of May, twenty teams had lights or were installing them. Attendance doubled and tripled; it was a financial boost that the minors badly needed.

Cities that continued to hold out were scorned. Four of the six teams in the Piedmont League had lights by mid-July. The two that did not, Henderson and Raleigh, were not drawing as well at home, and asked for a visitors' cut of the gate receipts while on the road. The other four teams not only refused, but told Henderson and Raleigh to install lights or get out of the league. So much for tradition.

But the majors held fast. The only owner who favored night ball was Sam Breadon of the Cardinals, and his trial balloon was popped by Phil Ball, owner of the Browns and of the stadium where both teams played. The Browns could have used a boost; they drew barely a million fans *that decade*. But Ball was not alone. In the face of declining attendance during the Depression, this astonishing denial of self-interest was sustained by all sixteen teams until 1935, when the Reds installed lights and played the first major league night game.

Of course, the major leagues did not intentionally discourage fans. Teams were attracting thousands of new patrons with Ladies' Days, a promotion so successful that the Chicago Cubs, for one, had to cut it back. One day in the heat of the 1930 race Wrigley Field was virtually taken over by 31,000 ladies, all admitted free. But the owners, then as now, feared that change would alienate the "true fan," whoever he might be.

In 1930, the Cubs' true fans included men prominent in Chicago's flashiest business, bootlegging. Al Capone was a Cubs fan, and so was his rival, Bugs Moran. The Cubs used to put on an entertaining pregame show, with fancy fungo hitting and a razzmatazz infield drill, and the gangsters came early to see it. "They used to come out and watch us practice," recalls Charley Grimm, the Cub first baseman. "They'd sit right behind our bench, and there was never a peep out of them."

One day, however, Capone peeped at Gabby Hartnett, the Cubs' catcher, and Hartnett walked over to Capone's box to autograph a ball. A newspaper photographer happened to catch them, and the picture—the Cubs' star catcher smiling alongside the country's most notorious gangster—appeared in newspapers throughout the U.S. Commissioner Kenesaw Mountain Landis was outraged; he summoned Hartnett for a scolding and ordered the league presidents to forbid any conversation between players and spectators. Landis also told the teams to stop announcing the next day's starting pitchers, since that information was useful to gamblers, but sportswriters successfully protested that stricture, pointing out that if the Judge really wanted to keep gamblers in the dark he should keep the schedule a secret, too.

There was plenty to gamble on. The National League was enjoying a tight race among the Dodgers, Cubs, and Giants, and in August the Cardinals crowded in. They had improved their pitching by trading for Burleigh Grimes, who frightened batters by throwing at them and got them out with a spitball, mean but legal. The spitter had been banned in 1920, but seventeen pitchers who already used it in the majors were given a grandfather clause. By 1930, only four were left; Grimes, at thirty-six, was the youngest.

The Cardinal hitting was fearsome. George Watkins hit .373, a record that still stands for rookies, but he was platooned in right field with veteran Ray Blades, who hit .396. Landis made the Cards keep a young catcher, Gus Mancuso, who had run out of options, and injuries to Jimmie Wilson, the regular catcher, forced them to use him. Mancuso merely hit .366.

These players, however, were not the Cardinal stars. Frankie Frisch, Chick Hafey, Jim Bottomley, and Taylor Douthit combined to drive in 411 runs.

But the Cardinals were somewhat undisciplined. They returned home in early August from a discouraging and raucous road trip, Manager Gabby Street having fined several players for what *The Sporting News* called "indiscrepancies," and seemed out of contention. On August 9 they were twelve games out, in fourth place. But they took a home series from the Dodgers and took heart for the stretch drive with Brooklyn, the Cubs, and the Giants.

Zigging and zagging, the Dodgers lost nineteen of twenty-seven games, falling to fourth place, and then won eleven straight to regain the lead in September. All four contenders were thundering. With ten games to play the Cards crept to within a game of the Dodgers, and came into Brooklyn for three games. The Cubs, only a game and a half back, meantime tangled at the Polo Grounds with the Giants, who trailed by five and a half.

The Dodgers had the home crowd and the momentum of their winning streak, while the Cardinals suffered the sudden disappearance of one pitcher and a freak accident to another. The vanishing pitcher was Flint Rhem, of Rhems, South Carolina, a hard enough thrower to have won 20 games in 1926 and a hard enough drinker to have been farmed out in 1929. The Cardinals restored him to grace in 1930, and Rhem went into the Brooklyn series with six straight wins.

Rhem did not return to his hotel room the night before the first game, did not show up at the ballpark the next day, and became an object of concern. He reappeared a day later, and immediately was pressed by newsmen as to his whereabouts.

"He was befuddled," recalls his roommate, Bill Hallahan. But Rhem was not without imagination, and he seized upon a newsman's chance question to spin a tale appropriate to the era. *I was idling outside the hotel*, went Rhem's tale, *when this big, black limousine pulled up. A fellow beckoned me over, and when I came alongside these guys pulled guns and forced me into the car. They drove me to a secret hideaway and forced cups of raw whiskey down my throat. Oh cruel fate.* "Imagine kidnapping Flint Rhem," says Hallahan, "and *making* him take a drink!"

The same night that Rhem disappeared, Hallahan caught two fingers of his right hand in a taxi door. The injury was to his glove hand, and the next day, as Hallahan puts it, "I had the catcher throw the ball lightly." Hallahan threw the ball hard enough himself to have a no-hitter for 6⅔ innings. But the Cards had as much trouble with Dazzy Vance, who fanned 11. The game was a rare classic of pitching and defense, with Dodger bumbles thrown in.

Herman stopped a Cardinal rally in the fourth with a brilliant catch. With two out in the Cardinal sixth, Sparky Adams was perched on third. He dashed for home and had it stolen, but Vance cut short his windup and fired the ball at Hafey, who was batting. It hit him: Dead ball, batter to first, runner back to third. Watkins, the next batter, fouled out.

In the Dodger eighth, batter Finn missed a hit-and-run sign: the runner, Harvey Hendrick, was out at second. Finn then singled, tried to stretch it and crashed into Charlie

Gelbert, the Cardinal shortstop. Gelbert was knocked cold; Finn was safe but woozy. He tottered off second base and Hallahan picked up the loose ball and tagged him out.

With runners on first and second and none out in the home ninth, the Dodgers worked the right combination: a bunt, followed by a single. Trouble is, the bunt was popped to catcher Mancuso, who doubled the runner off second, and the single was wasted.

The Cardinals broke the scoreless tie in the tenth as pinch-hitter High doubled, went to third on Hallahan's bunt, and scored on a single by Douthit. In the home half, Brooklyn loaded the bases with one out; Lopez grounded hard to the left of Adams, who was then playing short. Adams knocked the ball down, picked it up, and flipped it to Frisch, who made a lightning pivot and barely nipped Lopez at first. Ebbets Field, recalls Hallahan, lapsed into sudden silence. The race was tied. The Giants meantime shoved the Cubs back, 7-0, on a three-hitter by Carl Hubbell.

The Cards won the next two with the Dodgers, and now had a two-game lead with seven to play. They won six of them, one a smooth 9-3 effort by Rhem at Baker Bowl. The Dodgers kept losing and finished fourth, behind the Cubs and Giants.

Pitching had largely decided the final games, and it dominated the World Series as well. Lefty Grove and George Earnshaw of the Athletics won the first two games, yeilding only three St. Louis runs; the Cards' Hallahan and Jesse Haines won the next two, the A's scoring only once. Neither team scored in the fifth game until Foxx homered off Grimes in the ninth. Earnshaw, having pitched seven innings of that game, came back to pitch all nine innings of the sixth and final contest, won by the A's, 7 to 1. The team batting averages were among the lowest on record—.197 for Philadelphia, .200 for St. Louis.

But who can blame the lumbermen if, after a long season of unprecedented exploits, their arms at last grew weary and their bats slow? Put October out of your mind; 1930 was The Year of the Hitter.

An occult story of star-crossed swingers.

A Tale of Two Sluggers: Roger Maris and Hack Wilson

Don Nelson

If you were asked what Hack Wilson and Roger Maris had in common, your reply might be: "Wilson holds the record for home runs in the National League, Maris has the American League record." That would be correct.

But are there other things? You might also say: "Roger holds a significant *major* league record—for home runs in a season—and Hack set one too, for runs batted in."

Fine. Anything else? "Well," you might go on, "each had his troubles after his big year (1930 for Wilson and 1961 for Maris), never getting anywhere near his great year again, and each retired at a relatively young age." You might also add, "and both were outfielders."

These similarities are the ones most readers would cite, but they are only the beginning.

Both players started their careers slowly, made a meteoric dash to fame, and then took a fast slide to retirement. Both

DON NELSON, former newspaperman and long-suffering Cub fan, has done extensive research on home run hitters.

spent 12 years in the big leagues. Both reached the majors in their 23rd year. Wilson played his last major league game in 1934 at age *34*; *34* years later, in 1968, Maris played his last season, also at age 34.

Each had his second-best home-run output the year before his big campaign and each hit exactly 39 home runs in that year. More coincidental yet, each had a teammate club one more homer in the season previous to the Big One. Rogers Hornsby hit 40 for the Cubs in 1929. Mickey Mantle cracked the same number—40 for the Bronx Bombers—to lead the league in 1960.

Similarities enough? No. I'm just warming up. When Maris clouted his 61, teammate Mantle also had his greatest home-run season—hitting 54. Wilson also had a teammate enjoying his greatest long-ball year—Gabby Hartnett connected for a career-high 37 round-trippers the same year Wilson lifted 56. The Maris-Mantle total of 115 homers is the American and major league season record for two players on the same club. Wilson and Hartnett's 93 are the most ever hit by two Naitonal League teammates in a season.

I mentioned Wilson's major league record of 190 RBIs in 1930. Hack led the league that year and also the year before, when he drove 159 across. Maris also led the league in the year before THE year and topped that with 142 to lead the league and set a personal high in 1961. Neither ever led the league in RBIs in any other year.

Not surprisingly, Maris and Wilson set several other personal highs in their record-shattering years. Besides home runs and RBIs, Wilson had his highest batting average and most games played, at-bats, runs, home-run percentage, bases on balls, slugging average, and hits. Maris also had personal highs in games, at-bats, runs, home-run percentage, bases on balls, slugging average, and hits, though he did match his at-bat total the next season. Maris tied for the league lead in runs, in addition to his HR and RBI titles. Wilson also had league leaderships besides HRs and RBIs in 1930 (home-run percentage, bases on balls, slugging average), but two of them weren't the most coveted achievements— Hack led the league in striking out and outfield errors.

To continue. Both were about the same threat to poke it out of the park: Hack's career homers-to-at-bats ratio was 1 to 19.5; Rogers rate was 1 homer for every 18.5 official plate appearances. They had about the same totals for walks (Wilson 674, Maris 652) and strikeouts (Maris 733, Wilson 713).

Both started and closed their careers with teams other than those with which they achieved stardom—Maris was with the Indians and the A's before putting on the Yankee pinstripes; he was traded to the Cardinals for his last two years. Wilson began as a Giant and closed out with the Dodgers and Phillies (he spent a year in the minors before he called it quits). Each played for pennant winners other than his principal team—Maris on the '67 and '68 Cards; Wilson on the '24 Giants.

Perhaps most puzzling about the careers of both men is that their historic feats have failed to win them lasting admiration, even among their own fans. Wilson's achievement of 56 homers, though a National League record that has endured for 52 years, couldn't have been too thrilling at the time, coming so soon after Ruth had blasted 60 (and also 59 and 54 twice). Besides, Hack came off as somewhat of a heavy. At 5'6" and 190 pounds with a size 5½ shoe, he was no Frank Merriwell glamourboy, and he had problems with booze. Maris was considered by some to be more of a villain than a hero for his 1961 triumphs. Many pointed out that Rog had the benefit of a 162-game schedule and expansion teams to face in cracking Ruth's mark. And, to add insult to injury, he had the audacity to overshadow the long-ball feats of a latter-day Yankee favorite—Mantle—at the same time he was violating the immortal Ruth's 60-homer record.

It remains to be seen if Maris will ever have his name enshrined in the Hall of Fame. Wilson's name waited more than four decades to be cast in bronze at Cooperstown.

Certainly not everything about these two ill-fated athletes

supplies such fascinating parallels. Wilson hit for a higher career average (.307) than Maris (.260). Maris never batted .300 in the majors—.283 in 1960 was his best. Wilson topped the magic .300 mark five times; his best year was his big year, 1930, when he averaged .356. However, considering the eras in which they performed, their relative batting averages are not too far apart. During Wilson's career, the average National Leaguer batted .283. In Maris's time, the average ballplayer batted 33 points less (.250). Wilson was 8.5 percent better than the average batter of his time, Maris 4 percent better than his peers.

There are many other differences, statistical, physical, temperamental. But this piece is about similarities. Ready for some more?

Wilson had more home runs in his one great year than in his first four major league seasons or his last four; he hit more than half of his career homers in the three consecutive seasons of 1928 through 1930. Maris's home-run career fits the same mold: he had more round-trippers in 1961 than in his first three seasons and as many as in his last five; he also hit almost half of his career home runs in three consecutive campaigns—1960 through 1962.

Wilson closed out his career with only 15 four-baggers in his last two seasons (9 and 6) and Maris followed suit with 14 (9 and 5).

And then there was ... What? "Stop!" did you say? "Hold it! That's enough!" O.K., if you say you're convinced of the connection; but there's more....

As in Harry Perkowski, the brightest star in this lad's firmament.

I Remember Harry

Robert Cole

That summer of 1949, at twelve, I got closer to baseball. I carried a ball and glove in the car in case I met someone who wanted to play. I judged people by their baseball connections: if they didn't have any, they weren't interesting to me. One of my grandmother's neighbors, Mr. Martin, took on new stature when I learned that he was the famous Horsey Martin who pitched softball for Appalachian Electric Power Company in the City League of Beckley, West Virginia. I wouldn't have guessed: he looked just like an ordinary guy—square, ruddy face, wore gold-rimmed glasses, never said much. But now I always spoke to him. He still never said much.

If I wanted to play baseball, there was only one place in Beaver I really could count on it; up on Tank Branch Hill with the Wills boys, Jack and Jeep. Almost no one else would play—they called it hardball, and it hurt your hands—

ROBERT COLE is an associate professor of English and is writing a book about growing up in West Virginia.

so the three of us would go up the road from the Wills home and climb over the fence into Old Man Wolfe's field. Sometimes we could con another boy or two into playing, but we rarely had more than a pitcher, two fielders, and two batters. So we played a simplified version of the game, called Straight Base, or Move Up. If you hit the ball, you had to run through the pitcher's area and be safe at second base, or lose your bats. If you got to second, you had to get back home on the next batted ball, or you were forced out. There was no first base, at least not off at a ninety-degree angle to home. When you made out, you were "last man in the field," and all the other fielders moved up a position closer to batting. However, a fielder could go directly to batter if he caught a fly.

Usually we "threw easy" to each other, like batting practice, so we could hit the ball. That was the most fun. But one day Bobby Meadows, a big boy from down the road, wanted to play and impress us with his fastball. It wasn't that fast, but it was too fast for us, and he looked at you with disgust if you didn't swing, although a lot of his pitches weren't within reach. That day was no fun. Nor was it if Paul Pendleton was there: he was a blank-looking little blond boy who wouldn't swing at any "dead pitch" because his brother Mason told him not to. That meant I couldn't use my Gene Bearden knuckleball.

Lots of times we didn't play Move Up, but just shared the joy of chasing flies. I hated to waste any chance to catch one. It irritated me greatly to see the fungo-hitter try to hit a throw as it bounced in from the outfield, because he almost always sliced it off to the side, and we just had to waste time chasing a foul ball. No one liked chasing grounders, and anyone (such as I) who couldn't consistently hit fungoes took a lot of heat. We also shared the suffering of stoved fingers, usually thumbs, when we let a fly hit wrong on our tiny gloves.

As summer went on, nature shut our games down. Old Man Wolfe didn't mow his field, and by late July the outfield grass was knee-high. Chasing a fly was like splashing after a ball in a pool. We would have to retreat to Jack's front yard and just "pass some ball." There wasn't another convenient field big enough for baseball. On Sunday drives with my family, I began a quest for the ideal available field, evaluating all the vacant lots and pastures I saw. "There's a good one, grassy and level," I would think, or "we could play there: no one could hit it out," or "too bad that one's got a stream running through it," and so on, adjusting sizes, building fences, trimming grass, landscaping, and laying out diamonds in my mind.

I was particularly enamored of a field near Hedricktown, the shanty part of Beaver. This field was long and wide and dignified and sloped gently up toward a small hill. Part of the slope now was covered with small evergreens, but it was easy to imagine the baseball field they said used to be there, where the old town team played and people had picnics and watched on Sunday afternoons. What happened to it, I wondered. Why did it stop? Why can't it come back? Is everybody hiding something about baseball? I felt so alone. It was only about a hundred yards from the main road, but somehow I never walked over to inspect it closely. It was just *there*, like the background landscape in a comic strip, the cactus in "Red Ryder" or the stick palm trees in "Popeye" or the "Katzenjammer Kids."

At home, the most relief I could get from my itch for baseball was to throw a ball up in the air and catch it. My oldest brother was only seven, not worth throwing to. He wasn't interested anyway. At least once a week I might have the treat of a visit from Bill Brown, the deliveryman for Kester's Dry Cleaners. He had been a friend of Dad's for a long time, and always spoke to me in a friendly way, but paid more attention to me when Dad told him I had become a baseball fan. Bill was a fan of long standing, and loved to share his memories with me, but wasn't condescending. He would drive up in his bright red panel truck and stop on a summer day and talk baseball. He was a bald, tanned man with a heavily lined face that held a grin a long time as he told me baseball stories. His gold teeth would show, too, as we sat in the shade of the front porch and talked. He looked like I thought a baseball manager should. Bill used to take the C & O excursions to Cincinnati and see the Reds. Once he said he saw Eddie Miller, playing shortstop for the Reds, run way down the left-field line and catch a foul fly over his shoulder. "They had these wooden folding chairs down there for the bullpen crew to sit on when they weren't working," Bill said, "and Eddie caught the ball just before he got to the chairs. He caught it, and whirled around and sat right down in one of the chairs. People gave him a big hand."

I liked that story because Eddie Miller, now near the end of his career, was a utility infielder for the Phillies, my NL favorites because of young Robin Roberts. I could see Miller making the catch. It was a sunny day, an afternoon game. Bill also told me that while most people thought of Ralph Kiner only as a home run hitter, he once saw Kiner hit five straight singles in a game. "Little humpback liners," Bill said, "just right over the infield and sharp down into the grass—zing! zing!" He made a quick horizontal and downward motion with his cupped hand. He said Kiner could have been a percentage hitter if he had wanted to be, but there was more money in hitting home runs. I knew Kiner's famous remark about singles hitters driving Fords and home-run hitters driving Cadillacs.

Although the major leagues played on into October, local baseball and softball tended to wrap up by mid-August, because so many of the players and coaches had to turn to preparing for the really big sport in the area—football. High school practice started the Monday closest to the middle of August. Bones Bragg was going to be a freshman at Shady Springs High School that fall, so he went out for football. One day that August of 1949 I was playing in the front yard when I saw Bones strutting down the railroad track, coming home from football practice, carrying his cleats over his shoulder by the laces, neatly tied together. He said he was the starting center on the freshman team, and invited me to do some pushups with him. I didn't know how. He put on his cleats, dropped down in the yard and briskly dipped through a dozen or so. I tried, but couldn't lift my body off the ground. "Jesus, Bobby," Bones warned me, very seriously, "you're gonna have to learn to do pushups if you want to play football." Yeah, I said. Bones had wounded my confidence again.

Seventh grade started and as a veteran, I began to assume some position of authority on the recess softball field. I also followed the major league season through the World Series, and although I wasn't excited about the Series, I hated to see the season end. I wasn't prepared for the delightful surprise that followed for me a week later. Harry Perkowski, the Reds' rookie, was going to pitch in Beckley! The lead on the story in the Raleigh *Register* read:

> Local fans will get a chance to see a big leaguer in action Sunday. The occasion will be a game between the Eccles Admirals, champions of the Raleigh County Baseball League, and the Raleigh Clippers, who claim the Southern West Virginia Negro title, Sunday afternoon at 2:30 at Clipper Park on the Stanaford road.

Boy, this game had it all—the only local boy in the big leagues, the best team in the county league (whose games Dad wouldn't let me attend because all the teams were from coal towns, and he thought the crowds would be too rough), and a hotshot black team. My first baseball game. The ballpark was out behind Beckley Open Air Theatre. My best friend Jack Wills and I went, and the day was miserable, cold and damp. To my surprise, there wasn't a very big crowd. We stood along the sidelines behind the dugout between first and home, because we'd read that was the best place to watch a game. Actually the "dugout" was just a small structure with a roof and chickenwire sides, and benches inside. It enabled us to watch the players closely, and I didn't like what I saw: all they did was clean mud from their spikes and smoke cigarettes constantly, taking a few puffs off one and then throwing it on the ground, like the way Dad used to drop cigarettes and ashes on the floor at

home when he'd rest on the couch in the middle room in the
evening when he got home from the mines. I thought
players were not supposed to smoke.

Even Harry Perkowski smoked. But he pitched beautifully, and we were perfectly located to watch him, because he
was a lefthander. We were so close and he looked so big in
his Cincinnati road uniform and blue cap with the red
pointed "C." He was so smoothe and longstriding in his
follow-through, so attentive to his work, so straight and
square in his posture. The other players would watch him
and talk among themselves. He pitched five innings of
scoreless ball, allowed three hits—one by Sonny Watts of
the Birmingham Black Barons—struck out five, walked
none, then moved over to first base. Okey Mills, the county
sheriff and the Admirals' star pitcher, finished up, and he
held on for the win, 5-3.

Harry, a strong lefthanded hitter, helped with the scoring,
too, hitting a towering home run in the fifth. The bat
whipped into an uppercut and the ball, white, shot high,
very high, darkening, angling sharply up from the cold mud
of the field, up toward the chill gray glare of the sky, a little
dot disappearing black into the woods beyond center field.

The *Register* next day said the fences all were 500 feet
away, but Bob Wills, the sports editor, asked Pat Salango, a
Stanaford engineer, to measure the home-run distance with
his engineering tape. Salango said it was 420 feet to where
the ball cleared the fence and 453 feet to where three
eyewitnesses said Harry's homer landed. Bob looked in the
record book and deduced that the homer would have left all
but four of the fourteen major league parks at their longest
point from home plate. Best he could find, Babe Ruth
supposedly hit a 500-foot home run during spring training in
1913 and Jimmie Foxx hit one 550 feet in a league game.
"So, after all," Bob concluded, "history wasn't made
Sunday. But—that boy can still wallop the apple." And I
had been there.

And on top of that, I was going to meet Harry Perkowski.
Montgomery Ward's had hired him to work in the sporting
goods department for the winter, and one Saturday soon

after the home run, Dad, 35, took me uptown to meet Harry, 27. We got there early in the morning and Harry was along in sporting goods, wearing a brown suit, looking tall and strong. The space vanished between us. "Harry, this is my boy," Dad said, smiling with his lips bunched together. Harry, looking serious, reached out and politely shook hands with me. Seconds stretched. Words floated in jello. We left. "I met Harry Perkowski," I boasted to Jack Wills. No one else would have cared to know.

The Thomson Homer? The Merkle Blunder?
Larsen's Gem? The ancient scrivener
picks 'em.

Baseball's Greatest Games

Frederick G. Lieb

In addition to 1976 being the Nation's Bicentennial, it also
is a big year for celebration in each of America's major
baseball organizations. The venerable National League, being
born in New York, February 2, 1876, is celebrating its
proud centennial. Its once upstart junior, the American
League, is accepting congratulations on surviving 75 tem-
pestuous seasons.

With changes in frontiers and franchises in the early years
and later in the last generation, baseball fans have attended
thousands of games and have seen even more ballplayers. In
the parade of games, which particular game stood out above
all others? It had to be a game of vital concern to the game's
statistics, but even more it had to be a contest that touched
all the gamuts of human emotions, intense partisan loyalty,

FRED LIEB wrote this piece in mid-1976. Had he lived to update it in
1987, might he have included the deciding game of the 1986 World Series?
Or Game 6, played the night before? Or the deciding game of the 1980
National League Championship Series? Or the 1978 American League East
playoff? Lieb's reporting career lasted some 70 years—JT.

the deepest of hatreds, bribery, a threat of mayhem and even a suicide of a major league executive. All of these things were wrapped up in the emotions of one game.

For my No. 1 game of the last 100 years I must pick a contest played at the old New York Polo Grounds early in the present century. It was a post season playoff between John McGraw's scrappy New York Giants and Frank Chance's brilliant, wily Chicago Cubs, winners of 116 NL games in 1906, 107 in 1907, and a strong contender with New York and Pittsburgh for the 1908 pennant.

Of course, picking the greatest game must depend a lot on personal opinion or prejudice, also on how many games you have seen or know about. I am sure that by my picking the 1908 Cub-Giant playoff game as No. 1, some of the younger fans will say: "The old geezer picks a game we know nothing about. We haven't even heard of it."

Present-day fans can only guess of the heated atmosphere in which this game was played. It came at a time when baseball still was undisputed king of American sports. In the spring and summer, baseball received more than three-fourths of the space in the nation's sports pages. It yielded somewhat to college football in the fall, but in winter, baseball still got a third to a half of the space alloted to sports.

Golf and tennis then were largely amateur events, getting real space only when they had their annual championships. Pro football was played mainly in Ohio and western Pennsylvania. College football centered around Yale, Harvard, and Princeton in the East and Michigan and the University of Chicago in the Middle West. Basketball was a lesser sport played by high schools and colleges between the football and baseball seasons. Big championship boxing matches were fought in mining towns in Nevada and other out-of-the-way places and not in major cities.

As a consequence, the baseball world championships and the two major league pennants were the most cherished sports prizes. A lot of people did not go to ballgames by today's standards, but among the sporting fraternity, they knew all the players, and what they did from day to day.

The 1908 playoff was not a ballgame between respected opponents such as the Reds and Red Sox in the 1975 World Series, but it was war between the cities of New York and Chicago, the cities, teams, and followers. All over the country, fans backed either the Cubs or Giants, with the majority supporting Frank Chance's well-oiled machine.

The hatreds and ill feeling all started with an earlier Chicago-New York game at the Polo Grounds, September 23, 1908. At the time the top contenders, Giants, Cubs and Pirates, were running almost neck and neck. In this particular game, the score was 2-2 in the New York half of the ninth inning. There were two out, Harry "Moose" McCormick was the Giant runner on third base and Fred Merkle, the rookie, was on first base, when little Giant shortstop Al Bridwell smacked a clean single over second base, permitting McCormick to score the apparent winning run. The crowd surged on the playing field, as that was the quickest way to the exits leading to the trolley cars and the Sixth Avenue "L" trains.

However, things still were happening on the ballfield. Artie Hofman, skillfull Cub center fielder, fielded Bridwell's hit and threw in the general direction of second base. The alert Cubs had observed that young Merkle, instead of running down to second base after Bridwell's hit, had dashed off to the center-field clubhouse. New York's iron man, Joe McGinnity, struggled with shortstop Joe Tinker for the ball thrown in by Hofman. Joe, suspecting that the Cubs were after a force play on Merkle at second, won possession of the ball and threw it deep into the left-field bleachers.

Then there was another odd development. Floyd Kroh, a second-string Cub pitcher, rolled another ball on the ground from the Cub bench to Johnny Evers, standing at second base. Johnny claimed a force play on Merkle, and umpire Hank O'Day, standing near the bag, called Merkle out, nullifying McCormick's run.

The Cubs were ready to go to bat in the tenth inning, but by this time most of the 20,000 people who had watched the game were on the playing field. The Giants' management made no effort to clear the field, and Charley Murphy,

Chicago club owner, immediately called for a 9-0 forfeit victory. However, John T. Brush, Giant president, and manager John McGraw, ridiculed the antics of the Cubs after Bridwell's "winning hit," and insisted their team had won fairly on the playing field. They dismissed Merkle's failure to tag second as not being relevant. When the winning run is scored, "that's the end of the game."

As Merkle's failure to touch second became more and more damaging to the Giants' cause, he became "Bonehead" Merkle, an unfair nickname that followed him to the end of his career. However, I always have felt that Manager McGraw was partly to blame. A fortnight before the Merkle play in New York, Evers had tried the same play in the ninth inning of a game the Cubs lost in Pittsburgh. The umpire in chief was Hank O'Day. As the winning Pittsburgh run was scoring from third base a young player named Gill also failed to tag second with two out. When Evers and Chance argued that the side had been retired by a force play on Gill, O'Day said, "I had my back turned to the play, and did not see it. But, if such a play comes up in the future, I will look for it, and call it accordingly."

With this warning from O'Day, McGraw should have drilled all of his players, especially the youngsters, to be sure to touch the bag ahead in all situations.

League president Harry Pulliam ruled the September 23 game a 2-2 tie, and ordered that it be replayed the day following the last game of the schedule if it were needed to determine the winner. The league board of directors supported Pulliam in this decision, but it was stubbornly fought by John Brush of New York, who still considered the game of September 23 a Giant win and that "neither Pulliam, nor the board of directors could steal this victory from the Giants."

The National League ended its regular season on October 3, in the West, and October 7, in the East, as there then was Sunday ball only in Chicago, St. Louis, and Cincinnati. As the western clubs finished on a Sunday the Cubs were 98-53, and the Giants were 95-53. They still had to play three games with Joe Kelley's Boston Braves. Kelley had been a teammate of McGraw's on the Baltimore NL champions of 1894-5-6. One Boston win in the three games would kill off the Giants' chance to get into a playoff, but the Giants swept all three games without using their ace, Christy Mathewson, by scores of 5-1, 5-1, and 8-1. Both top contenders now were 98-55, and the October 8 game therefore was not only a replay of the Merkle game but also the playoff for the pennant.

Jim Johnstone and Bill Klem were assigned as the National League umpires. While Klem was walking on Madison Avenue near his hotel on the night before the big game, a man emerged from one of the brownfront houses with a fat roll of bills in his hands saying to Klem, "The Giants mustn't lose tomorrow."

Klem pushed him away and said, "Get away from me, you bum." As Klem walked through one of the subterranean passages under the old wooden Polo Grounds stands the next day, he again was approached by the man with the big roll of bills. Again, he muttered, "Take these, Bill; the Giants mustn't lose." "Get out of my way; you stink," said Klem.

Of course, Klem was not to be corrupted. He was an umpire who regarded his craft as something almost sacred. An investigation after the playoff game came up with a statement that the attempted briber was a part-time trainer and early osteopathic doctor of the Giants named "Doc" Cramer. The National League ruled that Cramer would be barred for life from all National League parks.

Most of the seats at the Polo Grounds then were unreserved, and crowds gathered around the Harlem field as early as daybreak. Though the game was scheduled for 3 P.M., the New York police closed the gates to all but reserved ticket-holders at 1:30, and even those with reserved seats had difficulty in getting in. They jammed Eighth Avenue and streets near the Polo Grounds. Some of the most daring somehow scaled the fence and climbed into the center-field bleachers.

Others produced some sort of a battering ram, and knocked several boards loose in the center-field fence. Fans poured through the gap in the fence until some of the grounds crew, aided by New York firemen, repelled the freeloaders by squirting water on them with fire hoses.

When it came time for the Cubs to take infield practice, Chance led his players on the playing field while the Giants continued with their batting practice. McGinnity, who was batting out fungoes, refused to yield his position at the plate. It was then that McGinnity and Chance had their confrontation. There was some pushing, and both men swung. It later developed that this was all according to Giant plans. The strong McGinnity was supposed to pick a fight with Chance, and work him over to the point that he would be unable to play. It didn't work, as Chance protected himself and in the game whacked out two doubles and a single and drove in two runs.

Even though McGraw rested Mathewson through the three-game Brave series, the big righthander was overworked and tired. He already had won 37 games for the Giants in 1908. That morning he told his wife, "Jane, my arm is as heavy and stiff as a board. I've got to tell McGraw I can't work, and to pitch Hooks Wiltse or Red Ames." However, when Matty told McGraw of his ailments, the Little Napoleon replied, "You've simply got to pitch, Matty. Sore, or lame arm, you still are the best I have. I wouldn't entrust this game to anyone else." So Big Six was the Giant starter.

Chance's starting pitcher was his lefthander, Jack Pfiester. He was a Giant hoodoo, and was called "Jack, the Giant Killer" because of his ability to beat New York. But, this day he did no Giant-killing. He got in trouble in the very first inning when the Giants picked up an early run and should have had more. Chance quickly turned to his old reliable, Mordecai Brown, to silence the Manhattan bats. The former coal miner gave up only four hits and one run the rest of the way.

The Cubs struck hard against Mathewson, in their big third inning, when they did all their scoring. Joe Tinker led off the inning for Chicago. Though Joe was only a .260 hitter, he was Christy's most difficult out. He started the victory ball with a triple over Cy Seymour's head. Kling quickly brought home Tinker with a single to left. Brown sacrificed Kling to second, and Sheckard lifted an outfield floater for the second out.

Then came an unhappy ten minutes for New York's beloved Matty. He made a mistake by walking Johnny Evers, and then Frank Schulte and Frank Chance crashed successive doubles, bringing in Kling, Evers, and Schulte, four runs for the inning.

The Cubs spent the rest of the game in defending their lead. Mathewson allowed no further scoring in his next four innings, and Wiltse pitched runless ball in the eighth and ninth.

New York fans had one last time to shout. They almost raised the roof of the old wooden grandstand when in the seventh they filled the bases with none out on singles by Art Devlin and McCormick and a base on balls to Al Bridwell. But the promising inning flickered out with only one run. A limping Larry Doyle (he was just recovering from a broken leg) batted for Matty and raised a dinky little foul to catcher Kling. Devlin scored on Tenney's sacrifice fly but the crowd gave a cry of despair when Tinker threw out Herzog for the third out. After getting out of this tough inning, ''Brownie'' retired the Giants in order in the eighth and ninth innings.

The Cubs won the game, 4-2, making it three straight flags, and they went on to beat Detroit in the 1908 World Series, four games to one. But it didn't end the bitterness, backbiting and vicious criticism of league president Harry Pulliam, who disallowed what the Giants considered a legitimate 3-2 victory, and made possible the playoff defeat, and loss of the pennant.

The National League and the Giants had offices in the same building, the St. James Building at 26th Street and Broadway. The two offices became hostile camps. Pulliam was booed when he walked along Broadway, attended the theater, or sporting events. ''I won the 1908 National League fairly and honestly on the ball field, but was skeedaddled out of it in the league's head office,'' McGraw protested, and his fellow members of the Lambs Club all felt the same way.

Pulliam took this sharp criticism through the winter of 1908-09, but when it carried into the 1909 season he fretted and worried. His physician in New York told him to take a trip to Atlantic City, to forget all about baseball, and let John Heydler, the league secretary-treasurer, run the every-day duties of the office. In a fit of despondency on July 4, 1909, Pulliam took his own life by firing a bullet into his brain in his Atlantic City hotel room.

I am sure many fans will be surprised that I did not pick as my first choice the final game of the 1951 NL playoff series between the New York Giants and Brooklyn Dodgers at the Polo Grounds. I'll admit that this game, known as the Bobby Thomson home run game, was more spectacular in itself. However, in my mind, it did not have the intriguing background, the intense national rivalry, and the lasting ramifications.

I don't mean to minimize the Giant-Dodger rivalry, which was substantial in the New York area. In 1951, the Giants, managed by Leo Durocher, trailed Brooklyn by 13½ games in mid-August, but thanks to a 15-game winning streak in September, they tied the "Bums" on the last day of the season. This necessitated a three-game playoff. The Giants won the first game in Ebbets Field 3-1, but the Dodgers stormed back with heavy artillery at the Polo Grounds, winning 10-0 behind Clem Labine.

In the third game, also played in New York, it was a 1-1 pitching duel for seven innings between Sal Maglie and Don Newcombe, the Brooklyn ace. However, the Dodgers apparently tore the game apart with three runs in the eighth, and they began counting their World Series dollars.

Newcombe hastily retired the Giants in the second half of the eighth, and three runs behind in the ninth, the Durocher cause looked rather hopeless. Don had yielded only four hits up to this point, but there was a glimmer of hope when Alvin Dark led off the Giant ninth with an infield hit. Another single by Don Mueller sent Dark to third. After Monte Irvin popped out, Whitey Lockman doubled to left, scoring Dark. Mueller suffered an ankle injury sliding into third, and was replaced by Clint Hartung.

At this point, Dodger manager Chuck Dressen had to make an important decision—to let Newcombe stay in the game or to bring in one of several hurlers warming up in the bullpen. He decided to yank Don and signaled for Ralph Branca, who, a few years before, had been Brooklyn's top hurler. Ralph did little pitching. He served over one called strike to Bobby Thomson, but the Manhattan Scot drove the next pitch high into the left-field bleachers.

It was "the shot heard round the world" as the score quickly changed from 4-1 Brooklyn to the dramatic final count of 5-4 New York. It was one of the historic blows of the first 100 years of big league baseball.

If the fan is a pitching nut, he may prefer the double no-hitter on May 2, 1917 between Cincinnati's righthanded Fred Toney, the "man-mountain of Tennessee," and the equally large lefty of Chicago, Jim "Hippo" Vaughn. In the regulation nine innings, neither of these heavyweights gave up the semblance of a hit at Wrigley Field. The break came in the tenth inning, when the weak-hitting Larry Kopf opened with a roller to the right side which got between two former New York Giants, Larry Doyle at second, and Fred Merkle at first. Vaughn then disposed of Greasy Neale with an outfield fly to Cy Williams for the second out. But Williams then muffed Hal Chase's line drive, and Kopf streaked to third. With Jim Thorpe, the Indian football and track star at bat, Chase stole second. Thorpe hit a high chopper in front of the plate which bounced high for Vaughn. Seeing he could not catch the speedy Thorpe at first, Vaughn threw home, which caught catcher Art Wilson off guard. The ball went through him and Kopf scored for a 1-0 victory. Thorpe was credited with a hit and an RBI. Toney pitched another hitless frame for a 10-inning no-hitter.

Among the other great games, I would have to include the October 2, 1908, pitching duel between Addie Joss of Cleveland, who pitched a perfect game, and Ed Walsh of the White Sox, who fanned 15 while giving up only four hits. Joss won, 1-0. Another contest involving a perfect game was Don Larsen's gem against Brooklyn on October 8, 1956. Not to be forgotten was the strong lineup the

Yankee hurler was facing that day—players like Robinson, Hodges, Snider, Furillo, Campanella, and Reese. Another outstanding World Series game was the one featuring the 1960 home run by Bill Mazeroski which gave the Pirates the title over the Yankees.

Three All-Star Games also have high spots on the writer's list of outstanding games. First is the familiar 1934 contest where the Giants' brilliant meal ticket, Carl Hubbell, struck out Ruth, Gehrig, Foxx, Simmons, and Cronin in succession. But with Mel Harder's fine relief pitching, the American Leaguers still pulled it out 9-7 at the expense of Van Mungo and Dizzy Dean.

The second mid-summer classic I have fond recollections of was the July 8, 1941, game where young Ted Williams broke up the game with a three-run homer to give the American League a 7-5 win. I can still see Ted dancing around the bases with all his youthful exuberance when he hit that homer in Detroit.

An All-Star homer dearer to National League fans was one hit in old Comiskey Park, Chicago, on July 11, 1951. At that time the American League had won 12 games to 4 for the NL, and it looked like the usual pattern would be followed with the AL leading 3-2 after eight innings. The late Arthur Daley, then the sports columnist for the *New York Times* and a National League partisan, said sadly in the Chicago press box, "No matter what the National League does, it just doesn't seem possible for it to win any of these games."

Hardly had he made the remark than Pittsburgh slugger Ralph Kiner tied the game with a homer into the left-field stands. Five innings later, Red Schoendienst hit another four-bagger in the same general area to give the Nationals a 4-3 win. It marked the end of AL dominance in All-Star play. From that time on, the NL has dominated to the extent that the Junior Circuit has won only six games in a quarter-century. The 1951 game was the turning point.

In conclusion, I should be allowed one sentimental choice, or so it may seem. Actually, this was a historic game in that it virtually assured the Yankees of their first pennant. It was a contest between the World Champion Cleveland Indians and the challenging New Yorkers on September 26, 1921. It was the last meeting of the two clubs for the season, and followed a 20-5 thrashing which the crew of Miller Huggins took the day before.

A sellout crowd of 40,000 packed the Polo Grounds to see Babe Ruth hit two homers and a double and George Burns hit a triple and three singles to lead the Yankees to a come-from-behind 8-7 victory. There was great tension and pressure, particularly in the ninth inning when the Indians loaded the bases. Yankee club president Jake Ruppert couldn't take it and retreated from the press box. He missed the most dramatic play of the game as the count went to 3 and 2 on batter Steve O'Neill. He could barely see the tricky underhand delivery of Carl Mays in the evening dusk and fanned on a pitch that was almost in the dirt. From the yelling of the crowd, Ruppert knew his club had triumphed. That put the Yanks a game and a half up, a lead they held for the rest of the final week of the season. It gave them the right to meet their landlords, the Giants, in the historic 1921 World Series.

Considering the way the Yankees dominated the American League and baseball in general over the next 40-odd years, the September 26, 1921, triumph over the Indians merits inclusion among the outstanding games of the last 100 years.

BASEBALL RHYME TIME

Eddie Gold

Rod Carew, Vida Blue, and Big Klu
Connie Mack, Stan Hack, Max Flack
Guy Bush, Emil Kush, Heinie Manush
Joe Rudi, Lyle Judy, and Howdy Doody

Ty Cobb, Scotty Robb, Rusty Staub
Rip Sewell, Bob Buhl, Joe Kuhel
Hank Bauer, Vic Power, Hank Sauer
Tris Speaker, Roy Meeker, and a streaker

Lyn Lary, Charlie Berry, Gaylord Perry
Jimmie Foxx, Johnny Knox, Billy Cox
Bill Terry, Max Carey, Larry Sherry
Mel Ott, Dick Drott, and I forgot

Tommy Tucker, Earl Brucker, Johnny Rucker
George Case, ElRoy Face, Hal Chase
Ernie Koy, Dummy Hoy, and Nap Lajoie
Or is it La-sho-aye and Bordagaray

Gene Dale, Larry McPhail, Bad News Hale
Ray Narleski, Hank Majeski, Johnny Pesky
Bucky Harris, Dave Ferris, Roger Maris
Dick Sharon, Henry Aaron, and Red Barron

Boccabella, Campanella, and Don Gardella
Ferris Fain, Sugar Cain, Johnny Sain
Alvin Dark, Fred Clarke, Dolly Stark
Poffenberger, Raffensberger, Wally Berger

Pete Rose, Billy Loes, Mike de la Hoz
Boots Day, Carlos May, Pete Gray
Herman Franks, Howard Shanks, Ernie Banks
Bunny Brief, George Strief, and good grief

Lou Brock, Wes Stock, and Ray Kroc
Buddy Myer, Eddie Dyer, Jim McGuire
Wally Post, Lou Tost, Eddie Yost
Gus Bell, George Kell, and William Tell

Ford Frick, Sammy Vick, Elmer Flick
Dick Hall, Gabe Paul, Chick Stahl
Bobby Doerr, Ernie Shore, Herb Score
Alex the Great, Bennie Tate, and Watergate

Dizzy Dean, Dick Green, Harvey Kuenn
George Dauss, Les Moss, and Buck Ross
Don Baylor, Rollie Naylor, Dummy Taylor
Henry Sage, Satchel Paige, and old age

Tom Seaver, Buck Weaver, Sam Leever
Walter Johnson, Stan Bahnsen, Evar Swanson
Ralph Garr, Jim Barr, Ray Starr
Billy Sunday, Rick Monday, and Tuesday Weld

Bobby Tolan, Gary Nolan, Cozy Dolan
Norm Cash, Billy Nash, Herb Hash
Harry Brecheen, Frank Gustine, Claude Osteen
Joe Lutz, Clyde Kluttz, and aw nuts

Billy Southworth, Jimmy Bloodworth, Jim Duckworth
Bob Feller, Hod Eller, King Kong Keller
Frank Hayes, Willie Mays, and Van Robays
Dom diMaggio, Vince diMaggio, and the other one

Mordecai Brown, Turk Lown, Clyde Shoun
Bill Veeck, Dave Schneck, Boom Boom Beck
Boog Powell, Dixie Howell, Bama Rowell
Branch Rickey, Bill Dickey, and Mantle Mickey

George Halas, Pat Corrales, Jerry Morales
Hank Schenz, Joe Benz, Jewell Ens
Cot Deal, Bob Veale, Greasy Neale
Duke Snider, Rollie Zeider, and apple cider

Wally Pipp, Ewell the Whip, Leo the Lip
Tony Piet, George Myatt, Whitlow Wyatt
Jake Atz, Matt Batts, Jigger Statz
Vinegar Bend, and this is the End!

It was not fiction after all.

Zane Grey's Redheaded Outfield

Joseph M. Overfield

"Zane Grey possesses no merit whatsoever either in style or in substance," wrote Burton Rascoe, the brilliant but acerbic New York literary critic. And this was the view of another critic, Heywood Broun: "The substance of any two Zane Grey books could be written upon the back of a postage stamp."

The public disagreed. According to the authorized biography of Grey written by Frank Gruber in 1970, the 85 books he wrote sold 100 million copies. Millions more saw the 100 movies based on his books.

Most of Grey's books were about the American West, but those he wrote about deep-sea fishing and on his world travels were widely read as well. Often forgotten is the fact he wrote numerous baseball stories that gained wide popularity among young readers. Grey's short story "The Redheaded Outfield" is one of the most famous and widely read

JOSEPH M. OVERFIELD, frequent contributor to SABR journals, wrote *The 100 Seasons of Buffalo Baseball.*

baseball stories ever written. Published by the McClure Syndicate in 1915, it was reissued in 1920 along with ten other baseball stories under the title *The Redheaded Outfield and Other Stories.*

It is not surprising that Grey wrote about baseball. He started to play as a youngster in Zanesville, Ohio, where he was born January 31, 1875. It has been suggested that he was forced to excel in sports to overcome the stigma of the name his mother had given him, Pearl Gray. Eventually he dropped the Pearl and assumed his middle name, Zane, and at the same time changed his surname from Gray to Grey. As a teenager he was recognized as one of Zanesville's better young pitchers. Equally adept as a ballplayer was his younger brother, whose unusual first name, Romer, seems somewhat prophetic for one destined to attain a degree of fame as an outfielder in professional baseball.

When the Gray family moved to Columbus in 1890, the brothers' baseball horizons broadened. Both joined the Capitols, a strong amateur nine, for whom Pearl soon became the star pitcher. A scout for the University of Pennsylvania watched him defeat Denison College of Granville, Ohio, whose star pitcher was Danny Daub, a future major leaguer. Penn offered him a baseball scholarship, and to satisfy his dentist father he decided to enter the dental school. After barely passing his entrance examinations, he began his college career in 1892. His graduation in 1896 was by the slimmest of margins. Undistinguished as he was in the classroom, he more than made up for it on the diamond. He played college baseball for four years, first as a pitcher and then as an outfielder. In 1896 he helped Penn defeat the New York Giants in an exhibition game, and then in the last game of the season he hit a home run with one man on in the last of the ninth to defeat the University of Virginia.

Helped financially by his father and by Romer, who had already started his professional baseball career, Grey set up a dental practice in New York City in 1896. Since the income from his practice was small, or possibly because he much preferred baseball to dentistry, he continued to play baseball in the succeeding summers. The entire story of

Grey's professional baseball activity is somewhat shrouded in mystery. Biographer Jean Karr writes that he played in the Eastern, Tri-State, and Michigan State Leagues, but cites no years and no cities. Gruber's book paints another picture. He wrote: "Pearl was sorely tempted to turn professional but he knew it would be the end of his dream of becoming a writer." According to the Grey obituary in the *Sporting News*, he played for Wheeling in the Iron and Oil League in 1895, Fort Wayne of the Interstate League in 1896, and Toronto of the Eastern League in 1899. SABR members Vern Luse and Robert Hoie have uncovered some pertinent data. Luse found an item in *Sporting Life*, April 15, 1896, reporting that Pearl Zane Gray had signed with Jackson of the Interstate League. Hoie has found he played for Newark of the Atlantic League in 1898, batting .277 in 38 games.

The haziness of his baseball career notwithstanding, his exposure to the game was such that it was only natural he should write about it. His first substantial check came from *The Shortstop*, published by A. C. McClurg of Chicago in 1909. Another success was *The Young Pitcher*, in which the author, transformed into "Ken Ward," is the hero and brother Reddie Grey is the shortstop. A few years later he wrote *The Redheaded Outfield*, starring Red Gilbat, Reddy Clammer, and Reddie Ray of the Rochester Stars of the Eastern League.

Two of the redheads were trouble personified. "Gilbat was nutty and his average was .371. The man was a jack-o-lantern, a will-o-the-wisp, a weird, long-legged, redhaired phantom." Clammer was a grandstand player "who made circus catches, circus stops and circus steals, always strutting, posing, talking, arguing and quarreling." Reddie Ray, on the other hand, "was a whole game of baseball in himself, batting .400 and leading the league." "Together," wrote Grey, "they made up the most remarkable outfield in minor league baseball."

The story revolves around a single crucial game between the Stars and the Providence Grays, a game in which the Stars' manager Delaney (first name not given) flirts with apoplexy before it is over. First, Gilbat is playing ball with some kids four blocks away and is rounded up only as the game is about to start. In an early inning Clammer is forced to make a one-handed catch (a no-no in those days) because his other hand is filled with the peanuts he is munching on. Then Gilbat, enraged by some remarks about the color of his hair, leaps into the stands to battle the hecklers and is put out of the game. In the sixth Clammer crashes into the wall in making one of his circus catches and is knocked cold. "I'll bet he's dead," moans Delaney. He revives but is through for the day. With no substitutes available for Gilbat or Clammer, the Stars are forced to play the last three innings with just one outfielder, Reddie Ray, "whose lithe form gave the suggestion of stored lightning." It comes down to the last of the ninth, the bases are full, the Stars are down by three and Reddie Ray is at the plate. He smashes one to right-center for an inside-the-park home run and victory for the Stars. "My Gawd!" exclaimed Delaney, "wasn't that a finish! I told you to watch them redheads."

Such was the Redheaded Outfield in fiction. In fact, it was the outfield of the 1897 Buffalo Bisons of the Eastern League, not of the Rochester Stars. In the story Gilbat, Clammer, and Ray make up the redheaded trio; in fact, their names were Larry Gilboy, Billy Clymer, and Romer (R.C. or Reddie) Grey, the author's younger brother. In the story the harassed manager is one Delaney; in fact, the manager was Jack Rowe, a hard-bitten veteran of the baseball wars who had been a member of the famed Big Four (with Dan Brouthers, Deacon White, and Hardie Richardson) of Buffalo's National League days. Such a dramatic game as described by Grey was never played by the 1897 Bisons. Closest to it was a game played against Scranton on August 5 when the Bisons rallied in the last of the ninth for a comeback win. Clymer and Grey participated in the rally with hits, but the tying and winning runs were driven in by non-redheaded third baseman Ed Greminger.

In the story Grey calls it the greatest outfield ever assembled in the minor leagues; in fact, that would be stretching the truth. But who can say it was not the most unusual? People who know about such things tell us there is one chance in nineteen of being a redhead, which makes the emergence of three redheads in one outfield on one minor league team the longest of long shots.

Perhaps not the greatest, but they were good nonetheless. "Fast and sure, both in the field and at bat," wrote a Buffalo reporter. The headline in the *Express* after the Bisons' opening-day win at Springfield was: "REDHEADS GREAT PLAYING!" In the game account we are told that "the redheaded outfield distinguished itself by covering every inch of ground," and that "Gilboy stood the fans on their heads with a spectacular onehanded catch off the bat of Dan Brouthers." In game two of the season, Bill ("Derby Day") Clymer was the star, "catching seven balls that were labeled for hits." On May 8 at Scranton, Gilboy made an acrobatic catch, called "far and away the best catch ever seen at Athletic Park." After a game at Wilkes-Barre, a writer called them great, "as good as any outfield in the game," then added: "Clymer and Gilboy were really sensational. They made some of the most startling plays ever seen in Wilkes-Barre. Both have evidently been with a circus."

When the Bisons opened at home on May 16 against Rochester, they were in first place with an 8-3 record. The highlight of the first game was a miraculous one-handed catch by Clymer, which he topped off by doing a complete flip-flop. On Memorial Day Clymer provided the one bright spot in what the *Express* described as an "execrable game" by the Bisons, by snaring a long drive off the bat of McHale of Toronto and then crashing into the fence, just as in the Grey story. According to the *Express*, "It was the most thrilling out seen here this season." Clymer was applauded to the skies when he came immediately to the bat (as so often happens after a spectacular fielding play), and he responded by slashing a hit to left. Not to be outdone by Clymer and Gilboy, Reddie Grey, on June 26 in a game at Rochester, raced to right-center to make a one-handed catch of a sinking liner hit by Henry Lynch. His momentum was so great that he turned head over heels after he made the catch.

And so it went all season, with visiting players and managers marveling at the play of the three redheads.

And they were far from slouches at the bat. Gilboy, while not a long-ball hitter (one triple and two home runs for the year), was a gem of consistency. He hit safely in twenty-eight of the first thirty games and then after a couple of blanks proceeded to hit in fourteen straight games. For the season he totaled 201 hits (second only to Brouthers' 225), scored 110 runs, hit 44 doubles, stole 26 bases and batted .350. Reddie Grey, called by the *Express* writer "the perambulating suggestion of the aurora borealis," played every inning of the Bisons' 134 games, batting .309, with 167 hits, 29 doubles, 13 triples and 2 home runs. In a game against Scranton in which he was the hitting star, he was, in the quaint practice of that day, presented with a bouquet of flowers as he came to the plate. He responded by doubling to left. Clymer, the most brilliant of the three in the field, was the weakest with the stick. He batted just .279 on 154 hits, but his extra-base totals were strong—32 doubles, 5 triples, and 8 home runs. Five of his homers came in a twelve-day period beginning on August 12 and caused the *Express* writer to inquire: "We wonder what oculist Clymer has seen?" Clymer's fielding average was phenomenal for those days—.969 with just 14 errors. As for the others, Grey fielded .915 and Gilboy .913.

Spurred by the redheads, the Bisons were in the pennant race most of the year, holding first place as late as August 14. A late-August slump, however, saw them drop to third by the end of the month. This was where they finished, a disappointing ten games behind first-place Syracuse and four games behind Toronto. As the team began to fade, so did the early-season euphoria. After a loss to Toronto, the *Express* said, "There are players goldbricking and the fans know who they are." And then the next day, after another loss: "The infield played like a sieve. Could some players be playing for their releases?" First baseman and captain

Jim Fields was abused so severely from the stands after making an error that he asked Manager Rowe for his release, which was not granted. In September, after three straight losses to Springfield, the *Express* writer, warming to the task, wrote: "The Eastern League is a beanbag league, just where the Bisons belong. They are playing the type of baseball that made Denmark odiferous in the days of Hamlet."

The 1897 season, which had started on such an optimistic note, came to a merciful end on September 22 with gloom and pessimism pervading the atmosphere. Owner Jim Franklin complained that he was losing money ("This has been no Klondike for me"), the press was vitriolic, the fans were disgruntled, the Eastern League was rocky, and the Western League of Ban Johnson was casting covetous eyes on Buffalo. (Actually, Buffalo did join the Western League in 1899.)

But spring has been known to wash away the depressions of falls and winters, and so it was in Buffalo as the 1898 baseball season approached. But what of the fabled redheaded outfield of 1897? Surprisingly, it was destined for a one-year stand. Clymer, who had been with the Bisons since 1894, was the first to go, being shipped to Rochester on March 11. Five days later the *Express* announced: "A Chromatic Deal—Grey for White." In an even exchange of outfielders, Reddie Grey had been sent to Toronto for Jack White. Only Gilboy remained. Not only was he coming back, but he was to get a raise, as well. Word from his home in Newcastle, Pa., was that "he had spent the winter as one of the leaders of the gay [old connotation] society." When he arrived in Buffalo in early April, the *Courier* noted that "the most prominent thing on Main Street was Gilboy's summer dawn hair, topped with a white hat."

Billy Clymer remained in the game for many years as a player and manager, returning to Buffalo in 1901, 1913, 1914, and from 1926 to 1930. This writer recalls him clearly, as he managed the 1927 Bisons to a pennant— strutting, chest out, argumentative, flamboyant, just as Reddy Clammer had been in the Zane Grey story. Clymer's managerial record is remarkable. He managed twenty-three complete seasons and parts of six others, all in the minors, compiling 2122 wins and 1762 losses for a percentage of .546. He won seven pennants and had an equal number of second-place finishes. Counting only the complete seasons, his record shows just three second-division finishes. He died in Philadelphia, December 26, 1936, at the age of 63. The Macmillan *Encyclopedia* shows he played just three major league games, those with Philadelphia of the American Association in 1891.

Reddie Grey played in the Eastern League with good success until 1903, performing for Toronto, Rochester, Worcester, and Montreal. With Rochester in 1901, he led the league in home runs with 12. In *The History of the International League: Part 3*, author David F. Chrisman picked him as the league's most valuable player for that year. According to the Macmillan *Encyclopedia*, Grey never played in the major leagues. This is disputed by SABR member Al Kermisch, who maintains that Grey played a game for Pittsburgh on May 28, 1903, but was confused with another Grey and therefore has not been listed as a major league player. Once out of baseball, he followed his father and brother into dentistry, but eventually gave it up to become his brother's secretary, adviser, and companion on his world travels. A strong fraternal relationship existed between Romer and Zane throughout their lives. Zane never forgot that it was R.C., along with his father, who helped him financially when he was setting up his dental practice in New York and that it was R.C. who gave him encouragement and monetary assistance when he was struggling to establish himself as a writer. Zane showed his esteem for his younger brother by naming his first son Romer. R.C. died in 1934 at age 59, one year before Zane too passed on.

Little is known about the third member of the redheaded triumvirate, Lawrence Joseph Gilboy. He lasted with the Bisons only until May 27, 1898, when he was released outright because, in the words of owner Franklin, "He was worse than useless when he got on the lines." He signed with Syracuse, played only a few days, was released, played for Utica and Palmyra of the New York State League and for

Youngstown of the Interstate. There is no record that he played after 1898. It was a strange and abrupt ending to a career that had started so brilliantly. There was a note in the *Express* that he was entering Niagara University to study medicine. The school cannot find that he ever enrolled.

Such is the story of three minor league outfielders who would have long since been forgotten, were it not for the color of their hair.

What baseball means to Japan—and humanity.

Where the Twain Shall Meet

Merritt Clifton

When a team of Japanese collegians defeated their American counterparts to claim the 1984 Olympic gold medal for baseball, stunned American fans realized what the Japanese have felt for years: Baseball is as truly theirs as ours. Japan's upset victory had even greater impact upon Americans than the initial victories by Taiwan, South Korea, and Okinawa in the Little League World Series some fifteen years ago. Then, at least, disgruntled U.S. fans could claim that the Asiatic teams consisted of older players hiding behind their small stature; and certainly the Asiatic Little League squads were selected from among the best players in entire nations, not just the best in extended neighborhoods. Olympic baseball, however, is just one or two steps from top-rank professional baseball. If the American game is still intrinsically superior, at this level the edge should show, even granting that the single-game elimination format of

MERRITT CLIFTON, freelance writer and small-press publisher, is the author of "Relative Baseball" and "A Baseball Classic."

Olympic play permits flukes and does not force the teams to call upon their depth. Americans may still produce more and better second-line starting pitchers, relief pitchers, punch-hitters, platoon outfielders, and utility infielders, but up front, the Japanese Olympians proved themselves equal, if not superior.

Thus far, no American major league club has ever lost an exhibition series to Japanese professionals. (The San Francisco Giants, playing mostly AAA farmhands, went 3-6 in their March 1970 tour.) However, the Kansas City Royals had to beat the Japanese champion Yomiuri Giants six games to two to salvage a 9-7-1 overall record on their 1981 tour. The Royals claimed they started poorly because of a three-week layoff between the end of the 162-game American League season and the beginning of their visit to Japan—but the Japanese players had been waiting around even longer since the end of their 130-game season. Like most other American baseball authorities, the Royals still describe Japanese baseball as the equivalent of American Double-A minor leagues. They point out that even Double-A teams occasionally beat the big leaguers in exhibitions. But sooner or later some cocky major leaguers are going to arrive in Japan expecting to clobber quasi-minor leaguers and really get their ears pinned back. The Olympics should be taken as a warning that Japanese baseball has not only established itself as a cultural tradition, but also matured at a top-flight level.

The past two decades of Japanese play represented a Golden Age, setting standards for the future much as the 1920s and 1930s set enduring standards for the American game. Since the 1920s, as documented in Thorn and Palmer's *The Hidden Game of Baseball*, the average American major leaguer has risen to the levels of natural ability and acquired skill once possessed only by stars. Thus today's American stars stand out much less than did Babe Ruth, Ty Cobb, and Walter Johnson. Likewise, though Japanese baseball no longer boasts players as dominant as home run king Sadaharu Oh was during the 1960s, this is because the average player has improved. The single-season and career records Oh and others set during the 1960s and 1970s may stand as long as the records of Ruth, Cobb, and Johnson because in Japan as in America it is no longer possible for any one player, no matter how good, to be that much better than all the rest.

It wasn't always so. Just a few generations back, the Great American Pastime was as foreign to Japan as the automobile and electronics industries. Japanese players were obviously smaller, slower, awkward, less understanding of the nuances of the game. But as with automobiles and electronics, Japan imported knowhow, worked hard, and put forth an impressive product.

"After the war," Japanese professional baseball commissioner Takeso Shimoda told the *New York Times,* "we had to start from zero. We had to improve the technical level of Japanese players. . . . We had to hire American players. It succeeded. Now there's not much difference between American and Japanese players, technically."

He might have been speaking of cars or television sets, as an executive for Honda, Nissan, Sony, Sanyo, or Mitsubishi. Yet Shimoda wasn't speaking of a business success so much as of a cultural transformation, of a process that more or less replaced institutionalized emperor-worship with the transient idolatry that fans individually accord to favorite star athletes. Where Japanese boys once memorized the sayings of philosopher-emperors, since the middle 1960s they have memorized the statistics on the backs of Kabaya-Leaf baseball cards, just as their American counterparts who, with rare exceptions, long since ceased memorizing passages from the Bible.

The economic incentive behind Japan's rapid industrialization is clear enough, but why should baseball have come with it? Why should baseball have become a national preoccupation while other American sports and other facets of American culture haven't? What particularly attracts the Japanese en masse to baseball and even bubblegum cards, but not to football or drag-racing?

Golf has been adopted among the Japanese economic elite because the nation's few greens provide an internationally acceptable place for informal business discussion. The young, upwardly mobile Japanese likewise play handball, squash, and tennis, and run marathons but, as in America, none of these successful transplants has become a major spectator sport, televised every day and discussed wherever men gather. Boxing, hockey, and basketball have been transplanted as spectator sports, but enjoy distinctly minor status.

Baseball possesses a uniquely national character in both Japan and America in part because it came first, ahead of the other leading spectator sports. But it also fills a cultural role that the other sports can't. Battalions of American sociologists and historians have tried to figure out just what baseball means, without reaching any consensus. However, historically it is clear that the rise of baseball was coincidental with that of industrialization in both the United States and Japan. It is further clear from the overseas birthplaces of many of the pioneer players that baseball in America caught on quite rapidly with recent immigrants, who might have been expected to stick with the sports brought with them from Europe. European-style football, rugby, cricket, and rounders all require less space to play, for one thing, and less equipment. They're easier for spectators to understand (all but cricket). Yet they faded into virtual oblivion, while the largest immigrant centers became the founding cities of the U.S. major leagues.

Sociologist Ken Hogarty, of the University of California at Berkeley, may have pinpointed the key difference between baseball and most other sports in his unpublished doctoral thesis (1977). According to Hogarty, the primary conflict in baseball is *individual versus society*, whereas the primary conflict in most other sports is *nation versus nation*. The model for most other sports is war, Hogarty observed, with the individual subordinate to the group, while baseball he compared to the classical western. The lone cowboy-outlaw, the batter, rides into town to confront a hostile posse of nine. Usually, society triumphs and the anarchic cowboy is buried in his dugout, the symbolic Boot Hill. Sometimes, however, the cowboy-outlaw shoots his way into the bank, first base. Sometimes his gang then shoots him back out of trouble with a succession of hits that finally bring him home. Once in a while, a particularly valiant cowboy shoots his own way clear through town with a home run. The umpires, in Hogarty's view, represent God rather than human authority. Dressed in their dark suits, they arbitrate justice.

Hogarty's model clearly explains why baseball should have appealed to U.S. immigrants. Often as not, they came to America in rebellion against authority back home. Many had themselves been outlaws, of one sort or another. They could identify with the ambitious batsman/gunslinger who takes 'em all on. And, as they gradually gained property and responsibilities, they could identify with the home-team defense, too.

In football, basketball, hockey, soccer, tennis, even chess, the object of the game is capturing territory, plundering or violating a protected treasure—goal-nets and basketball hoops mix sexual and territorial symbolism so thoroughly as to leave no doubt how the reproductive and territorial drives are connected. Such sports date back to the very beginnings of society, to the first time tribal groups engaged in symbolic rather than literal mass combat to determine who would drink first at a watering hole. They survive because we retain our tribal instincts, expressed now as nationalism and political partisanship.

But, particularly since the Declaration of Independence asserted the rights of the individual as equal to those of the state, we no longer think of ourselves first as parts of a greater whole. We are each "me" before we are Christians or Jews, northerners or southerners, blue-collar or white-collar. The rise of baseball historically parallels the rise of individualism, concurrent with the collapse of the village-based, semi-tribal agrarian economy. Alexander Cartwright and Henry Chadwick devised baseball even as Ralph Emerson and Henry David Thoreau distinguished individualism from mere selfishness, the first philosophers to openly salute those "marching to the beat of a different drum." Their colleague Walt Whitman saluted baseball for expressing the same independent American character that Emerson and

Thoreau defined. Unique among sports, baseball not only permits but demands that each player briefly emerge from among his teammates to stand alone. Every player must belong to the team on defense, but each must hit his own way on base. This balance of social and individual responsibility must have appealed greatly to young men who didn't really wish to be outcasts forever, but did wish to make the most of their own abilities in whatever field of endeavor.

But that was nineteenth-century America, not Japan. Japan has received no recent waves of immigrants seeking freedom and opportunity. Throughout recorded history, Japan has maintained a society that has been regimented, if not entirely socially stratified.

Indeed, historically Japan would seem much more like Europe than like America, so that one might expect the Japanese game to have followed the European course. A game called baseball developed from rounders and cricket in England even earlier than it emerged in America—again concurrent with industrialization—but became a girls' game, which novelist Jane Austen mentioned in *Northanger Abbey*, written ca. 1803. It faded from popularity as Victorian mores discouraged women's participation in competitive sports, and vanished by 1850.

Reintroduced repeatedly, baseball did finally catch on somewhat in Europe after World War II, with Little League and adult weekend clubs now scattered among all the western nations. Italy boasts one low-caliber professional league including several American ex-major leaguers, while The Netherlands recently sent pitcher Win Remmerswaal to the Boston Red Sox, the first major leaguer to spend his entire amateur career in Europe.

Europe is now well into evolving a postindustrial economy, however. Baseball is at most a successful minor sport, not a significant cultural influence as it has been in Japan for decades. If the evolution of baseball in Europe could be compared at all to baseball history in America, it must be placed at about the Civil War level, the point at which troop movements and the new transcontinental railroads first spread the game from coast to coast, north and south.

Baseball in Japan, by contrast, is today about as well established as it was in the United States in 1919, by which time it was already undeniably the Great American Pastime. American professional baseball was exactly fifty years old in 1919, the Cincinnati Red Stockings having become the first admittedly salaried team in 1869. The first Japanese professional team, the Yomiuri Giants of Tokyo, was chartered almost exactly 50 years ago, on December 26, 1934. The Hanshin Tigers of Osaka followed a year later, on December 10, 1935. The Chunichi Dragons of Magoya were assembled on January 15, 1936. The Hankyu Braves of Nishinomiya came together just eight days later. Nineteen thirty-six brought formation of Japan's first fully professional baseball league. Expansion began when the Nankai Hawks became Osaka's second professional team on March 29, 1938. Postwar, these original five teams gradually grew into the present two leagues of six teams each, paralleling the development of our American and National Leagues.

When the Yomiuri Giants formed, baseball had been played in Japan for about twenty-five years. A team of American major leaguers first visited in 1912, beating a nine of U.S. missionaries. Babe Ruth led several subsequent visits, leading to the almost annual tradition of one U.S. team or another visiting in the fall. Each time Ruth visited, he and his teammates noted larger crowds and better players, an observation continued to this day.

Like the 1869 Cincinnati Red Stockings, the Tokyo Giants drew together top players from various locales—in the Giants' case, their talent was drawn from college and athletic club teams. They barnstormed against these same colleges and athletic clubs, in the absence of any organized professional league, and having most of the best players they naturally won most of their games. Even after other professional teams organized and the first Japanese major league was formed, the Giants were able to maintain their advantage, winning over thirty championships. Only two other Japanese teams have won as many as ten.

Here Japanese baseball history first diverges from American, and a difference in the cultural traditions appears. Our

Red Stockings soon disbanded, with their players moving to other cities, principally Boston and Washington. But the Giants remained together. Other teams similarly started from scratch. Instead of raiding one another to achieve parity, they patiently developed their own talent. The principle became established that Japanese players would generally remain with their clubs for life. To this day, trading and otherwise moving from club to club is rare in Japanese baseball, just as Japanese factory workers rarely move from firm to firm. Japanese club owners, usually large industrial consortiums, are expected to provide lifetime employment for their players in one capacity or another, while players are expected to remain unswervingly loyal to their bosses.

These expectations of loyalty have recently become a point of conflict between the Japanese teams and imported American players, a conflict of great symbolic significance that may influence the future direction of all Japanese society. On the one hand, imported American players are viewed as mercenaries, and are clearly treated as such, hired, fired, and blamed for team failures with an abandon management would never display toward native players. On the other hand, the imported players are expected to conform at least outwardly to the same rules as the natives: to respect their supposed betters and keep their mouths shut, just as if they could expect similar long-term rewards for good behavior.

Grafting on an almost feudal system of team loyalty was only part of how the Japanese adapted baseball customs to suit the traditions of their own society. Baseball took root in Japan at precisely the time when most other foreign activities became suspect, the period during the late 1930s when tariff wars with Great Britain and the United States were raising tensions that culminated in World War II. As Japanese baseball promoters realized immediately, the game would have to take on a nationalistic character to survive.

To a great extent, this influenced the style of play. In the heyday of American jingoism, between the Spanish Civil War and World War I, the American game endured the "deadball" era, a phase in which managers tried to replace

the freewheeling Wild West style of offense that characterized the '90s with team play emphasizing the sacrifice bunt.
The sacrifice was lauded by sportswriters while players
swinging for home runs were derided as "rutting sluggers"
with more muscle than either brains or character. Baseball
in Japan entered a similar phase, with several significant
differences. Despite the patriotic emphasis on conformity
during the American deadball era, Americans still prided
themselves on being rough-and-ready. Thus American pitchers continued knocking batters down with inside fastballs
and American baserunners threatened fielders with their
spikes at every opportunity. While sublimating offense, the
American deadball era might have featured the most violently
aggressive style of play ever. The Japanese, on the other
hand, pride themselves on courtesy. As recently as the
mid-1960s, pitchers apologized for accidentally "dusting
off" batters, and no Japanese player ever physically challenged another. Players even bowed to the umpires who
called them out. Deadball play in Japan stressed the sacrifice without any form of self-assertion emerging until after
World War II.

Thus, even as jingoistic generals urged a return to the
code of the samurai and other unique cultural traditions,
baseball was not only tolerated but even encouraged. Baseball and military preparations were perhaps the only two
realms in which Japanese leaders urged the population to
learn from the West right up to the outbreak of war. Shortly
before Pearl Harbor, when most foreigners were being
hustled from the country, former major league catcher-
turned-spy Moe Berg was not only allowed in but was
welcomed with the red carpet, was allowed to take photos
from a tower overlooking Tokyo, and was further permitted
to take them home again, to be used in directing American
bombers. Berg recalled in his memoirs that his having
played on one of Babe Ruth's teams that toured Japan
served him much better with the Japanese authorities than
either his passport or his ability to speak Japanese.

Nor did the war itself curtail Japanese enthusiasm for
baseball. Americans who flew on General Jimmy Doolittle's

1942 raid against Tokyo recalled feeling guilty about dropping their bombs after passing over children at a sandlot ballgame. Japanese troops on the Pacific islands shouted "To hell with Babe Ruth!" at American invaders, but the invaders usually found shell-pocked baseball diamonds ready for play just as soon as they finished mopping up.

If baseball were only another game providing some sort of moral lesson, it probably wouldn't have caught on so strongly, certainly not at that time. But the nature of the lesson had special appeal. Although Japanese baseball was played in a fashion tending to promote traditional values, it added the notion that there are times in life when it is not only necessary but also good and praiseworthy that each individual step forward and do something conspicuous. Though ostentation was discouraged, the spotlight was unmistakably focused upon the man at bat, upon his individual contribution to the greater whole. Here, at least, the small fish in the big sea were not permanently anonymous. Here also, they received the opportunity to perform so well as to become big fish. The promise of social mobility endemic to America was rather new to Japan, but equally appealing—and all the more noticeable, because in Japan hardly any other field of endeavor overtly offered it. The peasant who accepted industrialization might indeed become richer, but he would still be a peasant, whereas the humble batsman who excelled might become exalted as a samurai.

Perhaps the most significant clue to what baseball means in Japan lies within the event that prompted Commissioner Shimoda to address *The New York Times*—an event highlighting essential differences. A few months before the Olympics, xenophobic Japanese baseball fans including Shimoda raised a hue and cry against the foreign players they once enthusiastically hired and copied. Foreign players should be banned, they argued, for corrupting the character of their national sport. Their definition of that character emerges from the origin of their wrath.

Former U.S. major league infielder Don Money touched off the uproar by signing with a Japanese team for more money than any of his native teammates were making, reporting to the team out of playing condition, griping incessantly about the Japanese training discipline, and finally leaving the team without permission in mid-pennant race. Money claimed he jumped the club to receive treatment for an injury from his own doctor back home, but Japanese baseball people weren't convinced. Many other disillusioned American players have used the same excuse as a means of escaping their Japanese contracts. Foreigners were nearly banned a decade ago, in 1973, when Joe Pepitone jumped the Yakult Atoms with a purported injury best diagnosed as acute culture shock.

Money was an irritant, both as an individual and as an economic factor, but Money in either sense wasn't the primary issue. The primary issue for most Japanese fans was that players like Money and Pepitone violate the fundamental tenets of their society by overtly placing their own interests above those of their team. Their actions are discourteous and disloyal. They set a poor example for Japanese youth. American sports columnists reported that Money and Pepitone were simply too individualistic to suit the Japanese, an unfair oversimplification. Money and Pepitone were criticized not for being individualistic so much as for being selfish.

Nor would their conduct have been any more acceptable in the American major leagues. Pepitone, in fact, wound up in Japan after similarly jumping his contract with the Atlanta Braves. During his career, Japanese baseball actually offered him more leeway than the American leagues did, since the standard Japanese contract for foreign players lasts only two years. At that time, players in the U.S. leagues, like native Japanese players, were purportedly bound for life to the teams that owned their contracts. In actuality, American players have always moved rather freely and frequently from club to club, through trades often self-initiated. Nonetheless, in either nation, Pepitone was expected to honor his contract by playing ball to the best of his considerable ability. In both nations, Pepitone was notorious as a playboy, often criticized for letting off-the-field pursuits interfere with realizing his on-the-field potential. American teams put up with Pepitone for a decade because he still hit better with a hangover than most players who were cold sober. In Japan, however, he hit .163, erasing any claim to special privilege.

Money's case was somewhat different, in that U.S. baseball norms have changed since Pepitone's time. Since 1976, about midway through Money's career, American professional baseball has offered veteran players several means of openly choosing their own teams, through requesting or refusing trades and playing out their contract options. The most significant change from past practice is that today players can change clubs without their former clubs receiving compensation: can in effect sell themselves, instead of being sold by club owners, and pocket the proceeds. But even under this new system, contract jumpers have never been tolerated. A U.S. major leaguer who simply breaks his contract is heavily fined, as Dick Allen was for abandoning first the Phillies and then the White Sox. If less valuable than Allen, one of the game's all-time great sluggers, a contract-jumper in the U.S. might also be suspended, or unconditionally released, ending the team's obligation to pay him. Over the last thirty-five years, such cases have usually been resolved through retirement or trade, rather than confrontation such as happened in Japan in the Money and Pepitone cases.

American fans would certainly boo a Money or Pepitone for jumping his club, just as they booed Allen. The issue in either nation is not "individuality" but honor. Antagonistic toward the Americanization of traditional Japanese society, the xenophobes emphasize the imported players' mercenary status—warriors with no sense of honor, who unlike the samurai fight only for pay, and then only when they feel like it. After all, the American and Latin American players in Japan have already left other teams and countries, often under questionable circumstances. The very first American players in Japan actually were mercenaries, more or less. Former Boston Braves' pitcher Phil Paine became the first ex-major leaguer to play in the Japanese big leagues during 1953, while serving with the U.S. Air Force. Infielder Larry Raines made the U.S. major leagues in the mid-1950s as the best-known of many Americans who also played for Japanese clubs on leave from the U.S. military. Arriving under moral suspicion, meanwhile, was first baseman Don Newcombe, who drank himself out of a brilliant pitching career with the Brooklyn Dodgers. The first American stars to reach Japan, Newcombe and outfielder Larry Doby, played poorly for the Chunichi Dragons in 1962, becoming the focus of criticism directed at U.S. imports ever since.

Although American players have generally given honest effort and conducted themselves honorably, Japanese fans are aware that most view their two major leagues as a sort of Siberia, preferable only to the death of a return to the minors. American players go to Japan either because they're washed up, not good enough to stick in the U.S. major leagues, or because no American team will put up with them.

Faced with the end of their careers, many Americans do take advantage of the tough Japanese training regimen to get back into shape and play good baseball. George Altman and Willie Kirkland came off the American scrapheap to become superstars in Japan, thanking martial arts discipline for rescuing them from hard drink, fast women, and what appeared to be fast fade-outs after brilliant beginnings. U.S. minor leaguer John Sipin similarly developed his abilities through the Japanese approach, also becoming a superstar after scarcely getting a trial in the American majors. Former Kansas City infielder Tim Ireland, now with the Hiroshima Carp, speaks for many American players in observing that under the Japanese regimen, "you forfeit individual expression, but you gain in production and non-confusion."

Great comeback efforts are applauded and compliments from Americans accepted, even when they miss the point. But comebacks attributed to sobriety and proper conditioning also hurt Japanese pride somewhat, since Americans often take the successes of "failures" to mean Japanese baseball is inferior. Never mind that American stars often likewise emerge after interleague trades—Hall of Famers Carl Hubbell and Joe Cronin, for instance. No baseball expert claims the National League of the 1930s was inferior because the late-blooming Hubbell excelled for the Giants after failing with the Tigers, or that the American League was inferior because Cronin made it big with Washington and Boston after riding the Pirates' bench. The accusation that the Japanese game isn't quite as good persists because nonentities like Greg "Boomer" Wells keep emerging as superstars when Japanese clubs give them the first real chance to play regularly that they've ever had. How, then, to account for the inability of former stars like Reggie Smith or Warren Cromartie to handle Japanese curveball pitching? American scouts find it easier to consider the Smiths and Cromarties washed up than to accept that they've misjudged a Sipin or a Wells, or an Altman or Kirkland, for that matter.

The Japanese, meanwhile, are sensitive about being considered a nation of imitators, whose products are essentially inferior to the originals. They've worked hard for two generations to erase the "Made in Japan" stigma from cars, cameras, and electronic equipment. Thus when Americans take Japan's national pastime lightly, the "ban foreigners" approach is understandable. It's what the U.S. and Soviet Union do, more or less, in boycotting one another's Olympics . . . what half the world does in boycotting sports events involving South Africans . . . what every child does when offended by a playmate: "If you don't play nice, I'll take my toys and go home."

Ironically, the Japanese victory over the U.S. baseball team in the Olympics makes a ban on foreign players less likely. Japanese pride has been assuaged. Now that Japanese collegians, at least, have proved themselves peers of their American counterparts, fans can more easily shrug off the "inferior" rap whenever an American unknown hits a home run. The pressure on imported players to excel conspicuously might also diminish considerably, after decades of mounting. Having starred for the Hankyu Braves in 1964-68 and again in 1971-72, former infielder Daryl Spencer knows that pressure well, understanding thoroughly how it contributes to the present situation. Not only the fans but "the managers like to use Americans as scapegoats," Spencer recently explained to baseball historian Mike Mandel. "If the American has a bad year and the team doesn't do well, then the manager says, 'Well, our Americans didn't do well,' without regard to the performances of the other twenty-three on the roster.''

Smith and Cromartie particularly demonstrate this tendency. The Yomiuri Giants more or less expected them to replace Sadaharu Oh, the first baseman who hit even more home runs than Hank Aaron (868 to 755 before retiring in 1980) and Shigeo Nagashima, the third baseman whose lifetime batting average is the highest in Japanese baseball history. While the Giants dominated the Japanese game as the New York Yankees once dominated American baseball, Oh and Nagashima were the Japanese Babe Ruth and Lou Gehrig. Through their prime, the Giants alone among Japanese teams steadfastly refused to sign Americans. Their only imported players ever had been Hawaiian-born Wally Yonamine, Andy Miyamoto, Bill Nishida, Jun Hirota, and Fumiharu Kashiwaeda, all of pure Japanese descent, who formed their nucleus during the early 1950s. But tradition changed fast after Nagashima began declining. In 1975 the Giants jumped at a chance to sign infielder Davey Johnson, a perennial Gold Glove winner and All-Star with the Baltimore Orioles who had also hit 43 home runs as an Atlanta Brave only two years before. Past his prime, Johnson disappointed, but he did have a good year in 1976 as the Giants kept on winning despite Nagashima's retirement. Aware what might happen, however, if the Giants lost, Johnson fled back to the U.S. after his two-year contract expired, where he enjoyed one more standout season in 1977. The Giants next traded for John Sipin, who did effectively replace Nagashima during Oh's last few seasons. In 1980 they added outfielder Roy White, a regular on three recent pennant-winning New York Yankee ballclubs. White starred, but after both Oh and Sipin retired, he slumped, unable to carry the Giants' offense alone. For the first time, the Giants suffered three consecutive losing seasons. Nagashima, probably the most popular Japanese player ever, had become the team's general manager. He couldn't be blamed. Nor could Oh be blamed, now the Giants' field manager. The Giants dumped White, bringing in first Smith, then Cromartie a season later with fanfare designed to hide the bitter truth that almost their whole club was over 30, they no longer had a single standout pitcher, and hadn't developed a native star in at least a decade.

Smith had been a legitimate major league superstar in his prime with the Red Sox, Cardinals, and Dodgers, distinguished for home run power, speed on the bases, and one of the best arms in the history of baseball. However, he arrived in Japan at age 38 after a succession of injuries had left him unable to throw hard, run fast, or even swing the bat hard every day. Cromartie, in his early thirties, was a few years past career highs of 14 home runs and .304 in seven seasons with the Montreal Expos. He was a good player, but only a marginal regular. Smith and Cromartie couldn't possibly have lived up to their billing, even if they had produced as well as Oh and Nagashima did during their last seasons; the Giants couldn't reasonably have been expected to win. But blaming them for the Giants' collapse helps Yomiuri management, including Oh and Nagashima, to survive the fans' disappointment while rebuilding their team from the bottom up.

The expectation that American players should be supermen even extended to Masanori Murakami, the Japanese pitcher who played for the San Francisco Giants in 1964-65. Murakami joined San Francisco almost straight out of college, after only half a season in the U.S. minor leagues. Under normal circumstances, no one would have expected him to create a stir right away. But, recalls Spencer, "Murakami came back [to Japan] and he was the first Japanese to play in the major leagues in America and they had a big bally-hoo every time someone hit a home run off him in spring training. And the kid got really psyched out, and the other Japanese players kind of resented him. He had a miserable time of it for about three or four years. Finally he did have a halfway decent season, but he never became a star," despite lasting eighteen years in professional baseball. Ironically, reversing the pattern of American players, Murakami returned to the San Francisco Giants for his final comeback attempt. Had he succeeded, he might have proved himself that American and Japanese baseball are simply different, rather than "better" or "worse." Instead, he received his unconditional release during 1983 spring training.

Yet another Spencer anecdote reveals the depth of the Japanese inferiority complex concerning American baseball. As he told Mandel in *S.F. Giants: An Oral History* (self-published, 1979), "I got in a situation where I was going for the home run crown with this Japanese player. And I was ahead of him 32 to 26 in August. And my interpreter told me to forget the home run title; it had already been decided that I wouldn't win. I couldn't understand what he was talking about, but in our next series we went into Tokyo and we were playing in this real small ballpark, and I always hit a couple of home runs there in a three-game series. And they walked me eight straight times. The greatest pitcher in Japan at that time, a kid named Koyama, who could throw strikes blindfolded, he walked me four times on sixteen straight pitches. So they were getting the message to me that I wasn't going to hit any more home runs. And eventually the guy caught me."

The Japanese have never been particularly sensitive about Americans winning batting championships. Even before former American major leaguers arrived, Wally Yonamine won the 1951 Central League batting title. Larry Raines won the Pacific League batting title with the Hankyu Braves in 1954. No feelings were hurt because at that time the Japanese leagues did not even pretend to equality. Almost a decade later, playing at the same time as Spencer, former American minor leaguer Jack Bloomfield won back-to-back Pacific League batting titles for the Kintetsu Buffalos in 1962 and 1963.

Home run titles, however, have been a sore point, as has the whole business of home run hitting. In America, the self-sacrificing deadball era ended when pitcher Babe Ruth turned in his toeplate at the peak of his career and became a fence-busting outfielder instead. The deadball era in Japan ended almost the same way, when onetime pitching great Michio Nishizawa returned from World War II with an

injured arm, forcing him to become an outfielder-first baseman. Unlike Ruth, Nishizawa had never before been much
of a hitter. In fact, in seven previous seasons, he'd hit over
.223 just once and that was as a teenaged rookie in 1937,
when he got two hits in five at-bats. He'd hit only one home
run in his life. Grateful just to be playing ball again,
Nishizawa played conventional deadball for a couple of
years, then discovered he was big and strong enough to hit
home runs in bunches. The individual self-assertion inherent
in swinging for the fences made Nishizawa the target of
considerable criticism from the old guard, but most fans
loved him. When he retired in 1958, his career total of 212
homers and single-season high of 46 in 1950 were both
Japanese baseball records.

They didn't last long. Because Nishizawa's teams won,
and because his hitting packed the bleachers, Japanese
management immediately began seeking more fence-busters.
This, as much as a desire to better the overall caliber of their
game, was the real impetus behind the wholesale import of
American players from the early 1950s on. Even playing in
much smaller ballparks than the American norm, few native
Japanese had the size and strength to hit home runs before
the 1960s, when the improved nutrition of the postwar era
brought a generally bigger, stronger generation to maturity.
Meanwhile American players of average power, like Spencer, challenged league and team home run records, while
Americans with no power reputation at all frequently became sluggers. The handful of Japanese players who did hit
home runs consistently during the 1950s and early 1960s
became symbols of national pride: Futoshi Nakanishi of the
Nishitsu Lions and Kazuhiro Yamauchi of the Hanshin
Tigers, who arrived in 1952; catcher Katsuya Nomura of the
Nankai Hawks, who broke in during 1955 and played until
age 46 in 1980; Shigeo Nagashima, debut season 1958; Oh,
and outfielder Shinichi Eto of the Chunichi Dragons, who
came up in 1959. These were the few players whose power
complemented their other abilities sufficiently that even the
most critical Americans recognized them as authentic major
leaguers.

Whether or not Spencer accurately accuses Japanese baseball of a conspiracy to deprive him of a home run title, it is
a fact that although many Americans had spectacular home
run totals, few of them actually became home run champions until after Oh hit the home run in 1977 that put him
ahead of Hank Aaron as the all-time, all-world professional
leader. Only since Oh's triumph have any Americans won
multiple home run titles. Japanese players and fans today
can better accept former American reserves like Adrian
Garrett, Charlie Manuel, and Samoan-born Tony Solaita
outslugging today's native favorites, Koji Yamamoto, Masayuki
Kakefu, and Yasunori Oshima, because regardless of the
outcome of any single season's home run race, Oh at least
has done something no American shall rival for a long, long
time.

What will happen in Japan, following the Olympic victory, might parallel developments in the Japanese industrial labor
force now that Japan has established her reputation for
quality and productivity. As Americans gain greater tolerance, they might also be permitted off-the-field influence
equal to their influence on the diamond. Japanese players
might begin asserting themselves as individuals with confidence that they do have somewhere else to go if their
employers foolishly release them. Certainly American teams
have been interested in obtaining Japanese players ever
since Murakami held his own with San Francisco through
the torrid 1965 pennant race. Only custom has bound them
to Japan, while only pressure from the U.S. State Department has prevented American teams from raiding Japanese
talent in bidding wars. If the State Department believes
American teams can sign Japanese players without Japanese
fans' feeling as if their major leagues are being treated like
an amateur talent pool, if the international trade authorities
judge that Japanese as well as American talent can move
both ways without provoking more serious economic or
diplomatic retaliation, the custom of eternal loyalty to one's
team could quickly crumble.

There is an on-the-field precedent, one that Daryl Spencer
initiated in early 1964. "In Japan they don't say 'Spencer,'

they say 'Spen-sah,' " he told Mandel, "and when they talk
about 'Spen-sah,' they talk about his sliding first. . . . In
this one game, this same pitcher with all the control, the one
who walked me four straight times on sixteen pitches, well,
he walked me again to get to the next guy. That put runners
on first and second in the bottom of the eighth inning with
one out. And I yelled down to Gordon Windhorn," a fellow
American who was the runner from second, "that if this
guy hits a ground ball to just keep on running because I was
going to take the second baseman out." A conventional
play in American baseball, from Little League up, this was
unheard of in Japan, where rough tactics had always been
shunned. "Two pitches later he hit a ground ball to shortstop, the second baseman covered, I knocked him down,
and Windhorn scored the winning run. They argued for
about thirty minutes over that. Our players had never slid
hard like that before. But from that game on, all our players
started sliding hard. And in fact it changed the whole style
of play in Japan as far as making double plays. It used to be
that the player running to second base, if it looked like he
was going to be out, he'd just turn and head out to right
field," away from the relay throw. "No one would ever
slide. The second baseman would just stand on the base and
make the nice easy throw. And almost from that day on, all
the second basemen had to adjust because all our ballplayers
started sliding in hard. And of course all the other teams
started to do it, too."

During the middle 1960s, firebrands like Spencer, Don
Blasingame, Don Zimmer, and one-time Nankai Hawks
coach Pete Reiser also introduced fighting with the hitherto
sacrosanct umpires. Murakami reputedly threw the first
deliberate brushback pitches in 1966—one reason, perhaps,
why he was anathematized by most other Japanese players
of his generation. Rough-and-ready American-style baseball
still isn't universal, but by the middle 1970s Japanese
management was hiring retired American tough guys like
Clete Boyer, Jim Lefebvre, and Vernon Law to teach the
very tactics some of them once asserted would kill their game.

From the sanctimonious press response to Spencer and

cohorts, one would gather that Japanese fans universally disapproved of rude, individualistic aggression. Gate receipts tell a different story. The more colorful the American, at least on the field, the better the fans like him. If this admiration for the man who stands out and even makes himself obnoxious spreads to off-the-field behavior, and if this in turn inspires average Japanese citizens to become more openly self-assertive as well, the whole of Japanese society could begin changing.

As, indeed, it seems to be. No longer content with collective achievements, many Japanese are now agitating for higher personal standards of living, more freedom of choice in occupational and social matters, and less rigidity in their educational system. The rights of peasant farmers were recently advanced by student militants as equal in importance to Tokyo's need for a new airport, a development perhaps akin to the Boston Tea Party in challenging the status quo. Minority rights have never before meant much in a society stressing obligations over options. Many of the student leaders professed Communism, certainly not the ideology of capitalistic American ballplayers. Yet both Communism and anything-goes capitalism present radical departures from prevailing custom, and may simultaneously appeal to the silently frustrated Japanese baseball fan for the same reasons.

While increasingly individualistic baseball players may help inspire the forthcoming changes in Japanese society, baseball should help equally to ensure that these changes are not violent. Baseball in Japan, as in the U.S. and Latin America, may glorify the individual disrupter, but at the same time provides a safety valve for pent-up emotions, and also asserts a timeless, traditional pattern to events. Though longtime players and fans agree that no two teams are ever the same, each team always fields a lineup of nine, sends nine hitters to the plate in an established order, and makes three outs in an inning.

There is an added dimension to this pattern, one that does not meet the average fan's consciousness—a dimension equally significant to nineteenth-century New Englanders, Latin American Catholics, and Japanese Shinto-worshippers. It is a dimension as old and universal as humanity itself. At root, baseball is a fertility rite, a ritual symbolizing human reproduction from conception to birth. The infinite number of variations possible within the structured combat of two teams suggests the infinite variety of romantic and genetic possibilities between male and female.

But baseball's sexual dimension goes far beyond the genetic abstract. Pitchers stand on the mound, the sacred pedestal, as ovulating females, whose egg becomes vulnerable to the phallus-swinging batsman. Their objective is to avoid unwilling impregnation; they are protected from rape by their clans, behind them, whose own phalluses menace other women in their turn. Yet each pitcher is also carrying the child of her clan, the hope of victory, which must be nourished through nine increasingly difficult innings corresponding to the period of gestation. Today, though not in baseball's first half century, midwife relief pitchers may help her. Relief pitchers, interestingly enough, were at one time former starters past their prime: postmenopausal females. Pitchers are even treated as women off the mound, surrounded by eunuch or old-maid coaches in the bullpen-harem. Pitchers' arms are treated with the same sort of superstition as women's genitals.

Most telling, perhaps, is that young men generally become interested in baseball as they approach puberty, and are most intensely devoted to it in puberty, just before establishing their first liaisons with real rather than symbolic women. On the sandlot, whether in the U.S., Japan, or Latin America, young men usually experiment with the differing pitching and hitting roles, arguably a sublimated substitute for sexual experimentation.

As a fertility rite, baseball maintains a connection between past and present wherever it establishes itself, the green outfield recalling an agrarian society, the stooping motions of infielders resembling those of berry-pickers and fishermen, the running and throwing of outfielders continuing skills originally developed by hunters and herdsmen, while the squatting catcher could be weaving a basket or milking a cow. Baseball may have initially failed in Europe because many centuries of Christianity had finally erased any instinctive feel for fertility rituals connected to the land and role-playing, rather than to statues of the Virgin. But baseball caught on like wildfire in Latin America, where Christianity has both absorbed and been absorbed by native fertility-worship. American Christianity through the age of Manifest Destiny took as its first commandment, "Go forth and multiply!", while the Transcendentalists, Mormons, and others variously explored how that might be achieved. Adopting the baseball fertility rite may have relieved the nation of having to choose definitively among the rival religious possibilities.

And in Japan, where forms of fertility worship have always been practiced, undisguised, baseball simply fit in, as a modern variant filling the same psychological needs when some of the older forms began to seem quaint, not quite what a growing industrial power should be doing.

Ultimately, baseball heroes are gods and goddesses of the harvest, of the future, a self-regenerating pantheon whose ever-shifting structure parallels our own lives. We watch stars emerge, shine, then fade and die within the space of a decade or two—but they don't really die, since as coaches and managers they perpetuate their lineage, while new players take their places. Baseball helps America remain American by demonstrating daily where we come from, why we're here, where we're each going, in a manner understood subliminally if not overtly. Likewise, baseball helps Japan remain Japanese. As a sport and subject of international commerce, baseball may help the world become a smaller place, providing new channels of communication. At some point, baseball rivalry might help replace war. When better understood, baseball's universal patterns may help replace nationalism with new recognition of ourselves as individual members of a common species.

All of this may come about not because baseball is an international melting pot, but rather because baseball provides a model of balance between individuality and teamwork. The history of baseball in Japan and America alike demonstrates that the individual must not and cannot be forever repressed, yet the formula for victory requires that the individual must also cooperate with others. No matter how the Japanese have tried to diverge from the American pattern—tried to make their game enforce their own traditional values more than ours—similar patterns have emerged, not because baseball is a quintessentially American sport but because it is a quintessentially human sport. Had baseball begun in Japan, the American game would likely still follow the prevailing pattern—breaking from quasi-feudal beginnings where the players were samurais or knights eternally loyal to overlords, to cooperation of peers for mutual benefit. This is the stage just now arriving in both lands. Whether the Japanese know it or not, they too are baseball teachers: Americans have learned from them how to run effective college baseball programs, how to use martial arts exercises to improve performance, even how to make better equipment.

Mutual acceptance of one another as peers may still be a few years off, despite the Japanese Olympic victory. But it's coming. Once it happens, acceptance of Asiatic people as equals may gradually follow, as gradual acceptance of blacks has slowly followed the admission of black players into the U.S. major leagues. From there, perhaps, we may progress to accepting Latin American baseball as something more than a source of raw material for the U.S. majors—to considering Latin American people as equals. Who knows, we might even wind up with world peace, to which the ongoing performance of the Hiroshima Carp could contribute as much as the lingering memory of the Hiroshima bombing.

"Imagine what might have been," he said.

Dick Allen's 1972:
A Year to Remember

Mark Lazarus

Richard Anthony Allen. Just the mention of his name evokes surprisingly emotional responses from the baseball fans who saw him play. Some recall Allen's awesome natural talent, his intimidating presence on the field. Others regret his off-field difficulties, his seemingly wasted opportunity for greatness. When Allen burst onto the major league scene in 1964 as the National League's Rookie of the Year, he had it all: He could run, hit for average and power, field, throw, and he had that unusual gift of awareness on the field, the "sixth sense" that enables great players to make the great play when it counts.

If natural ability were the criterion for Hall of Fame election, Allen would be a sure thing; instead, he is on the outside looking in and figures to stay there. Still, despite devastating injuries to his right shoulder, wrist, and hand, a succession of disputes with management, media, and fans,

MARK LAZARUS lives in Philadelphia, where Dick Allen began; he has also written for *The Baseball Analyst*.

and a growing battle with alcohol, Allen still produced a .292 career average and blasted 351 homers. In 1976, Dick himself wondered, "The Lord gave me a talent, but only He knows how much. Imagine if I didn't have this [pointing to his shoulder] and this [pointing to his hand]. Imagine what might have been."

Nothing was left to the imagination in 1972. Dick Allen was not only *the* dominant player in baseball, but his impact on the game and the city of Chicago went beyond the confines of the diamond. The period 1972 to 1974 was known as the "Allen Era" on the South Side. The attendance figures bear that out:

1971	833,891
1972	1,177,318
1973	1,302,527
1974	1,149,596
1975	750,802

Roland Hemond, general manager of the White Sox, still believes that Allen saved the American League franchise for Chicago. If it had not been for those three years, we might now have the Pale Hose of New Orleans, Denver, or Toronto. Beyond the raw attendance numbers, Allen's popularity and his leadership of a mediocre team into contention brought the South Siders much-needed publicity and media exposure. In 1972, the Sox games were broadcast on radio station WEAW-FM, a station that could barely be heard in the Loop. The following year, they contracted with WMAQ, a 50,000-watt AM station that could be heard clearly (at night) in Philadelphia!

In April of 1972 fans endured baseball's first full-scale labor strike, forcing the cancellation of 85 games and creating an uneven schedule (one that in the end would frustrate Red Sox fans particularly, as Boston finished one-half game behind Detroit in the American League East). The ailing national pastime was in desperate need of a surprise team, an epic phenom, or the coming of age of a superstar. While Carlton Fisk did his best to fill the role of phenom (Rookie of the Year in the AL), and Steve Carlton rolled to a 27-10 Cy Young Award year with a last-place team, it was Dick Allen and the Sox who captured hearts and headlines around the country.

In retrospect, it is amazing that the Sox were in the pennant race. Their main competition was an Oakland A's team that was to win the first of their three straight World Championships. The Sox finished seventh in team batting (.238), eighth in ERA (3.12), and ninth in defense (.977). They outscored their opponents by only 28 runs (566-538), yet were twenty games over .500! Oakland outscored their opponents by 147 runs, but finished 29 games over .500. Using Bill James' Pythagorean Method of determining a team's won-lost record—($Runs^2/ (Runs^2 +$ Opponent's $Runs^2$)) = Won-Lost percentage—the Sox should have finished eighteen games behind the A's, but were only five and a half behind when the season clock ran out. Chuck Tanner did a phenomenal job of managing, maximizing his team's mediocre talents and winning the close games (evidenced by their 38-20 record in one-run decisions). The pitching staff was led by the big three of Wilbur Wood (24-17, 2.51 ERA), Stan Bahnsen (21-16, 3.60), and Tom Bradley (15-14, 2.98), who collectively started 130 of the 154 games. The ace of the bullpen was twenty-year-old southpaw Terry Forster (6-5, 2.25, with 29 saves); Goose Gossage, only six months older, was 8-1 but saved only 2 games.

The Sox leadoff men—Pat Kelly and Walt "No-Neck" Williams were platooned—hit a combined .257 and scored only 79 runs. Mike Andrews batted second and "ripped" AL pitching at a .200 clip and scored 58 runs. Bill Melton, the league's home run champ in 1971 whose big bat was supposed to keep opponents from pitching around Allen, was shelved by a back injury in June and provided a meager 7 homers. His cleanup slot was taken by Carlos May, who hit .308 but certainly could not generate the power to protect Allen. May, in fact, went from July 23 to September 20 without a homer. The rest of the lineup was a collection of has-beens, never-will-be's, and maybe-someday's.

The 1972 White Sox

PLAYER	AVERAGE	HR	RUNS	RBIs
Pat Kelly	.261	5	57	24
Walt Williams	.249	2	57	11
Mike Andrews	.220	7	58	50
DICK ALLEN	.308	37	90	113
Carlos May	.308	12	83	68
Bill Melton	.245	7	22	30
Jay Johnstone	.188	4	27	17
Rick Reichardt	.251	8	31	43
Ed Herrmann	.249	10	23	40
Rich Morales	.206	2	24	20
Luis Alvarado	.213	4	30	29
Ed Spezio	.238	2	20	22
Jorge Orta	.202	3	20	11
Tom Egan	.191	2	8	9
Jim Lyttle	.232	0	8	5
Tony Muser	.279	1	6	9
Buddy Bradford	.271	2	13	8
Chuck Brinkman	.135	0	0	0

Despite being pitched around (Dick tied for tops in the AL with 99 walks), Allen still piled up some very impressive stats. As late as September 9, he led all categories for the Triple Crown. Rod Carew's solid September edged Dick by .011 for the batting title, but Allen's domination of all other offensive stats was awesome. His 37 home runs led the league; only one other player hit more than 26 (Bobby Murcer, 33). His 113 RBIs also set the pace by a wide margin; only one other had more than 96 (John Mayberry, 100). Allen's margin in slugging percentage over Carlton

Fisk (.603-.538) was the biggest since Frank Robinson's Triple Crown in 1966. As further proof of Allen's dominance, I offer Bill James' Runs Created formula, computed for 1972. Taking into account steals, caught stealing, and bases on balls as well as hits and total bases, it is a superior measure of offensive contribution to either the batting average or the slugging percentage.

TOP FIVE, RUNS CREATED

Allen, CHI	128
Murcer, NY	110
Mayberry, KC	99
Rudi, OAK	98
Fisk, BOS	90

In the premiere issue of *The National Pastime,* Bob Carroll wrote a piece ("Nate Colbert's Unknown RBI Record," TNP 1982) detailing the group of players that drove in 20 percent of their team's runs in a season. At 19.96 percent, Allen just missed that plateau in '72. However, none of the eight "20 percenters" (Frank Howard did it twice) accomplished it in the pressure of a pennant race. Jim Gentile's Orioles finished third in '61, but fourteen games behind the M&M Yankees. Ernie Banks was the National League's MVP in '59, but the Cubs finished tied for fifth, thirteen games back. All of the others finished at least twenty and a half games out of first, with Wally Berger's 1935 Braves finishing an astonishing sixty-one-and-a-half out. Certainly the Braves would have finished last with or without Berger, but the 1972 Chicago White Sox were a different story.

The definition of Most Valuable Player was epitomized by Allen's one-man gang. In addition to his prolific hitting, he stole 19 bases and finished second, only .0004 behind Mayberry, in fielding percentage. Coming down the stretch, in August and September, he hit .305 with an on-base average of .431. Despite their obvious intent to pitch around Dick, the World Champion A's were ripped by Allen for an on-base average of .514 and a slugging percentage of .647!

The way to beat the Sox was to pitch around Allen in clutch situations. This was evident from his 53 walks in the 65 losses he played in, compared to 46 walks in the 83 wins. When granted the opportunity to swing the bat, Allen hit .343 in winning games, .265 in losses. And he loved to entertain the home folks. In old White Sox Park (as it was called in '72), Allen hit 27 of his 37 HRs and had 83 of his 113 RBIs!

Some memorable moments of that memorable year:

- On June 4, in the second game of a doubleheader against the Yankees, with two on and one out in the bottom of the ninth, Allen (pinch-hitting for Rick Morales) blasted a Sparky Lyle pitch into the upper deck in left for a dramatic 5-4 victory. I'll never forget listening to Phil Rizzuto's call on radio (on my way to a batting cage in Seaside Heights, NJ). All the Scooter could shout over the roar of the crowd was, "I don't believe it!!! I don't believe it!!!," over and over, never telling what actually happened. It was at least two or three minutes before Frank Messer grabbed the microphone and told us of Allen's blast! On the All-Star Game telecast that year, the network showed a replay of the homer. Roy White took one step back, then headed straight for the dugout. It was one of the few times that I ever saw Allen display emotion on the field. As he rounded first and realized the ball had disappeared in the upper deck, he pumped his right fist in the air in triumph. Of course, he was mobbed by his teammates at home plate. It was a great moment for Dick, the Sox, and all of his fans (but not for the three Yankee fans who were in the car with me!).

- July 31: Allen became the seventh player in history, and the only one since 1950, to hit two inside-the-park home runs in one game. The pitcher victimized by both homers was Bert Blyleven, and the center fielder who fell victim to Allen's torrid line drives was Bobby Darwin. Dick connected in the first inning with two on, and in the fifth with one on to lead the Sox to an 8-1 victory.

• August 23rd: Allen became only the fourth player in history to reach the center-field bleachers at Comiskey Park. Only Jimmie Foxx, Hank Greenberg, and Alex Johnson before, and Richie Zisk since, have been able to reach the seats. Again, Allen's was extra special. The blast came off Lindy McDaniel of the Yankees in the seventh inning with one on and cemented a 5-2 win to vault the Sox into first place. During the 1972 season, the Sox played all of their Wednesday home games in the daytime, and Harry Caray would broadcast from the center-field bleachers, soaking up the sun and suds with his compatriots. Allen's shot missed Caray by just a few rows. Unfortunately, I have never had the opportunity to hear Caray's call of the homer, which must have been great. To reach the bleachers, the ball must travel 440 feet to the back wall and clear the sixteen-and-a-half-foot-high wall. Allen's blast cleared the wall easily.

• September 7-12: In a seven-game stretch against West rivals Oakland, California, and Kansas City, Allen had 16 RBIs, including four game-winners!

In November Allen was named, to no one's surprise, the AL Most Valuable Player. During the winter a new contract was negotiated, calling for $225,000 per year for three years, making Allen the highest-paid player in the game at the time.

Dick was well on his way to another MVP-caliber year in 1973 when he broke his leg in a collision with Mike Epstein in June. In retrospect, this event seemed to burst the bubble as the pressures of the media, management, and fans became too much for Allen to bear. Despite a triumphant return to action in 1974, in which he led the league in homers and slugging, Allen announced his retirement on September 14. Over the winter the Sox traded his rights to

Atlanta, who subsequently dealt him to the Phillies in May of 1975. Although welcomed home warmly by fans in the city of brotherly boos, Allen's continued erratic behavior and eroding skills led to his release after the '76 season. Charley Finley gambled by signing Allen for '77, but a quick exit from the ballpark during a game in June prompted his suspension and final release.

Dick Allen was a complex man with some deep-seated psychological scars that affected his behavior. But the sight of No. 15 digging in at the plate, tugging his uniform at the shoulders and left leg, pushing his batting helmet down on his afro, outlining the outside corner of the plate with his bat, and waving that forty-ounce war pole, brought a tremendous surge of excitement to the game. Wherever he played, the anticipation of a titanic home run had the crowd alive with each at-bat. In Philadelphia fans would not leave the ballpark until after Dick's final at-bat of the game, no matter what the score. Dick Allen may not make it to the Hall of Fame, but he was a player with *style*, a uniquely fearsome batter who will be remembered not only for what he might have been, but also for what he *was*.

He built champions, managed them, and bequeathed them.

Frank Selee, Dynasty Builder

A.D. Suehsdorf

In the ten years from 1891 to 1900, only two National League managers won pennants: Ned Hanlon and Frank Gibson Selee. Hanlon is well remembered for leading the flamboyant, intimidating Baltimore Orioles to three flags (1894-96) and Brooklyn's Superbas, bolstered by six Oriole transfers, to two (1899-1900). Modest, retiring Frank Selee— *See*-lee, like the mattress—scored his five with the intelligent Boston Beaneaters and is virtually forgotten.

Consider what baseball's amnesia has obscured: Selee's winning percentage of .598—achieved in twelve years at Boston and three and a half with the Chicago Cubs—is the fourth highest in managerial history. Twelve of his players are in the Hall of Fame, and five or six others have Cooperstown credentials. His 1892 and 1898 Beaneater teams were the first to win more than 100 games in one National League season. His 1894 powerhouse, although

A. D. SUEHSDORF, an ostensibly retired writer from Sonoma, Ca., authored *The Great American Baseball Scrapbook*.

finishing third, still holds the single-season record of 1,222 runs scored, and was the only club between 1884 and 1920 to hit more than 100 home runs (103) in a season.

Actually, the Beaneaters were better known for finesse than muscle. Selee's particular talents as a manager were, first, a brilliant sense of players' potentials and, second, a masterful insight into baseball's strategic possibilities.

It was said of him that he could "tell a ballplayer in his street clothes." Yet this sixth sense was more than a judgment of athletic skill: It was an uncanny ability to divine the position best suited to the man. Although Arthur Soden, the autocratic boss of the Beaneaters, reputedly thwarted many of Selee's deals, Frank repeatedly succeeded in acquiring promising minor leaguers and unappreciated National Leaguers, as well as in positional shifts.

This acumen was reflected on the field, where the Beaneaters were known and admired for playing "inside baseball," for "outthinking" the opposition, for being the "most perfectly drilled scientific team" of its day. While Boston's stolen-base statistics are unimpressive, Selee was an early advocate of overall team speed as an offensive and defensive weapon. He is credited with developing—through Fred Tenney and Herman Long—the 3-6-3 double play, and he encouraged "headwork and signals" on the field to shift players according to the pitch and to coordinate base coverages. John Montgomery Ward, one of the game's standard-bearers and pundits, praised the Beaneaters extravagantly in Spalding's 1894 *Guide* for their clever and effective use of the run-and-hit play: The runner's bluff to see who covers second, his signal as to the pitch he will run on, and a punched hit into the hole left by the covering infielder. "I have made a study of the play of this team," Ward wrote, "and I find that they have won many games by scoring nearly twice as many runs as they made hits."

"The success of the Boston team," *Sporting Life* explained in 1893, "is due, more than any other thing, to . . . a manager who is a thorough baseball general . . . who knows what should be done and how to do it, and is able to impress his advice upon the men under his control."

Given the evolution of playing and scoring rules since Selee's time, plus the changing fashions in press reporting, it is difficult to interpret such accolades in contemporary terms. What *is* readily apparent, and what establishes Selee's place among baseball's great managers, is his architectural brilliance in fashioning the 1890-1901 Beaneaters and 1902-05 Cubs.

Selee was born in 1859, the son of a Methodist-Episcopal clergyman, and raised in Melrose, Massachusetts, where he was a member of the town's Alpha baseball club. In 1884 he left a job with the Waltham Watch Co. to organize an entry in the Massachusetts State Baseball Association. "I was without any practical experience as a manager or player," he wrote in a retrospective article many years later. But he raised $1,000 to provide a playing field with fence and grandstand, appeared in a few box scores as center fielder, and quickly asserted his natural talent for managing.

The Waltham team was short-lived. Manager Selee and some of his players joined the league's Lawrence franchise to finish out the season.

In 1885, with the league reorganized as the Eastern New England Baseball Association, he managed Haverhill to second place, but in mid-1886 he was released.

What he called "my real start in baseball" came in 1887, when he won his first pennant as manager of the Oshkosh (Wisconsin) team of the Northwestern League. Trailing league-leading Milwaukee by fourteen games on July 4, Oshkosh stormed back to win the pennant on the final day of the season, led by outfielders Dummy Hoy and Tommy McCarthy and pitcher Tom Lovett, future big-league stars. The following year, with the league renamed the Western Association (on its way to becoming Ban Johnson's American League), Selee shifted to Omaha and, after a fourth-place finish, won another pennant in 1889.

He came to Boston from Omaha, bringing with him his star pitcher, Charles "Kid" Nichols, eventually a 360-game winner. He also persuaded Boston to part with $700 for a promising Western League second baseman, Bobby "Link" Lowe, of Milwaukee.

Selee started with a Beaneater team riddled by ten defections to the new Boston entry in the Players League. The entire infield and outfield were gone, including the redoubtable Dan Brouthers and King Kelly, and three pitchers—two of no account, but the other, Old Hoss Radbourn.

The splendid John Clarkson and his batterymate, the veteran Charlie Bennett, stayed loyal. Scrambling, Selee went to the American Association for three infielders. From Baltimore he got Tommy Tucker, notable for playing first base with a fingerless mitt, and journeyman third sacker Chippy McGarr; from Kansas City for a then-whopping $6,300 he got "Germany" Long, one of the preeminent players of the century, who would be a fixture at shortstop for twelve years. At second he used utility man Pop Smith rather than Bobby Lowe, whose time would come. From other National League clubs he picked up pitcher Charlie Getzien, onetime Detroit whiz; Marty Sullivan, an Indianapolis outfielder; and partway into the season the veteran outfielder Paul Hines, from Pittsburgh. One of his better bargains was Steve Brodie, from Hamilton, Ontario (International League), who became the regular right fielder.

Over the season the Beaneaters made a respectable fight of it, holding second place as late as August. A September slump, however, dropped them to fifth with a 76-57 record. Embarrassingly, the Players League pennant was won by the Boston defectors.

In 1891 the Players League had collapsed and better players were available. Two of the prodigals, second baseman Joe Quinn and third baseman Billy Nash, returned. With Turner and Long they gave the Beaneaters a first-class infield. King Kelly, a shadow of his former self, returned to catch a final twenty-four games for Boston; Bennett was beginning to fade, too, particularly at the plate. Thereafter, Selee was always on the lookout for competent catchers. Bobby Lowe broke into the lineup as left fielder, Steve Brodie moved to center, and Harry Stovey, a hard-hitting star in the American Association, became the right fielder when his old A.A. team, Philadelphia, failed to reserve him after the Brotherhood disbanded.

A Cambridge lad, Joe Kelley played twelve games in the outfield and batted .244 before being passed along to Pittsburgh in the deal that brought righthander Harry Staley to Boston to replace the worn-out Getzien. These were the first games in a seventeen-year career that would lead young Joe to the Hall of Fame (principally by way of the legendary Orioles), but there is no evidence that Selee misjudged Kelley's talent; at the time he needed another pitcher more than he needed an undeveloped outfielder. Staley, despite a reputation for "lushing," won 20 games. These, plus Clarkson's 33, Nichols' 30, and Getzien's 4, were enough to win a first National League pennant for Frank Selee by 3½ games over Chicago.

Kelley is one example among many of how Selee cast his net outward from the Hub. In a day of rather more haphazard scouting (although of more geographically concentrated player pools), he was acutely aware of promising players throughout New England. Of the 118 men who played for him in Boston, nearly 30 percent were from Massachusetts, and 38 percent were from New England.

Between seasons the ten-year-old American Association expired and four of its teams were absorbed into the National League. Selee was home in Melrose, attending Elks meetings and running a haberdashery with Sid Farrar, the former Phillie first baseman and father of the glorious Geraldine. But he never lost sight of baseball opportunities, and in the reshuffling of players for 1892 Selee drew three aces. From the Boston Reds, Association successors to the Players League team, he plucked outfielder Hugh Duffy. From St. Louis he got pitcher Happy Jack Stivetts and outfielder Tommy McCarthy, whom Selee had piloted at Oshkosh. Duffy and McCarthy, close personal friends, quickly became known as "the Heavenly Twins" for their superlative play afield and at bat, while Happy Jack won 132 games in the next six years, including the first no-hitter ever thrown by a Boston pitcher.

Lowe complemented the Twins in the outfield. Brodie and Stovey were released. The infield was unchanged. Stivetts won 35 games, a nice bit of timing inasmuch as a sore arm had brought John Clarkson's distinguished Boston career to an end (he held on for another season and a half with Cleveland). In the National League's one and only split season, the Beaneaters won 102 games—the most ever to that time—and took the pennant by eight and a half games over Cleveland.

In 1893 the Beaneaters marched to their third straight pennant. The major change in the team was the evolution of Bobby Lowe into an infielder. Joe Quinn was traded to St. Louis for Cliff Carroll, who took Lowe's outfield spot so that Bobby could replace Quinn.

The glory years for the Orioles now intervened. The Beaneaters, with largely the same personnel that had won so handily in '93, faltered and sank to third, to fifth (tie), and to fourth. It was hard to say what went wrong. In 1894 Hugh Duffy led the league in average (the incredible .438), homers (18), and RBI's (145). Lowe became the first major leaguer to hit four home runs in one game. Five regulars had more than 100 runs batted in. Kid Nichols won 32 games—the fourth of seven straight 30-or-over years. And Boston broke in a rookie lefthanded catcher named Fred Tenney, whose glory lay ahead. Yet not only Baltimore, but the Giants, finished ahead of Boston.

By 1897 the Beaneaters were back on top of the heap with a .705 winning percentage, highest in their history, and in 1898, with their second 100-victory season, they won the fifth pennant for Frank Selee in a span of eight years. It is instructive to compare the lineups of 1893 and 1897 to see how the manager restored the team's viability:

1893		1897
Tommy Tucker	1b	Fred Tenney
Bobby Lowe	2b	Bobby Lowe
Billy Nash	3b	Jimmy Collins
Herman Long	ss	Herman Long
Cliff Carroll	rf	Chick Stahl
Hugh Duffy	cf	Billy Hamilton
Tommy McCarthy	lf	Hugh Duffy

	1893		1897
	Charlie Bennett	c	Marty Bergen
	Charlie Ganzel	c/ut	Charlie Ganzel
	Kid Nichols	p	Kid Nichols
	Jack Stivetts	p	Jack Stivetts
	Harry Staley	p	Fred Klobedanz
	Hank Gastright	p	Ted Lewis

Carroll was first to go. In 1894 he was replaced by Jimmy Bannon, an Amesbury boy nicknamed "Foxy Grandpa," who was a bleacher favorite after his purchase from St. Louis. McCarthy went next. Thirty-one in 1895 and coming to the end of his lovely career, he was injured late in the season and replaced by Tenney. Jimmy Collins, acquired from Buffalo (Eastern League) as an outfielder, played a few games on Bannon's turf, played them badly, and was virtually hooted off the team by the foxy one's partisans. Selee loaned Collins (a common practice then) to Louisville, a constant tailender since its entry from the American Association. There, in the obscurity of twelfth place, the future Hall of Famer learned to be a third baseman.

This was not lost on Frank Selee. Before the 1896 season began, he had traded Boston's long-time favorite Billy Nash to Philadelphia for Sliding Billy Hamilton and recalled Collins to Boston. He dealt McCarthy to Brooklyn, perhaps with a pang, but Tommy was heavenly no longer. And for $1,000 and a utility infielder of minimal skills he lifted Marty Bergen from Kansas City—the catcher he had been looking for since the loss of Bennett.

Nash had been team captain, a role of some authority, since returning from his Players League sabbatical, but he was past thirty, Collins was a fair bet to hold down third, and Sliding Billy, though thirty himself, had both the power and speed to more than make up for McCarthy's departure.

As the season progressed, Selee also collected two fine pitchers: Ted Lewis, a righthander, as he graduated from Williams College, and Fred Klobedanz, a lefty from Fall

River who had whetted Selee's appetite by holding Boston to five hits in a spring exhibition. Both would have short careers, but both would be substantial winners in the pennant years.

Finally, Selee resolved Tenney's role. Since signing on in 1894 he had been tried at catcher, but his throwing was erratic, and lefthanders were going out of style. Otherwise, he was an outfielder. Early in 1897, however, after three straight losses to Baltimore, Selee suddenly benched Tommy Tucker and pulled Tenney out of right field to play first. It was another marvelous, intuitive Selee move. Tenney was a natural: agile, graceful, surehanded. He played wide and deep, he stretched arms and legs to meet the throw and gain an inch on the runner, a novelty at the time that soon became the custom. The infield of Tenney, Lowe, Long, and Collins, although it played together only four years, was judged the nineteenth century's best by all who saw it.

Icing on the cake was Chick Stahl, a first-rate outfielder and career .300 hitter, who was drafted from Buffalo in 1896 and available to take the spot vacated by Tenney.

Let it not be said that Selee was infallible. Two of his misjudgments, both committed in 1896, were whoppers. Ed Barrow recalled, half a century after the fact, that Selee had said he "wouldn't give a dime for Wagner." And the authoritative Fred Lieb reminisced that Selee had visited Fall River to inspect the young Nap Lajoie and was not sufficiently impressed by his .429 BA to make a bid.

Anyone who didn't want Wagner for his hitting alone would have some explaining to do. For even in 1896, his second season in organized baseball, rumors had spread that Honus was a terror. One after another, National League managers bringing their teams in to New York to play the Giants found time to cross the river and watch Wagner perform for Barrow's Paterson club of the Atlantic League.

Cousin Ed did not explain what determined Selee to spend his dime elsewhere. An off-duty pitcher scouting for the Phils reported Honus as too awkward to play major league ball, and his ungainliness may indeed have been seen as a flaw. It is also fact that Wagner did not play the

majority of his games at short until 1903. Before then he
was a novice at every position. Even so, there was no
missing that bat.

As for Lajoie, the story of his rejection has several
versions, only one of which involves Selee. The others have
a pitcher who was impressively battered by Lajoie urging
Boston to grab him and being ignored. In fact, a number of
scouts inexplicably ignored Nap in spite of his terrific
hitting, so that the Phils, trading for a nothing outfielder,
got him as a throw-in. As for Selee, with stars of the caliber
of Tenney, Lowe, Hamilton, and Duffy at all the positions
Lajoie played, he can perhaps be forgiven for taking Fred
Klobedanz instead.

Selee's final maneuver for Boston came in 1898, when,
for another $1,000 and another utility infielder, he acquired
from Syracuse (Eastern League) a remarkable righthander,
Vic Willis, the Delaware Peach. In eight of his thirteen
seasons the Peach had 20 or more victories and a career total
of 248. As usual, it was a timely deal, Willis's 24 wins
coming as Happy Jack Stivetts reached the end of the trail.

Thereafter, Ned Hanlon, now in Brooklyn, took the 1899
and 1900 pennants, and Fred Clarke earned his first with
Pittsburgh in 1901. Boston slid to second, to fourth, and
finally to fifth with a .500 record.

Selee was cast adrift after twelve years, 1,004 victories,
and a .607 winning percentage. Clark Griffith, manager of
the Chicago White Sox, said, "That is a big mistake. Selee
is one of the few great managers in the business." He was
promptly hired by the Chicago Cubs, who had not won a
pennant since 1886 and had achieved the first division only
four times in the dozen years Selee was at Boston. In 1901
they had finished in sixth place, 37 games out.

For Selee it was the Boston experience of 1890 all over
again. Of the twenty-five players on the 1901 Cub squad,
only eight survived to start the 1902 season, and three of
those were soon gone. One of these, a utility infielder—
Selee's favorite trade bait—went to Boston for the distinguished veteran Bobby Lowe. A few were sold for cash.
Most were simply released. Five jumped to the American

League, all of them considerable players, especially the two
snared by Connie Mack: outfielder Topsy Hartsel and pitcher
Rube Waddell.

These actions left Selee with: two regulars, Frank Chance
in right field and Johnny Kling behind the plate; two
pitchers, Jack Taylor, the team's best, and so-so Jocko
Menefee; and a rookie infielder, Germany Schaefer.

Where to start? Selee had left Boston with Jimmy Slagle
in tow. The Beaneaters had acquired him from the Phils in
1901, and it is possible that despite 66 games in the Boston
outfield management did not realize how good he was. He
would grace the Chicago garden through 1908.

Frank Chance, who had been catching and outfielding for
the Cubs since 1898, looked more like a first baseman to
Selee, and turned out to be one. Like Tenney, he fit
beautifully. By July Bobby Lowe was at second. Schaefer
was stationed at third. Another rookie, Joe Tinker, drafted
from Portland of the Northwest League during the winter,
was transformed from third baseman to shortstop.

Late in the season there was an historic coming together.
Bobby Lowe was hurt and Selee asked an eastern scout to
grab an emergency replacement. The choice was a scrawny,
lantern-jawed, ill-natured, hard-playing runt from Troy (N.Y.
State League) named John Evers. He joined the club after
Labor Day, presumably a shortstop, but Selee had a shortstop and needed Evers at second. On September 15 was
executed the first Tinker to Evers to Chance double play.

For the outfield, Davy Jones—also known as "Kangaroo"
—was bought from the St. Louis Americans; later on he
would form a threesome with Ty Cobb and Sam Crawford at
Detroit. John Dobbs, a stopgap, was purchased from
Cincinnati.

Kling, already on deck, was an excellent catcher. Hence-
forth he would be catching more than 100 games a season.

Pitching was a problem. Selee got 22 wins from ace Jack
Taylor and 12 from Menefee. Nine other pitchers came and
went. One discovery worth keeping was Carl Lundgren,
fresh from the University of Illinois. All told, thirty-eight
men wore the Cub uniform in 1902. At the end of the

season Chicago (68-69) had advanced one notch to fifth place.

In 1903 there were only two changes in the day-to-day lineup. Schaefer, who had hit .196, was released and Dobbs was sold to Brooklyn. A pair of Detroiters took their places: "Doc" Casey, third base, and Dick Harley, right field. In a year Harley would be gone, but Casey would hold his position for the rest of Selee's term in Chicago.

The pitching was much improved. Taylor won 21, Lundgren 10, Menefee 8, and two Selee surprises, Jake Weimer and Bob Wicker, won 21 and 19. "Tornado Jake" was a twenty-nine-year-old rookie from Kansas City in the Western League. Wicker came from the Cardinals in an even trade for pitcher Bob Rhoads. In three seasons he would win 49 games for the Cubs. (Rhoads did little for the Cards, but eventually became a winner for Cleveland.)

(Interestingly, within a few years Weimer and Wicker were involved in trades with Cincinnati which provided the final building blocks for Chicago's soon-to-be champions. Shortly before the 1906 season, Weimer and third baseman Hans Lobert were exchanged for Harry Steinfeldt, the hot-corner man who solidified the Tinker-Evers-Chance infield. In June, Wicker and $2,000 were traded for the excellent Orvie Overall.)

As for 1903, the Cubs (82-56) leaped to third place. In December of that year Selee engineered perhaps the finest deal of his career: Jack Taylor and Larry McLean, a catcher who had played just one game for Chicago, were dispatched to St. Louis for the nonpareil Mordecai Peter Centennial Brown, the three-fingered one, and Jack O'Neill, a backup catcher of rather less talent than his young brother Steve. Actually, it took two years to prove what a steal it was. Steady Jack won 35 for the Cards, while Brown was scoring 33 for the Cubs. Thereafter, of course, Mordecai had six consecutive seasons of 20 or more victories as one of the superb righthanders ever.

Jack McCarthy, a Massachusetts boy, continued the game of Rotating Third Outfielder, replacing Harley. And Artie Hofman, lively "Circus Solly," who could play all infield and outfield positions, came aboard through a simple cash deal with Pittsburgh. Finally, near season's end, the Syracuse Stars were persuaded to part with their fleet outfielder, Wildfire Schulte.

All this talent combined to win 93 games (and lose 60) in 1904 and edged the Cubs into second place, though still 13 games behind the high-flying Giants.

In 1905 Selee made his final contribution to the future welfare of the Cubs, acquiring a strong-armed college-boy pitcher named Ed Reulbach. A star at Notre Dame, Big Ed also played summer ball under assumed names. At Sedalia, Missouri in 1901-03 he was "Lawson." Pitching for Montpelier, Vermont in 1904 he was "Sheldon." At times, scouts may have been excited to think there were three pitchers of Reulbach's caliber waiting to be signed!

In the 1905 outfield, Billy Maloney took Davy Jones' spot—as McCarthy had taken Harley's and Harley had taken Dobbs'. During the winter Maloney, McCarthy, "Doc" Casey, a pitcher, and $2,000 were shuffled off to Brooklyn for the long-sought perfect third outfielder: Jimmy Sheckard.

Selee was not there to pull it off. Never robust and frequently ailing, he was found in July to be gravely ill with tuberculosis. The Cubs had won 52 and lost 38 when he turned them over to Husk Chance and migrated to Denver, hoping there would be healing magic in the Rocky Mountains. He died there in July, 1909, aged fifty, and his passing was mourned by the baseball world.

Not everyone was prepared to credit his accomplishments, and, to be sure, Frank Selee had help. All teams are the achievement of many people. But for every player, newsman, or scout who had a bone to pick, there were many more who acknowledged his skills and counted themselves lucky that they had known him or played for him. His teams had won 1,299 games while losing 872. Eight of his Beaneaters are in the Hall of Fame. Duffy, Tommy McCarthy, Nichols, Hamilton, and Collins truly felt his influence. Clarkson and King Kelly were finishing careers earned without him, and Joe Kelley won his spurs elsewhere. Yet it can also be argued that Tenney, Lowe, Long, and Willis, who are not in the Hall, should be, and that Reulbach and Schulte should join Tinker, Evers, Chance, and Brown in the Chicago contingent.

After a third-place finish in 1905, the team Selee handed to Chance went 116-36 in 1906 to set a record never since approached. The Cubs also won pennants in 1907, 1908, and 1910 and were second in 1909. Their 570 victories against 258 defeats in that period gave them a phenomenal percentage of .688. It is impossible to know whether Frank Selee would have compiled the same record. All that can be said is that of the thirteen key players of 1905, eight still were regulars in 1910. The principal additions—Steinfeldt, Sheckard, Overall, and Jack Pfiester—arrived in 1906. Otherwise it was pretty much Selee's bunch that built up Frank Chance as The Peerless Leader and took him to the Hall of Fame, although in three years of managing other big-league teams, Chance finished no higher than seventh. Frank Selee has been forgotten, but his record is there for all to see.